# All Three Channels

## Arlene Francis as Actress, Women's Trailblazer, and Television Pioneer

**Jennifer Bitman**

BearManor Media.com

Published in the USA by
BearManor Media
1317 Edgewater Dr. #110
Orlando, FL 32804
www.BearManorMedia.com

Softcover Edition
ISBN-10:
ISBN-13: 979-8-88771-141-6

Printed in the United States of America

This book is lovingly dedicated to Peter Gabel.

May his memory be a blessing. 1947 - 2022

# Contents

# Arlene Francis: Leading Lady of the Airwaves

Arlene Francis was a career woman long before women were proud to claim this title. She rose to prominence as a stellar figure in American broadcasting just when traditional gender divisions reemerged after World War II. Although Arlene may not have set out to forward the place of women in the power structures of broadcasting, she succeeded in rising to the topmost ranks of admired radio and television personalities, on par with any male celebrity.

Her life spanned almost the entire 20th century (1907-2001), and her career mirrored the transformation of broadcasting from radio's entertainment dominance to the reign of television. Arlene and broadcasting advanced together, her personal talents ideally suited to the industry's demanding forms. She transitioned with grace from local radio to network radio, then to network television, syndicated television, and finally back to local and syndicated radio, where her voice was heard on the airwaves until 1991. And she accomplished this lifelong media journey all the while pursuing her career as a stage and screen actor.

As Jennifer Bitman's expansive biography affirms, Arlene embraced the discipline of hard work; she was unafraid to take chances and make adjustments at every turn in her career. In an interview with *The Salina Journal* at age 74, she explained, "You can't be static in your life. You've got to move on and readjust your sights as you grow older because the world changes…you must move with the times."[1]

---

1. Kenneth R. Clark, "Show for Over 50s May Be Syndicated." The Salina Journal. Oct. 20, 1981.

## From Radio to Television and Back Again

Not one, but two stars on Hollywood's Walk of Fame applaud Arlene's prominence in both radio and television broadcasting.

Her radio career began two decades before television arrived in American homes. During the 1930s, Arlene's deep-timbered voice was heard on more than 20 soap operas, and her gift for mimicry made her a versatile performer, landing her roles in *The March of Time*, *Cavalcade*, *Betty and Bob*, and *Forty-five Minutes from Hollywood*. With network radio centered in New York City, Arlene remembered in her memoir, "I'd run from one studio to another in the same day, changing my accent *enroute*."[2] In 1935, she hosted CBS's musical show *Hour of Charm*, which boasted an all-female orchestra.[3] In 1937, she became the "Voice of Fashion" in collaboration with *Vogue* Magazine. During the war years, she was the mistress of ceremonies for the popular radio show *Blind Date* (1943-46), during which GIs had two minutes to convince "glamour girls" on the other side of a partition to go out on a date.[4]

During the industry's changeover from radio to television after World War II, Arlene adapted without missing a beat. *Blind Date* moved to TV in 1949, launching Arlene's decades-long run on network television.

Across the 1950s, Arlene could be seen on television with every click of the dial—a vivacious panelist each Sunday on *What's My Line?* (1950-1967); a charming host for the GI talent show *Soldiers' Parade* (*Talent Patrol*) every Thursday evening on ABC (1953-1955); editor-in-chief for NBC's daytime experiment *Home* (1954-1957), designed to appeal to America's homemakers each weekday morning; and headliner for her own variety program, *The Arlene Francis Show*, daily on NBC (1957-1958). Arlene was also NBC's first choice to co-host the *Today* show, which she declined for personal reasons.

---

2. Arlene Francis with Florence Rome, *Arlene Francis: A Memoir* (New York: Simon and Schuster, 1978), 21-27.

3. https://www.oldtimeradiodownloads.com/variety/the-hour-of-charm. Accessed Sept. 12, 2022.

4. For more examples, see "Selected Radio Show Appearances of Arlene Francis" in this volume.

Arlene remained a familiar face in American homes into the 1960s, 70s, and 80s. When *What's My Line?* ended its run on CBS in 1967, she continued as a panelist on the syndicated version until 1975. In the early 1980s, she hosted *Prime of Your Life* (1981-86), a syndicated program that dismantled the misperceptions of aging.[5]

Overlapping her TV schedule, Arlene returned to local radio in 1960, hosting the weekday interview program *The Arlene Francis Show*, aired on WOR-AM, Manhattan's prestigious local station. When the program was finally cancelled in 1986, she appeared weekly with Joan Hamburg on the same station, and then, at the age of 81, presided over *Celebrity Hotline*, a weekend show carried by over 100 radio stations in 1988.

Arlene's tenacity and pluck allowed her to adapt to the everchanging backdrop of 20th-century broadcasting. In every decade, Arlene's personal talents seamlessly matched broadcasting's arduous requirements.

## The "Quick Queen of Television"[6]

One of Arlene's most durable qualities was her work ethic. In an interview in 1979, Eileen Prose asked her how she took care of herself to look so terrific. Arlene, 72 years old, responded with a laugh, "I work all the time. That's the best way to survive. Never to give up."[7] Jennifer Bitman discovered remarkable examples of Arlene's steadfastness even when she wasn't feeling her best.[8]

Arlene's innate aptitudes and well-honed performance style famously crossed media platforms: her eloquence and ability to improvise on live media; her sense of humor and playfulness, the well-known smile so photogenic on TV; the deep pitch of her well-trained voice, perfected on radio and on stage but welcome on television; her down-to-earth personality so valued in women—charming, vivacious, magnanimous;

---

5. For more examples, see "Selected Television Show Appearances of Arlene Francis" in this volume.

6. "Arlene Francis: The Quick Queen of Television," *Newsweek*, July 19, 1954, 50 and Cover.

7. Arlene Francis - YouTube. Accessed September 2, 2022.

8. Bitman 179 and 180.

and her association with New York sophistication and fashion at a time when broadcasting's elite were centered in New York City.

Arlene's practiced ability to improvise and speak off the cuff, no matter the circumstances, fit perfectly with live broadcasting, on radio or TV. In 1954, *Newsweek* praised this efficacious skill: "Pre-eminently, she can talk. She can talk wisely, wittily, and continuously."[9] Her natural talent for adlibbing, so useful in managing the uncertainties of live broadcasting, underpinned her success.

Even in later years, when she was able to pre-tape *Prime of Your Life*, Arlene took little interest in how the show was edited, trusting to the expertise of her post-production team.[10] Her spontaneous on-camera performance was her greatest pleasure. Ever fearless in performing in the moment, Arlene also preferred live theater to filmmaking,

Arlene's improvisations were laced with humor, wit, and playfulness. Her on-air disposition was vibrant and energetic; she freely smiled and laughed as she invented quips on the spot. After a speedboat ride at 125 mph on *Home*, she joked, "Sure makes a girl yearn to cross the continent in a cover wagon."[11]

In another example on *Home*, Arlene introduced an array of French hats by adorning them on the heads of mannikins rotating on a tabletop. Because of the speed of the rotation, soon the hat she picked up no longer matched the hat named in the script, until she finally snatched the wrong hat from the last mannikin.

"This girl doesn't seem to know what to put on this morning," she improvised. "And it's because they're French hats and she's not used to them. Are you, darling?"[12]

Sometimes her humor could be self-deprecating, which endeared her to audiences. In her book *That Certain Something: The Magic of Charm* (1960), she joked about the cancellation of the *Home* show. "I was born

---

9. "Arlene Francis: The Quick Queen of Television," 50.
10. See Bitman's telephone interview with Chris Salvador, November 20, 2020, 179.
11. See Marsha F. Cassidy, *What Women Watched: Daytime Television in the 1950s* (Austin, TX: University of Texas Press, 2005), 148.
12. *Ibid.*

in Boston, raised in New York, and died in daytime television."[13] In her memoir she wrote that whenever she was asked "How old are you?" she replied, "Five feet five and a half inches. Next question?"[14]

In Jennifer Bitman's interview with one of Arlene's last producers, Chris Salvador is remarkably perceptive about the physical qualities that further established Arlene as a queenly figure on radio and television.[15] He admired her precise diction, the pleasing low resonance of her voice, and her elegant body language.[16] Her regal posture, formal bearing, and well-trained voice and gestures became her trademark.

Arlene came to broadcasting during an era which valued "charm" on the airwaves,[17] and her brand of feminine charm was highly prized. Part of this elusive quality entailed politeness, genteel etiquette, and grace of movement and speech, but Arlene also projected genuineness and modesty. Her knack for laughter and her willingness to joke about herself created an accessible version of refinement that was widely appealing.

On the air, she radiated the highest form of etiquette, the talent of making others feel comfortable. As her son Peter Gabel best expressed it, at the core of her performance style was a "spontaneous confidence in her own charm, goodness, and authenticity."[18]

Over the years Arlene carved out a distinctive image in broadcasting as an urbane New Yorker with elan. As a stage actor, party hostess to the famous, and fashion icon, Arlene best conveyed this cultured figure on CBS's *What's My Line?* where she wore stylish ball gowns (and her legendary diamond heart-shaped necklace, a gift from her husband) and magnified the program's courteous tone and chic sophistication. On this stage, in a live broadcast every Sunday evening, Arlene's gracious charm shone the brightest.

---

13. Arlene Francis, *That Certain Something: The Magic of Charm* (New York: Julian Messner, Inc., 1960), 10.
14. Arlene Francis with Florence Rome, 11.
15. Bitman interview with Chris Salvador, 179-180.
16. *Ibid.*
17. See Cassidy, Chapter 4 and Chapter 6.
18. Email correspondence with Marsha Cassidy, Dec. 23, 2003.

## Arlene and Second Wave Feminism

It is not surprising that a woman named the queen of television in an era dedicated to traditional gender divisions would tell journalist Helen Bolstad in 1955, "I'm almost an anti-feminist."[19] The Women's Liberation Movement was still on the horizon, and the country, with television itself offering reinforcement, extolled the gendered breadwinner/homemaker model. During the 1950s, the decade in which Arlene excelled as "TV's busiest woman,"[20] social shifts had revived a womanhood centered on homemaking and raising children.

Yet in an era preceding the establishment of Second Wave Feminism, Arlene's career might well serve as an example of what has recently been called "accidental feminism,"[21] when incidental factors advance the status of women in the workplace, even though underlying institutional structures of patriarchal power remain unchanged. By 1960, Arlene had risen to acclaim in the most coveted positions in broadcasting, a network darling at parity with any male star.

The incongruity between her fame as a busy career woman and a homemaker devoted to domesticity met its greatest challenge on the *Home* show.[22] Journalist Alfred Bester wondered what such a "hip chick like Arlene" was doing on such a "square" show.[23] *Newsweek* said she was the ambiguous ruler of both "pots and puns."[24] Within the binary gender norms of the 1950s, Arlene presented a paradox on a daytime television program focused on domesticity.

Arlene's attempts to project a homemaker image on *Home* countered her public style as a chic New York actor, creating a dissonance on the program. At the same time, her intelligence and reputation as an erudite

---

19. *Radio TV Mirror*, July – Dec. 1955.

20. "Arlene Francis: TV's Busiest Woman," *Look*, 4 May 1954: 52.

21. Swethaa S. Ballakrishnen, *Accidental Feminism: Gender Parity and Selective Mobility among India's Professional Elite* (Princeton: Princeton University Press, 2021).

22. See Cassidy, Chapter 6.

23. Alfred Bester, "Antic Arts: At Home with Arlene Francis, *Holiday* (October 1956): 82.

24. "Arlene Francis: The Quick Queen of Television," 50.

figure served to expand the world of her homebound viewers. *Home* was modeled on a magazine format, interspersing segments on glamour, fashion, shopping, and cooking with political, cultural, and social topics. The program covered issues of "child psychology, housing projects, comparative arts, teenagers' problems and segregation," according to producer Phyllis Adams Jenkins.[25] Arlene interviewed guests that ranged from Frank Lloyd Wright to Helen Keller, from Billy Graham to John and Jacqueline Kennedy. In remote broadcasts, Arlene travelled to many corners of the country. After *Home* was cancelled in 1957, she expressed her hope for more expansive programming like this for women, "I'd like to see more women care— really care about politics, charity, and service work. . . ."[26]

In a confounding way, Arlene also offered viewers a validation of career achievements and what in the 21st century would be praised as an attempt to attain a work/family balance. When her homelife was featured in promotional articles, picturing Arlene enjoying dinner with her husband Martin Gabel or attending to her young son Peter's needs, these were not false portraits.[27] The public emphasis on Arlene's hectic schedule affirmed what career women know all too well in this century—having it all is exhilarating but exhausting. This ongoing feminist predicament had to be glossed over in the 1950s, when *Home*'s publicity tried to cast Arlene as "a homebody."[28]

Even though Arlene never identified herself as a Second Wave feminist, in many ways she adhered to fundamental tenets of women's equality, as Jennifer Bitman's research clarifies. She supported the competitive talent of women in the workplace and equal pay for equal work.[29] She even addressed the safety of birth control pills and laws about abortion.[30]

---

25. Correspondence with Marsha Cassidy, 1996.

26. Eleanor Darnton, "TV's Darling Arlene Francis Says Stage is Her First Love." *The Miami Herald*, Aug. 8, 1957, 30.

27. See Cassidy, 145-146.

28. Bester, 80.

29. Bitman, 152.

30. Bitman, 159.

Arlene's son Peter Gabel recognized that his mother "would never have associated herself with the anger" of Second Wave Feminism."[31] She told the *Miami Herald* in 1957 that social change should be attained "in a sensible, non-violent way."[32] Nonetheless, the personal became political when Arlene's daily WOR radio show was abruptly cancelled in 1983 and she recognized that charm alone could not undo the station's hierarchy of male power.[33] When the term "feminist" even in the 21st century can still connote rebellious bra-burners and strident complainers, Arlene's softer feminism suited both her nature and the times.

***

When I was researching my book *What Women Watched: Daytime Television in the 1950s*, I had the pleasure of screening rare episodes of NBC's *Home* show that featured Arlene as the program's poised and eloquent editor-in-chief. I smiled at her jokes and admired her confident flair. I respected that she knew when to be serious and when to be humorous. For background, I watched old episodes of *What's My Line?* and studied online interviews others had recorded with Arlene later in her life. Before long, I found myself liking Arlene and feeling that I knew her. Her charisma had endured beyond her lifetime.

Another great pleasure was meeting Arlene's son Peter Gabel in California, getting to know the personal side of Arlene through him, and appreciating his commitment to acknowledge the impact his mother had made on broadcasting and the theater. Today I am pleased again to collaborate with Peter, his partner Lisa Jaicks, and their son Sam, as well as with Jennifer Bitman, the author of this biography, to honor the legacy of Arlene Francis and to help record her eminence as a leading lady in broadcast history.

Marsha F. Cassidy<br>September 2022

---

31. Peter Gabel's unpublished interview with W. Gary Wetstein, 2018.
32. Darnton, 30.
33. See Bitman 185.

# Acknowledgments

Firstly, I would like to express my gratitude to Peter Gabel, his partner Lisa Jaicks, and their son Sam Gabel. Their support and cooperation have given this book a personal touch that it could not have had otherwise. Also, a special acknowledgement to Sam for his inspired title: "All Three Channels." Thanks also to my publisher Ben Ohmart and the team at Bear Manor Media for taking a chance on this book, and to Marsha F. Cassidy for agreeing to write the introduction. My deep appreciation to Nadine Gay and Dr. Michael Bader for their willingness to share their experiences and stories of Arlene's final years. To Christopher Salvador and Karen Lee Cohen, I express my gratitude for sharing their fond remembrances of working with Arlene during the 1980s. My thanks also to Matt Davis for his help in piecing together the Kazanjian family tree, to Arlene Herson for her kind permission to utilize quotes from her televised interview with Ms. Francis, and to Jackie Sanders for providing insight into the creation of the first documentary made about Arlene. I am also grateful to W. Gary Wetstein for permitting the use of quotes from his unpublished interview with Peter Gabel, to Neil Feria for providing several photographs from his extensive collection, to Angelina Diana for gifting Peter the cover photo he admired so much, and to Nancy Keller for her time and generosity behind the scenes. Finally, to Arlene Francis and Martin Gabel, I am thankful for the legacy of talent they have left behind for generations to enjoy. Through the memories of their family and loved ones, they will never be forgotten.

# Preface

While several deserving women have been called "The First Lady" of television, Arlene Francis could arguably top the list. She not only pioneered a medium dominated by men, but she singlehandedly attained many firsts throughout her enduring career. Her record of achievements reads like an encyclopedia, and her reputation like a love letter. Nearly two decades after her death, she entered my life in a most unassuming way, prompting an enlightening journey into an extraordinary life. By the time I was born in 1984, Arlene had been a fixture on American television for decades. She had built her career as a stage and radio actress in the late 1920s and 30s, made a name for herself in the world of broadcasting during the 50s, and at the same time, appeared in occasional film roles. Driven by an insatiable affection for work, Arlene also managed to spare twenty-five years as a regular panelist on *What's My Line?* (1950).

The classic game show was the perfect outlet for her exuberant personality, razor-sharp wit, and unreserved warmth. It was through the medium of television that the world would fall in love with her, but not everyone was fortunate enough to witness Arlene Francis's engaging personality in real time. As one belonging to a generation of millennials, I have had to look backward to discover her life and career. The process happened quite inconspicuously, as great things often do. When a local over-the-air station decided to run classic *What's My Line?* (1950). episodes after midnight, I just happened to be watching. That might sound simple enough, unless you also consider the fact that I had recently been gifted a new-used television set—one that was tuned into more than the five channels my old set begrudgingly offered. However, I soon had no use for any channel or any show besides *What's My Line?* (1950). At first, I couldn't figure out why I was becoming so fond of it. The premise was simple. It was lighthearted fun, complete with an old-fashioned charm missing from modern television, but there was something else that drew me in, something apart from the show's intrigue. I soon realized it was Arlene Francis.

Like she had done for decades, Arlene attracted viewers with a unique combination of elegance and approachability. She was the epitome of class and sophistication while at the same time exuding the comforting familiarity of your closest friend, and strikingly, here I was in the year 2019, never having known that this remarkable woman ever existed. It was unfathomable to me, and I yearned to know more about her, to sit across a table and listen intently while she told me all about her life experiences. Since that was impossible, I did the next best thing and read her 1978 memoir. After turning the last page, I felt that Arlene hoped to be recognized for more than just being a loveable game show icon. The theater was her first love, and I think it was important to her that she be remembered as an actress. Principally, it was a love for acting that inspired her and brought her before the public in the first place.

There is no question that the incredible scope of her career on radio, stage, film, and television was awe-inspiring, and it made me a firm believer that every person in the world should know who Arlene Francis was. So, I decided to try my hand at making that happen in the form of this book. I had already written one other biography. It was a satisfying experience, but I had no plans to write another. For me, writing has to have a purpose–it has to mean something deep down in my heart. When I finished reading Arlene's memoir, I knew that she had cemented a legacy and a career worth remembering. In life, she had done it all. Now, I felt compelled to do something for her.

I began conducting research and wrote this biography to help secure Arlene's place in the millennial generation and beyond. With the assistance of her son Peter Gabel, I gained insight into her life and career, interviewing some of Arlene's relatives, former colleagues, and others who played important roles in her personal life. Their recollections have helped create a more intimate portrait of a much-loved woman. This book was written for Arlene's family, and it is my hope that all who read it will become better acquainted with her through its pages. Even though I never had the pleasure of meeting Arlene Francis, I do feel I've gotten to know her, and I hope that after reading this book, you will too.

Jennifer Bitman
January 2022

# Chapter One

"She's one of the greatest human beings ever born"[34]

– John Daly


Arlene Francis made her debut in 1907. She entered the world on October 20th and was met by an audience of adoring relatives. Chief among this familial group were her parents, Aram and Leah Kazanjian. The two came from different ethnic and cultural backgrounds, but the influences that made them distinct, inevitably brought them together. By the time Arlene was born, they had settled in Brookline, Massachusetts, a town in Greater Boston. Early on, there were several indications that the Kazanjian's young daughter was a natural performer. Her inclinations toward the stage surfaced in childhood, and this emerging interest was disconcerting to her father, who held a generally unfavorable view of showbusiness. Arlene's penchant for acting clearly came from her mother's side of the family, and the influence was strong. Albert Davis was her maternal grandfather and one of her earliest sources of encouragement. He had been a Shakespearean actor in England, and his theatrical stories captivated his young granddaughter. At the age of seven, she began reciting poetry, and she performed with gusto, even if her only stage was the center of the family living room.

Arline[35] Francis Kazanjian was born on a Sunday. The front page of *The Boston Globe* that morning boasted fair weather and predicted more of the same in the days ahead. For the Kazanjians of Brookline, the future was ripe with promise. The birth of Aram and Leah's daughter

---

34. *TV Guide.* May 24 (1975).
35. This was the spelling of her name at birth.

was an event that far surpassed any current affairs. Paling in comparison was the record-breaking 475-mile voyage of the Army air balloon that landed in West Virginia that very day from St. Louis, and the small fire that erupted in Boston's Hollis Street Theater during a stage performance of *Salomy Jane* (1907). The triumph and turmoil of urban life in the 1900s were the background noise amidst which all citizens went about their daily business. Unbeknownst to any local residents, a new star had been born in Brookline. Little Arline's conventional upbringing would belie her extraordinary future, but her early foundation was firm. The pride and joy of her family, she grew up in an atmosphere of love and attention, fostering in her a natural flair for performance and a desire for recognition.

Her Armenian father was the head of the household, and she described him as honorable[36] and adorable.[37] "He was also immensely strict–and immensely kind," she said. [38] "He's a smash at being my dad."[39] Thus his journey toward that destiny began long ago. Aram Kazanjian was born in Turkey in 1875, and residential records place him in the Erzincan province.[40] The family was said to have been prosperous until the ravages of the Armenian massacres in the 1800s.[41] His mother was Gatik Ashekian,[42] and his father, Harttoun Kazanjian,[43] came from a line of coppersmiths.[44] Included in the family unit was Varaztad; he was presumably Aram's younger cousin (Arlene referred to him as "Uncle") and would later become a renown reconstructive surgeon.

———————————

36. *Radio TV Mirror* (1955)
37. *Arlene Francis, A Memoir* (1978) by Arlene Francis with Florence Rome p. 14
38. *Radio TV Mirror* (1955)
39. *That Certain Something: The Magic of Charm*, by Arlene Francis. (1960) p. 9
40. *The Historical Dictionary of Armenia,* by Rouben Paul Adalian (2010) and U.S. Passport Applications via Ancestry.com
41. *The Boston Globe* (1905). Bostonian's Picture Wins. Kazanjian's Study of "Modern Madonna" Takes Photographer's Annual Trophy
42. Marriage Records of Massachusetts. 1840-1815. Ancestry.com
43. Ibid.
44. *The Historical Dictionary of Armenia* (2010) by Rouben Paul Adalian

It was Aram who took an interest in the fine arts. In his teens, he attended the Royal Art School of Constantinople for five years[45] and furthered his studies in the art institutes of Paris. This occurred during a time of great unrest in his homeland, and he would later relate his memories of those events to Arlene. "…One night, [my father] dreamed that his family's house in Armenia had been burned to the ground. In the morning, he learned the terrifying truth."[46] Tragically, both of his parents had been killed in the Armenian genocide. Afterward, a 24-year-old Aram and his surviving relative, Varaztad, came to the United States. Unlike the many Armenian immigrants who settled in Watertown, Massachusetts, the two arrived in Worchester, in 1899.[47] Varaztad initially went to work in a wire factory[48] before being accepted to Harvard University.

Aram, however, continued to follow his artistic interests and began working as a portrait photographer. He opened his first studio in Boston and steadily earned the respect of his community. In 1905, he won the prestigious silver Goerz Cup and a prize of $100 for his photograph of a young woman and infant, titled "Modern Madonna." In spite of his success, Aram had not abandoned art. He found a way to incorporate the creative skill into his photography, and was known to paint a bird or a butterfly on the shoulder of his female subjects. One of Aram's early patrons was Leah Davis. She would eventually become his wife, and the mother of Arlene Francis, but back then, Leah was merely curious about the dark, "handsome"[49] and "mysterious"[50] photographer. "My mother and aunt went over to have their pictures taken; and sure enough, Father painted a butterfly on Mother's shoulder."[51] Soon, they were married. This union no doubt brought a renewed sense of joy to Aram. Although

---

45. Ibid.

46. *Arlene Francis: A Memoir* (1978) by Arlene Francis with Florence Rome p. 11

47. U.S. Passport Application for Aram Kazanjian via ancestry.com

48. *Arlene Francis, A Memoir* (1978) by Arlene Francis with Florence Rome p. 12

49. Ibid.

50. Ibid.

51. Ibid.

his past had been scarred by loss, his future looked promising, and his bride had a history all her own.

Leah Ethel Davis was born on April 15, 1886, in New York City.[52] She was described by Arlene as "a glorious blonde with saucer blue eyes and the fragile look of her English heritage."[53] That part of Leah's heritage came from her father, Albert Davis. He had been born in Manchester, Lancashire, England,[54] and after immigrating to the United States in the 1800s, he found work as a clothing manufacturer.[55] In his younger years, he had been an actor, touring the English provinces with a Shakespearean theatre group.[56] Eventually, he made a life for himself in America, and it was there he married Julia Weiner.[57] Together, they raised six children. Two of those children, Alberta and Benjamin,[58] were Albert's offspring from his union with Charlotte Watson,[59] an English singer[60] he likely met while traveling or performing abroad. Following Charlotte's untimely death in the late 1800s, the two children were reared in the Davis household, alongside the offspring born of Julia, which included a son, Joseph, and daughters Jane, Jennie, and Leah.[61] When Leah reached 21 years of age, she became the wife of Aram Kazanjian, and the couple produced their only child, a daughter they named Arline Francis.

Following her birth, the young family lived in Brookline, Massachusetts, for six years. Located in Norfolk County in greater Boston, Brookline began as a town of merchants and shipbuilders.[62]

---

52. United States Federal Census. Ancestry.com & Leah Kazanjian Family Tree provided by Peter Gabel via Matt Davis

53. *Arlene Francis: A Memoir* (1978) by Arlene Francis with Florence Rome p. 8

54. US Passport Applications 1795-1925 for Albert Davis via ancestry.com

55. 1910 United States Federal Census. Ancestry.com

56. *Arlene Francis: A Memoir* (1978) by Arlene Francis with Florence Rome, p. 8

57. Last name provided by Peter Gabel (Author's Note: Census records list the surname: Werner which is the German derivative of the Yiddish Jewish surname Weiner)

58. Matt Davis & The Davis family tree via ancestry.com

59. Ibid.

60. Charlotte's background was provided by Matt Davis

61. Leah Kazanjian's Family Tree provided by Peter Gabel via Matt Davis

62. Proceedings of the Brookline Historical Society at the Annual Meeting January 22, 1908. https://www.brooklinehistoricalsociety..org

Between the years 1875 and 1909, the burgeoning area's population grew from around 900 to over 25,000.[63] During Arlene's early childhood, the enterprising town continued to evolve. In an address to members of the Brookline Historical Society in 1908, its president remarked on the industrious advancements, noting the "modern development and the use of electricity…[seen] daily in the lighting of buildings and streets, in the moving trolley car seen on every hand." [64] Although her memories of living there were scarce, Arlene did recall traveling with her mother on one of the town's transport systems. Often, they would ride together to the florist shop Leah maintained near Symphony Hall. "One of my first memories is getting carsick each weekday morning on the trolley car riding to Boston with my mother."[65]

The number of married women voluntarily entering the workforce reached a high in the early 1900s,[66] and, as part of this growing community, Leah reconciled her domestic duties by bringing her little daughter to work with her. This daily routine was but a snapshot of life in those years. As a young child, Arlene spent a great deal of time with her maternal grandparents. When tired of playing at her mother's floral shop, she would stay with Albert and Julia at their house on nearby Huntington Avenue. She remembered her grandmother wearing "Queen Mary hats littered with flowers."[67] The two bonded during those early years, and Julia encouraged her young granddaughter's personality.

"She was a great listener, recalled Arlene, "laughing at my antics and rocking over my jokes. 'You and I are very close,' she would say."[68] They would venture to the public gardens or the Boston Common, one of the

---

63. Proceedings of the Brookline Historical Society at the Annual Meeting January 26, 1909. https://www.brooklinehistoricalsociety..org

64. Proceedings of the Brookline Historical Society at the Annual Meeting January 26, 1909. https://www.brooklinehistoricalsociety..org

65. *The Boston Globe.* Sept. 28, 1958. Once More, With Feeling. Arlene Francis Still Thrills to Hub Homecoming. By Arlene Francis, p. 94

66. *The Boston Globe.* Oct. 20, 1907. Enter the Wife, p 55

67. *The Boston Globe.* Once More, With Feeling. Sept. 28, 1958. Arlene Francis Still Thrills to Hub Homecoming. By Arlene Francis, p. 94

68. Ibid.

city's oldest parks. Sometimes, Arlene would join her grandparents on vacations, visiting Cape Cod and Martha's Vineyard, and occupying a seaside cottage in Hyannis Port. In this environment, she would let her imagination flourish through art, experimenting with decalcomania, a popular creative process at the time – that of spreading paint on paper and transferring it onto canvas or ceramics. "I fancied myself a magician and went about transferring pictures onto everything in sight."[69]

As a precocious and friendly child, she desired to explore the world around her, which at that time was the streets of Boston. The nearby Ginter Grocery Co. on Washington Street sold cakes of Ivory soap for 5 cents, while the local drugstore had bottles of Lydia Pinkham's Vegetable Compound[70] at the ready for female Bostonians.[71] One day, at the age of four, Arlene wandered from her mother's flower shop, sending Leah into a panic. After half an hour of searching, she found her daughter sitting on the next block, legs dangling over the curb, sharing a sandwich with a kindly street cleaner.[72] Leah doted on her charming young daughter, and Arlene recalled her making special dresses for birthday parties, and putting "enormous ribbon bows" in her hair. Because she had been born close to Halloween time, Leah would decorate with a theme. "She strewed the house with orange and black crepe paper decorations." [73] During one celebration, an incident[74] occurred involving Arlene and one of the guests who had been invited from the neighborhood. "I had shown my affection for her by biting her toe too vigorously." The child's mother was none too pleased, and "hinted that it would be well to keep an eye on me, since cannibalism was taboo, even in our Brookline circles."[75]

---

69. Ibid.

70. Arlene would later appear in a radio commercial advertisement for Lydia Pinkham's Vegetable Compound.

71. *The Boston Globe.* Oct. 20, 1907

72. *The Boston Globe.* Sept. 28, 1958. Once More, With Feeling. Arlene Francis Still Thrills to Hub Homecoming. By Arlene Francis, p. 94

73. Ibid

74. Ibid.

75. Ibid

Imbued with a healthy dose of the theatrical, she rarely missed an opportunity to partake in her favorite pastime – reciting poetry for her adoring grandfather. "[He] would always hear me through, no matter how many times I repeated it."[76] "He was plainly and simply marvelous as far as I was concerned… his white beard, top hat, and large theatrical gestures… made everything he said sound important."[77] The retired Shakespearean actor also recognized his granddaughter's talents, and fueled them with his undivided attention. "He would sit down, rest his hands on the cane in front of him, fix me with his eyes and say, 'All right, Arlene, center stage.'"[78] She would begin with a curtsy, and recite *Two Glasses*, the poem by Ella Wheeler Wilcox.

Later, she would remark on the unusual choice of poetry for a young child. *Two Glasses* tells of a man's struggle to choose between water and wine. Her performance always rendered her grandfather to tears, and his emotional response might have been influenced by a note of poignancy. "Although it wasn't even whispered in my hearing, Grandfather also did a bit of drinking."[79] This was one of the reasons why Arlene's father associated acting with an appetite for loose living. "For my father, wanting to go on the stage was perhaps a trifle better than going to work in a house of ill repute."[80] The only actor Aram knew personally was Albert Davis, and there were already a few strikes against him. "It was common knowledge that he had done a bit of 'walking out' with women who happened not to be my grandmother…and could boast more begats than the Bible."[81] Evidently, his wife Julia was tolerant of his ways, and when he brought Alberta and Ben into the household, "she was as gentle and kind to the children from the wrong side of the sheets as she was to her own."[82]

---

76. Ibid.

77. *Arlene Francis: A Memoir* (1978) by Arlene Francis with Florence Rome. P. 19

78. Ibid.

79. Ibid.

80. *Arlene Francis: A Memoir* (1978) by Arlene Francis with Florence Rome, p. 8

81. *Arlene Francis: A Memoir* (1978) by Arlene Francis with Florence Rome p. 10

82. Ibid AND this account was also supported by Matt Davis via Zoom call January 11, 2021

These children also happened to account for some of Arlene's favorite relatives, among them, her adoring aunt Alberta. The daughter of Charlotte Watson, she had grown into a lovely and talented young woman. Alberta married Herbert Cluxton,[83] a photography apprentice at Aram's studio,[84] and she was described as an exquisite beauty with dark curly hair and violet eyes.[85] "If she took after *her* mother, I can understand grandfather straying from the straight and narrow,"[86] Arlene once remarked. Alberta had most certainly inherited Charlotte's singing talents, and easily recognized a young Arlene's flair for the theatrical. She enthusiastically provided her niece with ample encouragement, even trying to convince Aram to let his daughter receive professional training. But the answer was no. Her solution to this opposition was to become Arlene's acting coach, and personally provide her with "surreptitious lessons"[87] in poise and voice projection.

These discreet lessons only increased Arlene's aspirations. Her early desire to perform had to have been pure influence and heredity, as she never so much as attended a show when living in Brookline, but the fantasy world of which she dreamed, very-much existed. "I do know that there were seven or eight theaters in Boston in my time [there], she recalled, "at least three vaudeville houses."[88] The city's theatre district was occupied by establishments like B.F. Keith's, located across the street from the Boston Common. The Park Theater on Washington Street showed popular motion pictures such as *Caprice* (1913), starring Mary Pickford,[89] and George M. Cohan's *Hello Broadway* (1915) played to packed houses at The Colonial in the spring of 1915.[90] At that time, an eight-year-old

---

83. Massachusetts marriage records 1840-1915. Date of marriage Dec. 25, 1915

84. Bulletin of Photography. Volume 18. Edited by Frank V Chambers and John Bartlett. January 5 to June 28, 1916.

85. Ibid

86. *Arlene Francis: A Memoir* (1978) by Arlene Francis with Florence Rome. P 10

87. Ibid

88. *The Boston Globe.* Sept. 28, 1958. Once More, With Feeling. Arlene Francis Still Thrills to Hub Homecoming. By Arlene Francis, p. 94

89. *The Boston Globe.* May 2, 1915. Attractions at the Theaters.

90. Ibid

Arlene had not yet experienced the excitement of live entertainment. "Theater-going was an excess I didn't engage in until we moved to New York."[91]

About five years later, the family took up residence at 1324 St. Nicholas Avenue in the Washington Heights neighborhood of Manhattan. It was around this time that Aram expanded his photography business, specializing in children's portraits and opening a studio in the Ehrich Galleries Building at 707 Fifth Avenue.[92] His services were advertised in many periodicals, such as *Vogue* and the *New York Times*, with a notice that read, "KAZANJIAN STUDIOS: Art Photography at your home or our studio." The business became well known for capturing portraits of juveniles as well as notable personalities, and it was also a training ground for aspirants such as Dorothea Lange. The future photographer, known for capturing the faces of the depression era, was one of Aram's early apprentices.[93] In addition to hours spent in the studio, Mr. Kazanjian kept up his interest in painting, and continued to fill canvases with bucolic nature scenes. Many of them were displayed around the Kazanjian home. Arlene recalled the walls being "completely covered by his paintings."[94] "My recollections of childhood are all tied up with trying to find a light switch."[95] In fact, Aram hoped his daughter might also become an artist, and during her school years, he sent her to the *Art Students League of New York*.[96] However, Arlene was more interested in the art of performing.

---

91. *The Boston Globe.* Sept. 28, 1958. Once More, With Feeling. Arlene Francis Still Thrills to Hub Homecoming. By Arlene Francis. P. 94

92. *R.L. Polk's and Co. Trow New York Copartnership and Cooperation Directory, Boroughs of Manhattan and Bronx.* 1919. Trow Directory, Printing and Bookbinding Company. AND *Rider's New York City and Vicinity Including Newark, Yonkers and Jersey City. A Guide Book for Travelers.* 16 Maps and 18 plans. 1918. Henry and Holt Company. [e google books] AND The New York Times advertisement. Dec 17, 1920.

93. *Dorthea Lange: A Photographer's Life.* (2000). By Milton Meltzer. Syracuse University Press. [google e-book]

94. *Arlene Francis: A Memoir* (1978). By Arlene Francis with Florence Rome, p. 12

95. Ibid.

96. Verso of image: Celebrity Art Reproduction. General Electric Company

When she was about 12 years old, her father discovered her sitting at the picture window in their apartment, playing the ukulele. "That might not sound like such a serious offense."[97] After all, a performer *does* need an audience, but that was precisely what worried her father. "He had a dark suspicion (absolutely correct as it turned out) that his only daughter had an unseemly, wild desire to, heaven forbid, go on the stage."[98] Aram's reaction to this interest was to send Arlene to Mount St. Vincent, a Catholic convent and boarding school. It was located in the Bronx's Riverdale neighborhood, and the Kazanjians moved into a large house nearby. Adjusting to life at the school was difficult at first. Not only was she lonely, but she also felt quite out-of-place. To begin with, she was not Catholic, nor was she reared in the traditions of any particular religion. "Daddy belonged to the Greek Orthodox Church . . . ." Her mother had Episcopalian ties, and she "had gone to a Presbyterian Sunday School, but only because it was convenient."[99] Added to this new experience was the fact that the convent would account for her first memorable school years. "While I don't recall going to any school in Boston, it is possible that I attended a nursery school. In the back of my mind there's a faint recollection of coming home one afternoon and telling mother that the school was locked, and that some men were throwing coal into the cellar."[100]

Getting used to Mount St. Vincent would take some time. "I couldn't bear being different,"[101] she recalled. "I'm sure all the other children and certainly the sisters were perfectly nice to me. But I was an outsider."[102] These feelings set Arlene on a mission to become likeable and obedient.

---

97. *Arlene Francis: A Memoir* (1978) By Arlene Francis with Florence Rome p. 9
98. Ibid.
99. *Arlene Francis: A Memoir* (1978) By Arlene Francis with Florence Rome p. 15
NOTE: "My grandmother purported to be Protestant or Episcopalian, but we discovered in 1993 the reality that she was Jewish on her mother's side." Email communication with Peter Gabel. March 26, 2020.
100. *The Boston Globe.* Sept. 28, 1958Once More, With Feeling. Arlene Francis Still Thrills to Hub Homecoming. By Arlene Francis, p. 94
101. Ibid.
102. *That Certain Something: The Magic of Charm,* by Arlene Francis (1960). P. 23

She would lie awake at night, trying to figure out clever ways to fit in. She also made an effort to become an exemplary non-Catholic student. ". . . saying my prayers, saying my rosary, confessing to sins I hadn't even committed . . . there was no way I was going to let a nun humph down her nose and say: That's what we get for letting a protestant in the place!"[103]

Later, Arlene's son, Peter, would offer some insight into this early period of adjustment. "I think mom's discomfort and feeling different likely was more connected to her being half Armenian."[104] Her ethnic features no doubt set her apart from the rest of the girls. She described her "dark eyes, dark hair, olive complexion . . . ."[105] It's just lucky for me that I never grew a mustache because otherwise I'm a dead ringer for Daddy."[106] To Arlene, her mother's fair skin and golden hair were ideal. In addition to her self-consciousness, she was also concerned with making friends. "I didn't just want people to like me—I was desperate for them to like me."[107] All of this sounds a bit far-fetched now, considering that Arlene Francis was not only one of the most elegant, attractive, and fashionable women of her time, but she was also one of the most likeable.

As an awkward adolescent, however, she was determined to win over her peers. Her playful and fun personality began to surface, and she had no trouble attracting friends. Included among them were a few admirers from the Horace Mann School for boys. One such suitor was Ashley De Wolfe. He was Arlene's first crush, and she referred to him "as the awakening of love's sweet young dream."[108] After asking permission from the Kazanjians, Ashley took a 16-year-old Arlene on her first date. They had lunch at the *Athletic Club* in New York City, accompanied by the De Wolfes. Afterward, the two took a walk in the park, and she rejected

---

103. *Arlene Francis: A Memoir* (1978). By Arlene Francis with Florence Rome. P. 15
104. Email correspondence with Peter Gabel. March 26, 2020
105. *Arlene Francis: A Memoir* (1978). By Arlene Francis with Florence Rome. P. 15
106. Ibid.
107. *That Certain Something: The Magic of Charm*, by Arlene Francis. 1960
108. *Arlene Francis: A Memoir* (1978) by Arlene Francis with Florence Rome. P. 16

his attempt to kiss her by saying: "Is this how I must pay for a lovely afternoon?"[109]

Her conservative attitude might have been influenced by her protective upbringing. Even a few years later, when asked to dances, her mother came along to chaperone. She recalled these experiences with humor and hindsight. "I was invited to West Point to a dance and, hold your breath, my *mother* came with me."[110] Looking back, she sympathized with her likely disappointed beau. "It couldn't have been much fun for him to walk a girl and her mother past kissing rock."[111] Despite her initial concerns, Arlene became a popular student at Mount St. Vincent. She also took part in the school's drama club.

The very place that her father thought would dissuade her from the stage, actually brought her closer to it. She performed as Petruchio in the graduation production of *The Taming of the Shrew* (1590). Her most convincing scene was one where she had to lift an actor in heavy costume, and carry her off the stage, "while she kicked and pummeled me . . . with a great deal of feeling . . . ."[112] However, it was all worth it for the compliment she received from one of the sisters. After the play, the nun and theatrical teacher had these words of advice for Mr. Kazanjian: "I don't think there is any point in denying your daughter what she wants most in the world."[113]

Her father wasn't convinced, and there would be no acting in her immediate future. Instead, after graduating from Mount St. Vincent, Arlene was enrolled in Finch's Finishing School. The building was located in the upscale neighborhood of Manhattan. An all-girl institution, women's activist Jessica Finch Cosgrave founded it in 1900.[114] It became a baccalaureate college in the 50s and eventually closed in 1976. However, when Arlene was a student, Finch was still considered a finishing school.

---

109. *Arlene Francis: A Memoir* (1978) by Arlene Francis with Florence Rome. P. 17
110. Ibid.
111. Ibid.
112. *Arlene Francis: A Memoir* (1978) by Arlene Francis with Florence Rome. P. 16
113. Ibid.
114. *The New York Times.* https://www.newyorktimes.com

Along with a formal education, it likely provided Arlene with a few lessons to file away for future theatrical use. Many prestigious schools at that time taught the Mid-Atlantic accent, a combination of American and British English, which was prominent among early stage and film actors.

During her time at Finch, she also explored an interest in writing poetry. "I contributed to the magazines at the colleges where I had beaux."[115] She adopted the pen name Spark Plug, and her poems appeared in periodicals like *The Cornell Window* and *The Columbia Jester*. Despite her popularity, Arlene didn't feel like one of Finch's socialite students. "The other girls already knew how to pour tea,"[116] she explained. Nevertheless, her social life continued to flourish, and she was asked to a number of gatherings and dances. One event, in particular, taught her a valuable lesson in being herself. She was invited to a party on Park Avenue, and was set on making a good impression. The idea was that she would take on the assumed identity of "Countess Kazanjian."[117] She later humorously recounted her arrival in "a little black hat with a nose veil and a violet dress. I must have been a mess!"[118]

One young man at the party saw through the disguise, but was kind enough not to reveal her to the rest of the guests. The experience taught her about the importance of authenticity. Part of being authentic meant not giving up on her dream of becoming an actress. It "never left me."[119] From reciting poetry for her grandfather to impressing the nuns in her graduation play, Arlene had consistently proven that she was certain about her desire to pursue an acting career. Eventually, her time at Finch's Finishing School came to an end. According to her own account, she emerged "partially finished,"[120] but she had fulfilled her obligations. Arlene was now a young woman of twenty, and it was time to focus on the future.

---

115. *Arlene Francis: A Memoir* (1978). By Arlene Francis with Florence Rome P. 18
116. *The American Magazine*. October (1954)
117. Ibid
118. Ibid
119. *Arlene Francis: A Memoir* (1978). By Arlene Francis with Florence Rome. P. 18
120. *Arlene Francis: A Memoir* (1978). By Arlene Francis with Florence Rome P. 20

# Chapter Two

"I started out with one goal: I wanted to be a serious actress"[121]
– Arlene Francis

Broadway welcomed Arlene Francis for the first time in the late 1920s, but her journey toward the stage did not come without opposition. After graduating from the convent of Mount St. Vincent, she made a decision to become a professional actress. Her father was resistant to her career choice, and as a young adult on the brink of independence, she was still sensitive toward his objections. However, her determination to act was persistent. Eager to make her mark, she attended drama school and began taking roles anywhere she could: on radio, in summer stock theatre, and even in a motion picture. New success also brought change. When her name was misspelled on an early radio contract, she decided it was lucky. As a result, Arline, with an I, officially became Arlene, with an E. During this evolving period, she would strive to achieve career goals and attain fulfillment in her personal relationships. Becoming an actress and being true to herself were parallel endeavors for Arlene early on. In 1927, her ultimate success on the stage was still elusive, although she certainly didn't lack ambition.

"I went from theater to theater, looking for a smiling face," she told the *Milwaukee Journal.* This enthusiastic approach to obtaining roles was backed by an education in the dramatic arts. Innately determined, she convinced her father to send her to the newly formed *Theatre Guild School.*[122] Her mother was supportive of the idea and declared that, at the

---

121. Arlene Francis Obituary. May (2001).
122. *The Milwaukee Journal,* 1940.

very least, the theatrical institution would provide an education in the social graces.[123] It was also the perfect complement to her acting goals. The curriculum was focused on the art of stage performance, and she received coaching[124] from director Rouben Mamoulian.[125]

During her time at The Theatre Guild, she was among a group of students selected to illustrate roles in a series called *The Daughters of Midas*.[126] The story, written by Anne Austin, was a dramatic serial published in newspapers. Arlene portrayed the leading lady, and photographs of her and the rest of the student-character cast, accompanied the story in print. As a young theatre pupil, she got the chance to exercise her acting skills. Later, she would offer some sage advice about what should be taught in drama schools. She asserted that young actors would benefit from learning how to handle the financial part of the profession. "That's what most thespians neglect, and yet it's the thing you deal with all your life—how to pay for the bacon and eggs."[127] Arlene spent one year studying at the Theatre Guild, and the school closed its doors after just three years.[128] Nonetheless, she had been refined by professional training.

Imbued with new confidence, her ambitions increased, paving the way for her first Broadway role. In December of 1927, the Theatre Guild's former director, Hamilton MacFadden, established a production firm, and Arlene landed a small role in the company's first play, *La Gringa* (1928). In a move contrary to his usual attitude toward the performing arts, her father, Aram, joined the production firm as one of six policy directors.[129] His motivations were perhaps a means of feeling more secure about his daughter's involvement in the play. When *La Gringa* (1928) opened at the Little Theatre on February 1, Arlene portrayed the part of

---

123. Ibid.
124. Verso of image [advertising Hour of Charm] circa 1935
125. *On My Way: The Untold Story of Rouben Mamoulian* (2013). by Joseph Horowitz.
126. *The Athens Messenger*, March 18, 1927
127. *Radio TV Mirror* (1955)
128. *One Naked Individual: My Fifty Years in the Theatre* (1977). By Cheryl Crawford.
129. *Brooklyn Life and Activities of Long Island Society* (Brooklyn, New York) Saturday, Dec. 31, 1927

a nun, Sister Felicidad, alongside Claudette Colbert. The storyline told of young Carlotta, played by Colbert, who is abducted from a convent in Mexico and forced into a phony marriage to a sea captain. While the play's religious setting was familiar territory for the convent-bred Arlene, she had come a long way from Mount St. Vincent. Now, instead of being an aspiring actress living in a convent, she was performing in a play set in a convent – quite the role reversal! The production ran for 13 performances, and first reviews praised Claudette Colbert and highlighted the efforts of few other players. The rest of the cast was called "good enough."[130] Perhaps Aram, too, was satisfied, maybe even hopeful that the experience had gotten acting out of his daughter's system. But Arlene's first taste of Broadway left her wanting more.

Soon, she began seeking other roles, but "When my father found out about it, he sent me to Europe."[131] In the summer of 1928, she and her mother, Leah, set sail for France.[132] They visited Dijon, a city known for its vineyards and mustard. While there, the closest they came to live theatre was attending a local circus. An article[133] later told of a memorable incident that occurred during their visit. Amidst the merriment of the Dijon circus, a lion escaped from its cage and caused a frenzy among the audience, especially the young children. While the animal was being contained, Arlene gathered together the startled youngsters and soothed them by singing a Chinese song. It was a tune she had learned in her youth, from a governess who had traveled the countries of Asia.[134] This unexpected performance demonstrated her good nature as well as her ability to entertain. A newspaper referencing the story mused: "If Arlene could quiet children faced by an uncaged lion, she ought to have an even chance with the theatrical critics."[135]

---

130. Daily News (New York). La Gringa is La Buncombe. Old Day Melodrama Nearly Saved by Claudette Colbert. Feb. 3, 1928
131. *The Milwaukee Journal* (1940)
132. New York Passenger and Crews Lists July 10, 1928. Ancestry.com
133. *The Jackson Sun.* (Jackson, Tennessee) Dec. 8, 1946. Arlene Francis, Wednesday Night Feminine Sleuth. P. 28
134. Ibid
135. Ibid

Even so, her pursuit of showbusiness was briefly upstaged by a new prospect. While in Europe, she and her mother had purchased inventory for a new gift shop: *The Studios D'Arlene*. In an effort to re-direct his daughter's career path, Aram opened the storefront on Madison Avenue. It was combined with an upstairs studio in which to conduct his photography business. This new arrangement suited her parents well, but Arlene was not content to work behind a counter. "The whole idea was to keep me off the streets until I could find a nice rich feller and get married."[136] Despite this intent, Arlene continued to seek out the stage. She recalled sitting in casting offices "unbeknownst to my father"[137] and waiting to be called upon. As a result, she landed a few small roles.

In January of 1929, she accepted a series of brief walk-ons in the play *Street Scene*, and the following summer, she appeared in tryouts of *A Very Great Man* (1929). The production, co-written by John Houseman and directed by Richard Whorf, cast Arlene in the role of a secretary. Houseman recalled his first impressions of the young actress, describing her as a "vivacious beauty."[138] However, the awkwardness she had felt during adolescence was reflected in the vanity mirror of show business, and she attempted to correct her own perceived imperfections, such as a sizeable gap in her front teeth. A removable device called a Jackson Brace made the necessary adjustments, and this boost in her morale couldn't have come at a better time.

In the fall of 1931, she and her mother vacationed in Hollywood, California. The Golden Age of the movies was in full swing, and the exciting atmosphere no doubt intensified her enthusiastic yearnings. Leah was not entirely opposed to indulging her daughter's early acting ambitions, and a meeting with film executive David Selznick was arranged through a friend. Arlene was hopeful that he might find a place for her in the movies. Nervous on the day of the meeting, she not only worried about being rejected for a part, but her feelings of self-consciousness began to rise. After removing the corrective brace from her teeth just

---

136. *Arlene Francis: A Memoir* (1978). By Arlene Francis with Florence Rome. P. 20
137. Interview with Arlene Herson. 1987. The Arlene Herson Show DVD
138. *Run-Through: A Memoir* (1972). By John Houseman. P.93

before entering Mr. Selznick's office, she was met by a receptionist and told to wait. As time dragged by, she became increasingly anxious, and began to imagine that her teeth were slowly moving back out of place. She recalled the excruciating scene: "I am in a state of panic. My teeth have started making the return trip."[139] Now, while trying to keep her "upper lip immobile,"[140] Arlene urgently pleaded with the receptionist to expedite her meeting with Selznick. "She must have seen the agony in my eyes . . . maybe she thought he was the father of my unborn child or something."[141] In either case, Arlene's anxious appeal landed her face-to-face with the studio executive.

After a brief appraisal, he agreed to place her in a small role. Her name began appearing in local publicity columns, and at least one news report predicted she would appear in Fox's *The Yellow Ticket* (1931).[142] But it was the *Universal Pictures* horror film, *Murders in the Rue Morgue* (1932), in which she made her film debut. The pre-code movie was based upon a short story by Edgar Allan Poe and starred Bela Lugosi as a mad scientist who conducts fiendish experiments. Arlene was cast as a prostitute and one of Lugosi's female preys. The part originally called for her body to float along the Seine River after a death scene. First, she had to master the art of floating. After practicing in a friend's freezing cold swimming pool (while wearing a borrowed overcoat to keep warm),[143] she was later informed that the floating scene would be cut, but alas, she was still featured in the movie, and received billing as a street woman.

During her time on the West Coast, she did more than just appear in a film. Arlene took part in a historical event in the field of aviation, and her picture was published in a Santa Cruz newspaper. She was asked to help publicize a *Varney* airplane flight,[144] and posed alongside Governor James Rolph Jr., his secretary, Betty Gerke, and a man dressed

---

139. *Arlene Francis: A Memoir* (1978). By Arlene Francis with Florence Rome. P. 19
140. Ibid.
141. Ibid
142. *The San Francisco Examiner*. July 7, 1931
143. *The Milwaukee Journal* (1940)
144. *Santa Cruz Evening News*, October, 1931

in costume as Father Time. They gathered to promote the takeoff of the first *Varney* plane on its one hour and fifty-eight-minute flight between San Francisco and Los Angeles. This marked a milestone for airplane travel in 1931. It also marked Arlene's first publicity gig. She was identified in the news caption as *Arlene Francis: New York stage actress*. That title was further solidified by her role in the Pulitzer Prize-winning play *Alison's House* (1931) at the Beverly Hills Community Playhouse. The production, which premiered on December 12, was the first to take place in the newly built theater[145] and gave Arlene a chance to appear on a Los Angeles stage. She had visited California in hopes of furthering her career as an actress, and no one could argue against her recent success.

In February, *Murders in the Rue Morgue* (1932) was shown at Lowe's State Theater in New York. An image of Arlene, in character, was used on the film's poster display. She and her mother were still vacationing in Hollywood at the time, and the film's release came as a complete shock to her father. Aram had known nothing of his daughter's first venture into motion pictures. "I suppose it was a bit sneaky, considering how father felt about acting,"[146] Arlene later recalled. He immediately sent a telegram ordering her to return home. At nearly 25 years old, she now had a film role to her credit, but the stage was where she truly longed to be, and unfortunately, Aram would have none of it. At this point in her life, Arlene might have considered blatantly disregarding her father's viewpoints and asserting more freedom in her decisions, but back then, "nice girls didn't move from the protection of their parents' roofs," she explained, "especially when those parents were as uncompromisingly old-fashioned as mine."[147]

Arlene also believed she understood the root of her father's reasoning. "You must know what kind of a man my father is. He came here from Armenia, where most of his family had been killed in the Turkish

---

145. *The Los Angeles Evening Post-Record*. Dec. 12, 1931. Alison's House Well Done. By Sid Hughes.
146. *Arlene Francis: A Memoir* (1978). By Arlene Francis with Florence Rome. P. 18
147. *Arlene Francis: A Memoir* (1978.) By Arlene Francis with Florence Rome P. 69

massacres. I think this intensified his desire to protect me from anything and everything."[148] Her father's opposition to her acting ambitions was only heightened by her appearance in a Hollywood horror film, and soon, Arlene was back to work at the gift shop. "I hated every moment of it,"[149] she admitted. Tending to the shop left her with limited time to pursue the theatre, and when her beloved grandfather, Albert Davis, passed away, her acting dreams almost died along with him. The loss of her grandfather brought "immeasurable sadness."[150] Having been an actor himself, he had always been a great source of inspiration and encouragement for her. Now, "He was no longer alive to talk to about my hopes and dreams."[151]

Anyone who knew Arlene knew that her determination could not be permanently stifled. A radio-actor friend of hers (disguised as a gift shop customer) approached her about an opening for an actress on a WOR[152] radio program called *King Arthur's Round Table* (circa 1933). The job required her to do a variety of accents and vocal impressions, including animal sounds. "I woofed and meowed on the spot,"[153] and she got the job. She also discussed the matter with her father. To her delight, he was accepting and deemed radio to be a respectable medium. With her father's approval, she excitedly made her radio debut. She recalled trying to steady her nerves before going on air. "I closed my eyes and breathed deeply, and a wonderful thing happened. A picture of my grandfather . . . giving me his undivided attention flashed through my mind. . .and suddenly I was serenely sure of myself."[154]

She was also a natural. Her speaking voice, with its beautiful depth and delicately cultivated inflections, had the ability to transform into the laughter of a child, the quacking of a duck, or even the grumblings of

---

148. *Radio TV Mirror* (1955)
149. Ibid.
150. Ibid.
151. Ibid.
152. Arlene would later become a major radio personality on WOR, hosting the Arlene Francis Show from 1960-1984.
153. *Arlene Francis: A Memoir* (1978). By Arlene Francis with Florence Rome P. 22
154. Ibid.

an elderly man![155] The satisfying simplicity of the work only magnified Arlene's certainty that she was meant to be an actress. Even years later, she would declare her radio debut to be a thrill unmatched by any accolade she had received since. Indeed, a note of inner realization had occurred on *King Arthur's Round Table* (circa 1933). ". . . Hardly a man is now alive who remembers it," she noted, "But I knew way down in my gut that as silly and unimportant as this show might be, it was the beginning of the only career in the world which held any interest for me."[156]

While Arlene kept working behind the microphone, her mother began helping out at the gift shop counter. However, the business could not stand against the economics of the Great Depression and eventually closed in the early 1930s. The failure of the shop left Arlene with mixed feelings. "I felt sorry, of course, that my father had lost a great deal of money. But I also felt free. At last, I had a chance to do what I always wanted to do."[157] Her time spent working there was not in vain, however. The experience taught her some valuable lessons for living. "Running that gift shop, I learned how to keep books, and I still do them myself, she later told *Radio TV Mirror*. I also learned there are 100 cents in every dollar and they all need to be earned."[158]

Her first taste of radio success led to more opportunities. Soon, she was making appearances in popular serials such as *March of Time* (1931). The CBS show featured dramatizations of current news stories, and *American School of the Air* (1930),[159] an entertaining and educational radio program, brought together teachers and radio actors. Its format offered 30-minute lessons in history, music, and science to school-aged children. The evolving world of radio in the early 30s also provided Arlene with an education in production. She recalled the actors huddled around microphones, taking hand-signal cues from the director.[160]

---

155. Interview with Arlene Herson. 1987. The Arlene Herson Show DVD

156. *Arlene Francis: A Memoir* (1978). By Arlene Francis with Florence Rome P. 22

157. Radio Television Mirror (1955)

158. Ibid.

159. Radio Mirror (1935}

160. *Arlene Francis: A Memoir* (1978). By Arlene Francis with Florence Rome P. 27

Many of the radio shows featured sound effects and the presence of a live orchestra.

This environment likely facilitated her meeting with composer Johnny Green, for it was around this time that the two began dating. The popular musician and songwriter had already made a name for himself, and his signature song, "Body and Soul," was on its way to becoming a jazz standard. Arlene recalled the talented gentleman as "madly attractive"[161] and described their relationship as "serious."[162] A native New Yorker,[163] he had attended the Horace Mann School for boys, and was accepted to Harvard University at the age of 15, where he established an orchestra.[164] After graduation, he began pursuing a career in music against the wishes of his father.[165]

He and Arlene had common ground in this respect. Both were working in careers driven by their own desires, and their personalities were also similar. Johnny Green was noted for having "an exuberant sense of humor"[166] and "magnetic charm."[167] When Arlene first met the young performer, he was working in a variety of capacities, among them composing scores for motion pictures. He would later go on to win multiple Academy Awards for his contributions to musicals, including *Westside Story* (1957) and *Oliver!* (1968).[168] In the early 30s, he was occupied with conducting a band at the St. Regis Hotel and would arrange a special table for his sweetheart in the audience. "He'd send loving looks in my direction as I waited for him to join me between sets or take me to supper when his night's stint was over."[169] The public began to notice their romance, and the two were mentioned as an item in the

---

161. *Arlene Francis: A Memoir* (1978). By Arlene Francis with Florence Rome P. 35
162. Ibid.
163. *Harvard Magazine* (2010). John Waldo Green: The Brief Life of a Complicated Musician. Sol Hurwitz.
164. Ibid.
165. Ibid.
166. Ibid.
167. Ibid.
168. Ibid.
169. *Arlene Francis: A Memoir* (1978). By Arlene Francis with Florence Rome P. 35

"Social Whirl" section of *Radio TV Mirror*: "Johnny Green is going places with Arlene Francis." She compared the events and ambiance of the time to scenes from a classic movie. "I loved every minute of it"[170]

She was also enamored with Broadway. While performing on radio, she continued to search for stage roles, and she landed a few of them, such as *I Loved You on Wednesday* (1935)[171] and a regional starring role in the Anne Rowe comedy *Bridges to Cross* (1935).[172] Each role was preparation for the next, and in the spring, she was an understudy for her friend Claire Trevor in *The Party's Over* (1933). Much of Arlene's participation in the play consisted of sitting in the Vanderbilt Theater watching rehearsals and "Praying that Claire would get a minor ailment so that I could go on and get discovered."[173] From her position in the playhouse, Arlene began noticing the presence of a "terribly attractive"[174] man. He wasn't an actor, and she became curious about him. She soon found out that he was Neil Agnew, an executive of *Paramount Pictures*. The studio had a stake in the play, and he was sent to observe the production.

Neil saw Arlene on stage at least once during a rehearsal. "He told me he liked my performance, and thought I ought to be playing the lead."[175] The two got better acquainted at a party for the cast and began spending more time together.[176] Dates with Neil were different than she was used to: fancy restaurants, gifts, and flowers. Neil was charming, and Arlene enjoyed his company immensely. "He was witty and cozy, and I loved being with him,"[177] she recalled. He was also fifteen years older than she was, but Arlene decided that the difference was "not exactly an insurmountable barrier."[178] If there was a blockade to their

---

170. Ibid.

171. *The Item of Milburn and Short Hills* (Milburn, New Jersey), Sept, 15, 1935. "Bridges to Cross" Next attraction at Lyric.

172. Ibid

173. *Arlene Francis: A Memoir* (1978). By Arlene Francis with Florence Rome P. 34

174. Ibid

175. *The Milwaukee Journal* (1940)

176. *Cosmopolitan Magazine* (1962)

177. *Arlene Francis: A Memoir* (1978). By Arlene Francis with Florence Rome P. 35

178. Ibid

relationship, it was Johnny Green. Arlene had told him about Neil, and he was considerably upset, but "Johnny and I mutually agreed that we weren't made for each other,"[179] and parted on friendly terms.

At this point in Arlene's life, work was a central focus. Radio continued to take notice of her talents, and she made several appearances on serials such as *Roadways to Romance* (1933) and *The Columbia Dramatic Guild* (1933).[180] The auditory medium not only gave her the opportunity to act, but it continued to provide a platform on which to showcase her vocal impressions. This unique ability was something Arlene fostered early on. Believing that versatility was an asset, she devised a system for practice. "I used to go to see almost every foreign actress performing in New York. Then I'd go home and read Shakespeare with all kinds of different accents."[181] Her efforts paid off. In 1934, *Radio Land* Magazine listed some of her most notable celebrity impressions, ranging from Lupe Velez to Jean Harlow. She also took on a Bette Davis role in the program *45 Minutes in Hollywood* (1934). Starring in the show's adaptation of *Of Human Bondage* (1934), it was during this performance that she began to refine her acting technique. For her most dramatic part, she asked for phone books to tear apart in order to work up the breathless emotion needed for the scene.[182] Arlene had always known what she wanted in a career, and she was steadily proving her ability to achieve it effectively.

By the summer of 1935, she was a regular fixture in radio listings, and it was around this time that a Canadian-born performer, also named Arlene Francis, began appearing on the New York broadcast of the program *Al Pearce's Troupe* (1928). Confusion quickly began to arise among the radio-listening public, resulting in the often-mistaken identity of both actresses. To remedy the situation, it was deemed necessary for one of the women to change their professional last name. According to news reports, the decision was made by drawing straws. As a result, the

---

179. Ibid
180. *Radio Mirror* (1935)
181. *The Pocono Record.* June 13, 1962. P 21
182. *Arlene Francis: A Memoir* (1978). By Arlene Francis with Florence Rome P 38-39

Canadian actress became known thereafter as Arlene Harris,[183] and the now one-of-a-kind Miss Francis happily accepted her next role.

Further appearances on shows like *Cavalcade of America* (1934), a CBS anthology series dramatizing historical events, brought her even more popularity. The program featured star players such as Agnes Moorehead and Orson Welles and led to performances alongside even more radio luminaries. In addition to appearing in soap operas like *Pepper Young's Family* (1934), she was added to the supporting cast of the *Beatrice Lillie* show (1935), where she took part in comedic segments called *Aunty Beasop's Fables* (1935).[184] Soon, she was working in five shows a week and running "from one studio to another . . . changing my accent en route."[185] She reveled in the fun and busyness of those early radio experiences, and described it as "the kind of fun when you're all in something together . . . it gave us a sense of camaraderie."[186]

To her further delight, Arlene's parents were also happy about her success over the airwaves, especially her mother, whom she called "my secret ally in my desire to be an actress."[187] Leah was a very proper woman,[188] "a lady down to her fingertips,"[189] Arlene remarked. The newfound ease both of her parents had with her career was due to the squeaky-clean nature of radio at the time. "It was clearly designed for family listening,"[190] but the excitement of working on radio only partially satisfied Arlene's desire to act, and she was constantly on the lookout for stage roles. "What I didn't mention to my parents was that I would have given up Pepper Young and his whole family for a decent role in a good show on Broadway."[191]

---

183. The Vancouver News Herald. (Vancouver British Columbia Canada) June, 28, 1935. Daily Dial Radio highlights for Today. By, Jack Scott.
184. Broadcast Weekly, 1935
185. *Arlene Francis A Memoir* (1978). By Arlene Francis with Florence Rome. P. 26
186. *Arlene Francis A Memoir* (1978). By Arlene Francis with Florence Rome. P. 27
187. Ibid.
188. Email communication with Peter Gabel. March, 26, 2020
189. Arlene Francis A Memoir, 1978. P. 27
190. Arlene Francis A Memoir, 1978. P. 25
191. *Arlene Francis: A Memoir* (1978). By Arlene Francis with Florence Rome. P. 25

In the meantime, she was asked to be the mistress of ceremonies for *Hour of Charm* (1935).[192] She joined the music-themed radio program in August. It had been originally hosted by Rosaline Greene, and it featured a chorus and an all-girl orchestra led by Phil Spitalny. Interestingly, *Hour of Charm* (1935) only provided 30-minute allotments of entertainment, but this new assignment proved that Arlene was on her way to becoming one of the most recognizable voices on the dial. Not only was she the first woman to announce the name of a network during a station break,[193] but her energy and attractive delivery destined her to be chosen as radio's "oomph girl."[194] In fact, listeners began expressing their admiration for her in letters to popular magazines. One such listener, Mrs. Hazel Kirk Beer, of Vineland, New Jersey, wrote to *Radio Television Mirror* Magazine: "Arlene Francis is just a name to me, but her voice tells me that she is a warm-hearted, fun-loving girl."

She was also greatly admired off the air. Her relationship with Neil Agnew was developing steadily, and he had proposed marriage to her. "He was devoted to me"[195] she recalled. And Arlene adored him. The adjectives she chose to describe Neil included "marvelous," "considerate," and "divine."[196] She accepted his proposal, but there was a quiet note of hesitancy on her part. "I had misgivings, but they were so terribly vague."[197] There was nothing about Neil she didn't like, but at the same time, she couldn't help but feel that something was missing in the relationship. Added to this flux of emotions was the fact that her parents were extremely fond of their daughter's fiancé. He would make a reliable provider and protector. Neil had "all the qualities my parents had prayed for in a son-in-law . . . He was the man of *their* dreams."[198]

On November 28, 1935, Arlene and Neil Agnew became husband and wife. In attendance were Arlene's parents and an officiating judge.

192. *Radio News* (1935)
193. Arlene Francis. News Clipping. Circa 1935
194. *The Yellow Jacket Newspaper*. December 7, 1939. The portal to Texas History.
195. Arlene Francis A Memoir (1978). By Arlene Francis with Florence Rome. P. 36
196. Ibid
197. *Arlene Francis: A Memoir* (1978). By Arlene Francis with Florence Rome P. 35
198. Ibid.

The ceremony brimmed with promise, but for the bride, there was also doubt. "I knew I was making a mistake even while the ceremony was in progress." However, there she was, in the presence of her mother, father and husband-to-be. They were all expecting a joyous scene, and how could she interrupt it. "What do you do?" she asked herself, "Tap the judge on the arm and say 'Hold the phone please. I've just had a blinding flash of intuition that this isn't going to work?'"[199] Arlene let the wedding unfold, and her vows that day included a silent prayer of hope and a pledge "to make a success out of my marriage."[200]

The drive toward success was something both she and Neil had in common. Less than a week before the wedding, he had been elected vice-president of sales for *Paramount Pictures*, Inc., where he succeeded George J. Schaefer.[201] Neil's promotion was part of a steady rise through the corporate ranks. He had been working with *Paramount* since 1920, and by the mid-thirties, he was appointed to several supervisory positions, such as sales manager for *Paramount's* New York division.[202] Neil was also admired by his peers, and had earned a reputation for being a gentle yet effective leader. A news report covering a company meeting in Hollywood, remarked on the delivery of his address on the future of motion pictures: "He says things quietly but gets a lot more emphasis than most persons achieve with stentorian tones and pounding on tables."[203] An asset to Paramount, his work demanded frequent travel, and just days after the wedding, he was expected at a sales meeting in Chicago.[204]

His new bride had an equally full itinerary. For all her radio efforts, Arlene was still getting her turn on the Broadway stages. She hadn't won a starring role yet, but any opportunity to be on stage was thrilling. In the fall, she appeared in the supporting role of Sue Barnes in Robert Rossen's

---

199. *Arlene Francis: A Memoir* (1978). By Arlene Francis with Florence Rome P. 36
200. Ibid.
201. *Motion Picture Herald*, November 20, 1935
202. Ibid
203. Ibid
204. *Motion Picture Daily*, November, 1935

*The Body Beautiful* (1935). The play, which told the tale of a burlesque dancer who chooses love over a chance at the big time,[205] opened at the Plymouth Theatre on October 31, 1935 but closed after only four performances.

Although hectic and sometimes unpredictable schedules kept both Arlene and Neil extremely busy, the couple still found time to build a life together. They enjoyed the comfort of their elaborate apartment on Fifth Avenue, and their country estate, *Kettletown Farm*, in Southbury, Connecticut. Neil also had a house built for Arlene's parents on the Kettletown property. "He was wonderful to my family," she recalled, "far beyond the ordinary son-in-law's responsibility."[206] When the Agnew's were at home, they threw lavish parties, many of which were attended by Neil's *Paramount* colleagues and friends. The executives who were at these gatherings were the foremost figures in their field. Arlene and her own group of friends were still striving toward success, but these distinguished guests had already achieved it. Not only were they more accomplished, but they were also of a different generation. She couldn't help but sense she was a bit out-of-place, and described feeling like a "bright youngster"[207] trying to charm her parents' friends at a dinner party.

Arlene never lacked charm or talent, and she was most at ease in her own element. In the fall of 1936, she performed as Tillie in Orson Welles's production of *Horse Eats Hat (1936)*. The play was staged under the *Federal Theatre Project*, a program established under the New Deal, that provided employment relief through funding for the arts.[208] Welles's exaggerated adaptation of the French film *The Italian Straw Hat* (1928), was a farce of substantial proportions. The suggestive dialogue, numerous props, stunts, and audience participation,[209] provided memorable moments throughout the play's

205. *The Complete Book of 1930s Broadway Musicals* (2018). By Dan Dietz.
206. *Arlene Francis: A Memoir* (1978). By Arlene Francis with Florence Rome P. 38
207. *Arlene Francis: A Memoir* (1978). By Arlene Francis with Florence Rome P. 39
208. The Federal Theatre Project. Wikipedia
209. Welles Net Theater: Horse eats Hat. https://www.wellesnet.com

61 performances. "Orson was beginning then, recalled Arlene, and he was full of originality."[210]

A passion for the arts drove nearly every actor's ambition, but few were as tenacious in their efforts as Arlene. On the day after Christmas of '36, she appeared as Princess Tamara Helene alongside a bevy of other actresses in the Broadway cast of *The Women* (1936). The Claire Boothe Luce script showcased the ladies of high society and presented women's issues on a notably entertaining platform. Still, any new stage performance was another chance for Arlene to do the work she loved, and accepting radio gigs was common practice between roles. In the summer of 1937, she appeared on the *Beatrice Fairfax Show* (1937)[211] for the Mutual Radio network. Ms. Fairfax was an advice columnist, and her inventive program consisted of dramatizing scenarios from the letters she had received. Arlene was chosen to perform some of the adapted presentations, and she played alongside actors Arthur Scott and Don MacLaughlin. The episode in which she appeared focused primarily on societal and domestic issues like unemployment and marital difficulties. A review in *Radio Daily* called her performance "excellent."[212]

The parallel efforts of radio and Broadway kept Arlene consistently active. On her 30th birthday, she performed as Sylvia Jordan in a George Abbot production of *Angel Island* (1937) at the National Theatre. It wasn't a leading role, but it was enough to fulfill her yearnings for the stage. Arlene would later admit to taking on as many projects as she could handle during those early years despite being newly married.[213] "Neil understood that facet of my character and was enormously supportive at all times,"[214] but the pace she kept was purposeful. It diverted her attention from addressing the doubts she still felt about her marriage.[215]

---

210. *New York Herald Tribune.* January 17, 1943
211. *Radio Daily.* September 2. 1937
212. Ibid
213. *Arlene Francis: A Memoir* (1978). By Arlene Francis with Florence Rome P. 54
214. *Arlene Francis: A Memoir* (1978). By Arlene Francis with Florence Rome P. 41
215. *Arlene Francis: A Memoir* (1978). By Arlene Francis with Florence Rome P. 48, 54

She was also unwavering in her pursuit of the theatre,[216] which meant staying close to New York. When Neil mentioned that his work for *Paramount* could prompt a move to the West Coast, Arlene made her opposition clear.[217]

However, there were other feelings she kept hidden. "I knew after I'd been married for two years that there was no possibility I could make the marriage work."[218] Neil was unaware of her discontent, and Arlene felt a sense of guilt for not expressing her concerns. In retrospect, she attributed her uneasiness about their union to her pre-marital need for independence and emotional maturity. "It seems to me that if I had had a little more time to be a young woman alone . . . to really grow up internally as well as externally, things could conceivably have been different."[219] Arlene placed no blame on Neil for her uncertainties, and the fact that he was an exemplary husband only made the situation more complicated for her. "Neil was the most gracious, considerate husband one could have, and it seems coldly ungrateful of me to have been so unloving" "How do you ask a man like that for a divorce? I found it impossible."[220]

Setting her personal issues aside, Arlene welcomed a constant stream of work. In November of 1937, she became a featured commentator on an RKO-Pathe news radio program in collaboration with *Vogue* Magazine.[221] Her official title was the *Voice of Fashion*, and the show also covered timely stories and highlights from the current issue of *Vogue*. The program's contemporary and sophisticated tone was enhanced by the music of a 50-piece orchestra. More importantly, the show introduced Arlene to female listeners. It was during this project that she first began her association with women's fashion. Noted for her sense of style, she would become something of a public appointed expert on the subject – a mantle she would carry throughout her career.

---

216. Ibid, p 48
217. *Arlene Francis: A Memoir* (1978). By Arlene Francis with Florence Rome P. 41
218. Ibid
219. *Arlene Francis: A Memoir* (1978). By Arlene Francis with Florence Rome P. 59
220. *Arlene Francis: A Memoir* (1978). By Arlene Francis with Florence Rome P. 41
221. *Motion Picture Herald.* November 13, 1937

By the late 1930s, Arlene was emerging foremost as an actress. She was heard on more radio soap operas, such as *Aunt Jenny's Real-Life Stories* (1937), for CBS, and *Stella Dallas* (1937), for NBC. Although still playing bit parts, she was becoming an increasingly secure fixture on radio. The versatility of her voice also made her available for product publicity, and she was asked to perform in her first commercial: a sales advertisement for *Lydia Pinkham's Vegetable Compound*. The bottled liquid mixture, invented by Lydia Estes Pinkham, was marketed as an herbal tonic for women. It was popular, but also incited controversy over its alcohol content.[222] The compound's proposed medicinal benefits ranged from the treatment of feminine ailments to an increase in fertility.[223] In fact, the popular slogan for Lydia Pinkham's compound was: "A Baby in Every Bottle."[224]

During the commercial, Arlene was to act in the role of a 40-year-old customer giving a testimonial. She had to convey to listeners that after taking the product, she went from having a dull, meaningless life to becoming a happy and peppy mother of four children. Arlene read the part with accuracy. But the company's president, Mr. Charles Pinkham, who had flown in to oversee the commercial, thought she needed to perform it with more feeling. He asked her if she had ever tasted the product herself. When she replied that she had not, he insisted she try it. Arlene had been assigned the role of advertising actress, but she clearly wasn't interested in becoming a consumer. "I was determined to avoid letting a drop pass my lips."[225] But Mr. Pinkham was adamant, and declared that it was her duty to taste it. At this point, Arlene began to fear losing the commercial altogether if she didn't relent. "I don't know what I thought it would do if I tasted it, probably make me the mother of four beautiful children and the life of the party."[226] Finally, while Mr. Pinkham "lovingly ladled out"[227] a spoonful, she came to her senses and

222. *Lydia Pinkham's Vegetable Compound.* Rainy Horwitz, May 20, 2015
223. Ibid
224. Ibid
225. *Arlene Francis: A Memoir* (1978). By Arlene Francis with Florence Rome P 136
226. Ibid.
227. Ibid.

made a decision: "Hanging onto my job was more important than the risk of premature motherhood."[228]

With that, she had completed another successful gig. The events of the late 1920s and 30s had carried Arlene from the Theatre Guild to the Broadway stages. Her introduction to the world of radio placed her in a position of popularity, and she had at last achieved her goal of becoming a working actress. But there was much more to come. Life was just beginning to open up for Arlene, and professional and personal changes were ahead. During her first commercial, Mr. Pinkham gave her one final admonishment and imparted a piece of advice for the future: "You're young and just starting out," he told her, "Never talk about something unless you know what you're talking about, and can actually describe it from experience."[229] In time, she agreed with him: "That's not such a bad rule for living, come to think of it,"[230] and in the life of Arlene Francis, new experiences were just around the corner.

---

228. Ibid.
229. Ibid.
230. Ibid.

# Chapter Three

"The First and Last Mrs. Gabel"[231]
    – Martin Gabel introducing Arlene on *What's My Line?*

Arlene Francis and Martin Gabel had one of the most enduring and endearing relationships on record. Their affection for each other was obvious, and when Martin made any one of his 112 appearances as a guest panelist on *What's My Line?* (1950) the viewing audience was treated to the couple's sweet exchanges, humorous back-and-forth banter, and a playful affection that was clearly on display. Off-screen, their love was deep and private. When they met in the late 1930s, more than a few obstacles stood in their way. Both were occupied with successful acting careers, motivated by an affinity for the stage. As a result, it was no surprise that the ambitious arts brought them together for the very first time. It didn't take long for the two to fall in love, but life was complicated. At the time, Arlene was Neil Agnew's wife, and that reality would force her to face her true feelings and make a decision that would change the course of her future. The union of Arlene Francis and Martin Gabel would be life-long, but they couldn't have known that at the beginning, on the set of a popular radio series in 1938.

Love stories were among the plots permeating radio soap operas in the latter half of the 1930s, and *Big Sister* (1938) was one of them. The CBS series, created by writer Lillian Lauferty, was broadcast daily from New York. Listeners tuned in from 11:30 a.m. to 11:45 a.m. to get their dose of the soapy serial. In those days, it wasn't unusual for a radio show to fill a fifteen-minute time slot. Its brevity, however, was replete with

---

231. *What's My Line?* May 19, 1963

drama, desire, and overcomplicated relationships. The plot revolved around a group of orphaned sisters being reared by the eldest. When one of the siblings requires the attention of the town physician, a complicated love triangle ensues between the dashing doctor and the longsuffering eldest sister. The series would experience a strong run from its debut in 1936 to its finale in 1952, and it succeeded with a competent group of revolving actors.

When Arlene joined *Big Sister's* (1938) cozy company, she rounded out the supporting cast by stepping into the bit roles of Judy La Rue and Lola Mitchell. Early endorsements described the character of Lola as being a "tempestuous backstreets girl."[232] Playing a part contrary to her own personality was something of a theme for Arlene, and would prove advantageous to her burgeoning skills as an actress. At the time, *Big Sister* (1938) was just one of many radio shows to which Arlene lent her talents. Nevertheless, this small, unassuming gig would have surprising significance to her personal future, and it would come in the form of Martin Gabel, a debonair young actor whose presence and resonant voice could steal the hearts of any soap opera devotee.

From an early age, Martin had aspired to become an actor. Born to Austrian Jewish parents on June 19, 1911, he grew up in the culturally diverse atmosphere of 20th century Philadelphia. The youngest child of Jacob and Rebecca Herzog Gabel, Martin joined a group of four older siblings. His sister Esther and brother Max had been born in Austria in the late 1800s,[233] while his sister Fay and brother Joseph arrived after the family settled in Pennsylvania.[234] Martin came along 14 years after Joseph's birth, giving him a unique placement in the family order. "I was a trial to my parents, he recalled. First, because I was determined to act; second, because my prime interest in school was to quit it and learn to act."[235] Martin's first performance was the lead in a school play

232. *Radio Guide.* September 24, 1938. P. 14
233. 1910 federal census
234. 1900 federal census
235. *The Philadelphia Inquirer* Magazine. March, 1957. West Philadelphia's Gabel.

at Bryant intermediate.[236] He also took up sports, and at fifteen, he was on a winning doubles tennis team that made it all the way to the state championships.[237] Later, he developed an interest in Shakespearean literature at Allentown Prep. Upon graduation, he enrolled at Lehigh University as an English major.

A well-liked and interested student, he was elected to the freshman cabinet.[238] He joined the Mustard and Cheese drama club and subsequently appeared in a few plays. Among them was *The Shannons of Broadway* (1930). He was selected from a group of eighty aspiring actors to be cast in the play,[239] and he also received a notable review for his performance as James Hutton in *Paris Bound*. An article in Lehigh's *Brown and White* college newspaper reads in part: "Much of the play's interest was held by Mr. Gabel's remarkable stage presence and clear enunciation, rarely witnessed on the amateur stage."[240] His talent was as evident as his ambition, and after three years, he left Lehigh University to attend the American Academy of Dramatic Arts in New York. During his time at the academy, Martin refined his acting skills and graduated in 1933 alongside a company of future notables such as Garson Kanin and Jim Backus.[241] For novice actors, it was a time of forward-looking ambition mingled with a society on the tail-end of the Great Depression.[242]

Martin's pursuit of acting was not pleasing to his family, especially his father, a jeweler by trade. "My father was a frustrated actor", Martin recalled. "I remember him reciting around the house the great speeches

---

236. Ibid.

237. Ibid.

238. Freshman Cabinet Members Elected. Brown and White Vol. 36 no. 16-13. November 1928

239. *The Morning Call.* May 8, 1930. Mustard and Cheese Gives 46th Show: Shannons of Broadway presented in Drown Hall at Lehigh.

240. Barry's Paris Bound Given by M & C Before Large Audience. Brown and White. Vol. 39 no. 22 – 18. Dec. 1931

241. American Academy of Dramatic Arts. Eighty Sixth Graduation Ceremonies. Tuesday, March 31, 1970. Transcript.

242. Ibid

of Jacob Adler, the Yiddish actor."[243] Eventually, Martin would realize his father's forgotten dream, and with dramatic passion in his blood, he made his professional stage debut in *Man Bites Dog* (1933). Two years later, he would appear on the Broadway stage in *Dead End*, prompting critic Percy Hammond of the *New York Herald Tribune* to boast that Martin Gabel "gave one of the top 10 performances of the year."[244] This acclaim, followed by appearances in *The Sky's the Limit* (1934) and *Ten Million Ghosts* (1936), led to more roles.

His performance as Cassius in the Mercury Theatre's modern-dress version of *Julius Caesar* (1937) was perhaps one of his most memorable. Orson Welles's adaptation of the Shakespearean tragedy was unique, resulting in a play that was described as "a parable of dictatorship, its actors in the grim, dark military costumes of fascism . . . It is not a stunt nor the desecration of a classic. It is a moving, exciting, and shockingly modern play."[245] Martin, with his resonant voice embodying the character Cassius, proclaimed boldly from the stage: "How many ages hence shall this our lofty scene be acted over in states unborn and accents yet unknown!" Reviews called his portrayal "perfection"[246] and "splendidly read."[247]

In the afterglow of such success, it was no surprise that he was starred in the popular radio serial *Big Sister* (1938). Martin played Dr. John Wayne, and he was one of three actors to take on the male lead. He was cast opposite Alice Frost, who assumed the female starring role in the late 30s. The show placed the fictionalized couple in a string of sensational scenarios and sent listeners into a frenzy. The enormous reception even prompted sponsors *Rinso* and *Lever Brothers* to manufacture lockets, containing pictures of Dr. Wayne and his

243. *The Philadelphia Inquirer* Magazine. March, 1957. West Philadelphia's Gabel.
244. American Academy of Dramatic Arts. Eighty Sixth Graduation Ceremonies. Tuesday, March 31, 1970. Transcript.
245. *Evening Star* (Washington, DC.) Nov. 21. 1937. Julius Caesar Season's Most Exciting Play. By, Richard Watts, Jr.
246. *St. Louis Democrat.* Nov. 16, 1937. Lyons Den. By Leonard Lyons
247. *Daily News* (New York). Nov. 13 1937. Julius Caesar in Overcoats Mercury's First Experiment.

bride. They could be easily obtained for 15 cents each and a *Rinso* box top.

Off the air, Martin was an eligible bachelor and a popular date among Arlene's circle of friends. Initially, the excitement surrounding Martin was something of a mystery to Arlene, who found herself downright intimidated by the seemingly serious actor. The two had only exchanged occasional pleasantries, and despite a jovial atmosphere on set, she recalled Martin as quiet and avoidant of the joking and lighthearted chatter that carried on between her and the rest of the cast. Indeed, the crossing of paths between Arlene Francis and Martin Gabel was brief during the run of *Big Sister* (1938). However, in keeping with the tradition of all good soap operas, their story was to be continued.

At the time, Arlene was busy pursuing her first starring role on Broadway. Director George Abbot was producing the stage play, *All That Glitters (1938)*, and the cast of characters was nearly complete. Abbot was still searching for someone to assume the role of Elena, a Spanish prostitute. Mr. Abbot's need for an actress was likely rivaled only by Arlene's burning ambitions for the stage, and her prowess and physical appearance were also fitting. Because of her past experience with voice impersonations, she would have no trouble using a Spanish accent, and her dark hair and olive complexion made her a potential candidate for the role.

An audition was arranged through Arlene's *Big Sister* (1938) cast member, Alice Frost. The exciting opportunity sent Arlene rushing from the *Big Sister* (1938) set and into Mr. Abbot's office. She was permitted in at once, bypassing the other waiting hopefuls. And, she won the role, opposite Allyn Joslyn. Clearly, her status as an actress was changing. Arlene's placement in a George Abbot production also seemed to change the way her father viewed her career aspirations. She recalled the shift in his perspective. "Father knew Mr. Abbot to be a responsible man, a gifted man, a good man. If a man of that stature believed I had talent and wanted me in a play, father decided it must be alright."[248]

---

248. *Radio TV Mirror.* July-December, 1955

*All That Glitters* (1938) opened at the Biltmore Theatre on January 18. The audience was treated to a light-hearted but inevitably doomed scenario; one in which a social outcast masquerades as a countess. The initial reviews were lukewarm, but Arlene's performance was favorably acknowledged by theatre columnist Arthur Pollock, who wrote: "Arlene Francis does well by the Spanish prostitute."[249] Early notices could not help but predict the play's success, due in part to a rousing applause following the curtain, an ovation that prompted the producer-director himself to take the stage for a brief bow on opening night. Arlene gave her all in the show's 69 performances, and George Abbot wasn't the only director who had taken notice.

Orson Welles decided to star her in one of his upcoming projects for the Mercury Theatre. She would appear in silent film-style segments for *Too Much Johnson (1938)*. The footage was intended to be part of a three-act Mercury film and stage presentation of William Gillette's nineteenth century play, and the film segments were to be shown as an introduction to each act. In the footage, Arlene's character, Clairette Dathis, is engaged in a love tryst with an undercover playboy, portrayed by Joseph Cotten. When her husband discovers evidence of their romance, he begins a fervent search for his wife's lover. For reasons not substantiated, Welles halted the film production of *Too Much Johnson (1938)*, and focused on other projects such as the Mercury Theatre of the air. The radio series became famous for performing adaptations of popular novels and plays, but it is perhaps best known for its presentation of *War of the Worlds* (1938), which sparked public panic due to its convincing portrayal of an alien invasion. Arlene made appearances in the company's less controversial productions, such as *The Affairs of Anatol* (1938) and *Around the World in 80 Days (1938)*, where she played the role of Madame Aouda.

By the fall of thirty-eight, she had her sights set on another *Mercury* production, and this one involved Martin Gabel. *Danton's Death* (1938) was being produced for the stage. It had been translated to English from its

---

249. *Brooklyn daily Eagle.* January 20, 1938

original German, and this would be one of the first English presentations of the Georg Buchner script to be performed in the United States. The already 100-year-old play was set during the French Revolution. Despite a small cast and a limited budget, Orson Welles was determined to stage a show rivaling that of Max Reinhardt's grand production in 1927. If ever there was a director for the job, it was Welles. Describing him as "the most imaginative theatre man I ever worked with,"[250] Martin later praised his innate abilities. "He combines imagination and a gift for execution to a degree that probably deserves the term genius."[251] To achieve the look of the Parisian masses, Welles bought hundreds of Halloween face masks. He had them sewn together to form a cyclorama, creating an illusionary backdrop depicting the "garish drama of the French revolution."[252] Martin had already secured the role of Danton, the perceivably heroic yet destructively tragic male lead. There was, however, an opening for one of the supporting female roles, and, as it were, the part called for the portrayal of another prostitute. Or, more eloquently described by Arlene as "a lady of the evening."[253]

She wanted the role, and decided to approach Martin about the possibility of his speaking to Orson Welles on her behalf. After all, Martin was an established Mercury Theatre member, with enough influence to recommend an audition. Arlene recalled seeing Martin enter the drugstore-coffee shop, located in Manhattan's CBS building. She had worked up the nerve and decided that this was as good a time as any to speak to him. Her hesitancy was easy to recall. "The real reason I was afraid to talk to him was because I thought he was a bit of a stuffed shirt… he was Mr. Star, and how!"[254] Thus began an uncomfortable conversation. It started with nervous ramblings from Arlene about why she was right for

---

250. American Academy of Dramatic Arts. Eighty Sixth Graduation Ceremonies. Tuesday, March 31, 1970. Transcript p. 19
251. Ibid
252. American Academy of Dramatic Arts. Eighty Sixth Graduation Ceremonies. Tuesday, March 31, 1970. Transcript p. 20
253. *Arlene Francis: A Memoir* (1978). By Arlene Francis with Florence Rome. P. 32
254. Ibid

the part, and how her previous experience playing similar roles gave her the advantage. It ended with a serious expression on Martin's face, and an underwhelming declaration to "think about" speaking to Orson Welles about her. So much for first impressions!

Little did they both know that this awkward exchange would be the start of something beautiful. As the record reveals, Martin was convinced enough to approach Welles, and Arlene was permitted to audition for the role of Marion, the ah, "lady of the evening." They soon found themselves at the center of Orson Welles's inventive approach to staging. He designed the set in such a way that cast members were assembled and positioned by means of an ensemble of stairways and risers. The most important feature for Martin and Arlene was a hollowed-out center circle, which led to a cellar below. For their dramatic scene, the two were to hold each other in a passionate embrace as a makeshift elevator lifted them from the basement to the surface of the stage, but it was in the obscured shadows of the cellar that the dynamics between them began to change. While waiting for their cues, the once quiet Martin began reciting lines not found in the script. At first, Arlene was not sure how to interpret his expressions of flattery, and she recalled brushing them off as an exaggerated jest. "When Martin would say, 'You silly little thing, don't you know I love you'? I would answer in kind and then laugh to show him that I wasn't serious either."[255]

In time, she began to see Martin in a different light, and was soon taken by the persuasive effects of his charm. "That terrific voice whispering sweet talk in my ear generated a lot of excitement."[256] However, as a married woman, these new feelings presented a complication. Her husband, Neil, was an admirable man, and one whom she held in high esteem. Arlene had entered into her marriage with a heart full of hope,[257] but those wedding day doubts never quite dissipated,[258] and

---

255. *Arlene Francis: A Memoir* (1978). By Arlene Francis with Florence Rome. P. 43
256. Ibid.
257. *Arlene Francis: A Memoir* (1978). By Arlene Francis with Florence Rome. P. 36
258. *Arlene Francis: A Memoir* (1978). By Arlene Francis with Florence Rome. P. 41

the future fulfillment she had wished for would take an unexpected turn. After rehearsals for *Danton's Death* (1938), Arlene and Martin got to know each other better over coffee and conversation.[259] Soon, this suave, erudite, and handsome man left her with no option but to fall in love.

Their emerging fondness for each other wasn't always easy to conceal. *Danton's Death* (1938) bit player, Betty Garrett, was a witness to their blossoming affection. Garrett was an understudy in the play, and later became well known for her role as Irene Lorenzo, the broad-minded neighbor on the '70s sitcom *All in the Family* (1971). In her 1998 autobiography, Garret recalled her perceptions on the *Danton's Death* (1938) set. "After a while, it was clear that Martin and Arlene did not realize we were there, and every evening they would get into position just a little earlier than the night before. It was not long before we saw that the love scene was not *acting* anymore."[260]

Reviews for the play were not quite as affectionate. An early notice in *Variety* called it "sketchy" and compared it to an amateur production. Arlene was not spared either, when she decidedly "failed to enliven a purely incidental part . . ."[261] It was Martin, however, who garnered praise from the critics. An early reviewer wrote, "He invests the character with vitality and conviction."[262] This was high praise, considering the fact that Martin was tense during his performance. The object of his apprehension was Orson Welles's unusual set design. That circular hollow in the center of the stage was ominous to him without the aid of his spectacles. Arlene recalled his trepidation. "Martin can't see worth a darn and he was sure he was going to fall in."[263] His fear was ultimately realized on opening night, and Martin would later describe the dreaded incident with a note of affection: "I fell down the stairs to the cellar and had to rush up to play

---

259. *Cosmopolitan Magazine* (1962)

260. Betty Garrett and Other Songs: A Life on Stage and Screen (1999). By Betty Garret. P. 44. Retrieved from Google Books.

261. *Variety* (1938)

262. *Ibid*

263. *Radio Life.* January 26, 1947. P. 5

the next scene, a love scene, with blood streaming down my face. But the love scene was with the girl who later became my wife, so the bleeding was worth it."[264]

*Danton's Death* (1938) was an undeniably momentous production. Although not outstanding in the opinion of early critics, the play was an important turning point for Arlene and Martin. It had served as the backdrop for their budding romance, and unwittingly ushered them into a relationship both professional and very personal. The moral dilemma regarding Arlene's marital status, however, disturbed them greatly. She knew that asking Neil for a divorce was inevitable. But he was unaware of any issues in their marriage, and she feared the shock and hurt a divorce would cause him. "It kept me awake nights worrying,"[265] Arlene recalled. She agonized over the guilt she felt at living something of a double life. "It was as though I lived at two different levels. One so deeply buried that most people, particularly the principles in the case, were not even aware that anything was amiss. The other, the smiling young matron, was so real that even I didn't recognize her for what she was—a facade."[266]

At the same time, Arlene found solace in her work, and she was selected to perform leading roles in the NBC radio program *There was a Woman* (1938).[267] In the series, she portrayed the wife of notable men, including Marco Polo and Alexander Hamilton, but in a reversal of stereotypically feminine roles, she began a job that would cement her status as one of, if not the first, female co-hosts of a game show on radio.[268] Presiding over the new NBC radio quiz show *What's My Name?* (1939) she worked alongside co-hosts Bud Hulick and Fred Uttal. The radio show originally aired as a replacement for Fred Allen's *Town Hall Tonight* in the summer of '39. The rules of the game were simple. Contestants were quizzed with

---

264. American Academy of Dramatic Arts. Eighty Sixth Graduation Ceremonies. Tuesday, March 31, 1970. Transcript p. 21
265. *Arlene Francis: A Memoir* (1978). By Arlene Francis with Florence Rome. P. 54
266. *Arlene Francis: A Memoir* (1978). By Arlene Francis with Florence Rome P. 38
267. *Radio Daily.* January 24, 1938
268. According to the author's research

clues about a notable person. Then, they had to guess that person's name. One dollar was lost for each incorrect answer, and the top prize was $10. *What's My Name?* (1939) was also Arlene's first experience with ad-libbing. Now that she was able to deviate from the confines of a scripted role, listening audiences were introduced to her natural wit and vivacious personality.

Named American Radio's *Woman of the Year* in 1939,[269] she made several guest appearances on shows such as *The People's Rally* (1939).[270] The radio program, hosted by Bob Hawk and moderated by journalist John B. Kennedy, was a combination of a quiz show and a debate panel covering topical issues. But Arlene couldn't stay away from the stage for too long, and true to her determined nature, she juggled hosting duties for *What's My Name?* (1939) while at the same time appearing in summer tryouts for a new play, *Michael Drops In* (1939). When the show opened at the Ridgeway Theatre in White Plains, New York, Arlene was relieved 15 minutes early from *What's My Name?* (1939) in order to make it to the theatre for a nine o'clock curtain.[271] The comedy, written by William Dubois, cast her in the role of Judy Morton, a small-town girl who finds forbidden love in the big city. *Variety* magazine called her performance "histrionically convincing and personally captivating."[272] The show made it to Broadway two days after Christmas, but closed in January after only eight performances.

Soon enough, Arlene found herself back on the NBC radio set. This time, she was starring in *Betty and Bob* (1932). The already popular soap opera had been broadcast from Chicago, but when production moved to New York, Arlene joined the serial in progress and stepped into the starring role of Betty. Van Heflin was among the actors who played her husband, Bob Drake. The show was an early success, and its plot revolved around the lives of a young couple. When Bob gives up his family fortune to marry Betty, the two embark on an uphill battle for a life of their

269. The *Australian Women's Weekly*. April, 1940
270. *Motion Picture Daily*. February 10, 1939
271. *Scarsdale Inquirer*, July 15, 1938
272. *Variety*. Circa 1939

own. The show tackled serious subjects such as pregnancy, divorce, and the death of the Drake's firstborn child. The series, written by Frank and Anne Hummert, experienced a steady eight-year run. But ratings declined, and even Arlene couldn't keep *Betty and Bob* (1932) together. It was cancelled in the spring of 1940.

Acting work was transient, and every new role offered the risk of success or failure. The next opportunity was *Young Couple Wanted* (1940), a play written by Arthur Wilmurt and staged by Martin Gabel. He and Arlene had not worked together in a play since *Danton's Death* (1938), and this production marked the first time Martin would direct Arlene on the stage. These early professional projects demonstrated the ease with which they collaborated. Yet life off stage was not as simple. Arlene continued to be torn between the realities of her marriage to Neil and her relationship with Martin. It would be sometime before the two could build the life they dreamed of together. For now, they would have to settle for opening night.

*Young Couple Wanted* (1940) opened on Broadway at Maxine Elliot's Theatre, but closed after only thirteen performances. The play's short run was not without some notes of praise, however. Because the cast was comprised of several radio actors, including Arlene, who played the role of Catherine Daly, the comedy was acknowledged by *Television and Radio Mirror*. A brief article read in part, ". . . The folks from radio were every bit as expert behind footlights as they are behind microphones."[273]

That was certainly true for Arlene, whose work in radio serials like the thriller *Beyond Reasonable Doubt* (1940) kept her consistently on the air. In the serial, she was cast as Gloria Wayne, a woman whose theatrical aspirations lead to murderous consequences. An article in *Australian Woman's Weekly* cited the parallels between Arlene's real-life ascent into the world of acting and that of the character Gloria Wayne. The newspaper feature itself illustrated just how far-reaching Arlene's career had become. "Miss Francis is well known to Australian audiences for her appearances in the *March of Time* (1931) series on the [movie] screen,"[274] it noted, but

---

273. *Television and Radio Mirror.* 1940
274. *Australian Woman's Weekly.* 1940

Arlene's primary aim was the stage, and her next project would take her no further than the National Theatre.

*Journey to Jerusalem* (1940) opened on Broadway on October 5. The play was based on the Christian gospel's account of Mary, Joseph, and a young Jesus traveling to Jerusalem for the Passover. In Maxwell Anderson's script, the biblical story was set against the metaphor of Nazi Germany. The evil of Adolph Hitler was typified by the role of Herod Antipas, played by Frederic Tozere. Arlene appeared as Miriam, the Virgin Mary, and Horace Braham was cast as Joseph. A fifteen-year-old Sydney Lumet played the role of Jesus, referred to in the play as "Jeshua". The production marked an interesting first for a stage play. It was selected to be preserved on reel by the *Theatre-on-Film* corporation of New York. The archival process would enable the 90-minute production to be screened at venues such as schools and religious institutions. *Theatre-on-Film* chose what they deemed to be Broadway's finest productions. And though *Journey to Jerusalem* only ran for 15 performances, it would make a lasting mark on history and prepare Arlene for the success ahead.

The early 40s also placed Martin in a position of achievement. During those years, he began a lengthy collaboration with producer Carly Wharton. Ms. Wharton was described as "one of the only successful female producers on Broadway."[275] Together, she and Martin took an interest in several productions, namely the profitable play *Life with Father* (1939)[276] Eventually becoming one of the longest-running plays of all time, Martin saw the script's possibilities from the beginning and approached Arlene about it. She recalled his wise insight and her not-so-wise rejection. "Before we were married, he brought me the script of *Life with Father* . . . he thought I should invest in it, and after reading it, I said, 'If you ask me, who's going to be interested in a play about a man getting baptized?'"[277] Arlene failed to reap the production's success, but Martin's discernment for a good script kept him in steady work.

---

275. *The Hobart Democrat Chief.* June 2, 1942
276. Ibid. and *The Alfred Hitchcock Encyclopedia,* by Stephen Whitty (2016)
277. *Arlene Francis: A Memoir* (1978). By Arlene Francis with Florence Rome. P. 69-70

In 1940, he optioned the play, *Everybody Comes to Rick's* (1940). Written by Murray Burnett and Joan Allison,[278] it would later be re-named and re-packaged as the film *Casablanca*. Initially, Martin's response to the script was to advocate for revisions,[279] believing that the play could not be staged without changes to the plot.[280] The production never materialized, and the writers took their script to Hollywood,[281] eventually selling it to *Warner Brothers* and prompting the making of one of the most successful films of the early 40s. But as a discerning stage director forging his own path, Martin knew what he wanted, and sometimes that resulted in a challenge.

When he and Carly Wharton produced the play *Charley's Aunt* (1892),[282] it resulted in Broadway success and a subsequent legal battle. In September of 1941, the two filed an injunction[283] to prevent showings of the latest film version, released by 20th Century Fox, claiming plagiarism. An article in *Variety* asserted that while Martin and Ms. Wharton did not own the screen rights to the play, they "claimed they did have a property right in novel technique, expression, treatment, and embellishment."[284] Opposing sides asserted that the alleged plagiarism, referred to as "original stage business,"[285] was already present in earlier versions of the play, predating Martin's and Ms. Wharton's production. The injunction was dismissed by Justice Kenneth O'Brien, with a decision reading in part: "Whether Gabel and Wharton acquired any rights by reason of their production, or whether 20th Century-Fox made use of stage business which would affect the property rights are not so clear that the court should exercise its power as to grant such drastic relief as is sought."[286]

---

278. *Casablanca Behind the Scenes* (1992). By, Harland Lebo
279. Ibid.
280. Ibid.
281. Ibid.
282. *Laird Cregar: A Hollywood Tragedy* (2014). By, Gregory William Mank
283. Ibid & *Variety.* September, 1941. Can't Protect Stage Business N.Y. Court Rules.
284. *Variety* September, 1941. Can't Protect Stage Business N.Y. Court Rules.
285. Ibid.
286. Ibid.

Despite the ruling, Martin forged ahead with other projects, and his next production, *Café Crown*, was an uninterrupted success. He served as co-producer of the play, written by Hy Kraft, and the story focused on the members of a Yiddish Theatre group meeting at a downtown restaurant.[287] It received favorable reviews from critics, with *Billboard* magazine calling the play "flavorsome," "funny" and, "amusing."[288] *Café Crown* (1942) also marked the directorial debut of Elia Kazan. It opened at the Cort Theatre on January 23, 1942 and ran for 141 performances.

While Martin's stage career progressed, Arlene continued to add more radio performances to her growing resumé of acting credits. She was heard on the show *Daughter of Uncle Sam* (1942),[289] a wartime entertainment feature. "Arlene Francis endows the program with a goodly portion of charm,"[290] noted *Variety*. Such critical praise led to several appearances on the CBS series *Second Husband,* (1939)[291] where she played the character Marion Jennings. Arlene was in great demand as a radio actress at this time, and more opportunities followed. Soon, she was added to the cast of the popular crime serial *Mr. District Attorney (1939)*, assuming the role of Miss Rand. Former law student Ed Byron created and co-wrote the series, which was inspired by politician and prosecutor Thomas E. Dewey. Arlene's success on the show garnered her further acclaim, and she landed a starring role in the new soap opera, *Helpmate (1939)*. Preceding veteran actress Fern Persons,[292] she was the first to be cast as the character Linda Harper, a disillusioned young woman newly married to a symphony composer. Arlene fondly recalled these early experiences, "running from soap to soap"[293] and trying to keep up with the exhilarating pace.

The heavy workload was a delight to her. She was fueled by boundless energy and the satisfaction that comes with being productive, and, she

---

287. *Great Shakespearean Set IV*. Edited by, Adrian Poole and Peter Holland. P. 163
288. *Billboard*. February 7, 1942
289. *Variety*. Wednesday, February 25, 1942. P. 26
290. *Variety*. Circa 1942
291. *Radio and Television Mirror*. October, 1939
292. Short-Lived Television Series 1948-1978, by Wesley Hyatt, 2003. P. 36
293. *Arlene Francis: A Memoir* (1978). By Arlene Francis with Florence Rome. P. 28

was the first to admit it. "For me, my work is my pleasure, so I have my holiday when I'm doing something that pleases me work-wise."[294] Arlene appeared in two more Broadway roles before the year's end. First, was *The Walking Gentleman* (1942), a murder-themed thriller. She played the character, Doris, for only six performances at the Belasco Theatre. According to a review[295] in *Billboard*, the intended thriller failed to stimulate the audience: "Beads of perspiration turned out to be on the characters rather than the customers,"[296] but Arlene was praised for "bringing dignity"[297] and "effect"[298] to her role. When the show closed in May of '42, short runs were becoming something of a regular occurrence.

That pattern would be broken with her next play, *The Doughgirls* (1942). Fortuitously, her participation in the play came by way of a prediction. "It was only a coincidence of course," she explained, "but a mind reader told me something at a party I went to."[299] As the story goes, all of the party guests wrote a question on a card. And the mind reader, led by intuition or indiscretion, blindly answered. Arlene's question was: "When shall I have my next [theatrical] engagement?"[300] In response, she was told to expect a stage role in November. What the mind reader didn't know was that the future role would end up being one of Arlene's earliest successes.

Nevertheless, her appearance in *The Doughgirls* (1942) seemed doomed from the beginning. While playing radio roles, Arlene would periodically frequent Broadway houses in hopes of being considered for upcoming productions. "Going to the theatrical offices and getting turned down isn't pleasant,"[301] but sometimes, Arlene risked rejection for reward. On one such occasion, she entered producer Max Gordon's office

---

294. Arlene Francis radio Interview on Keep in Touch with George Douth. 1966.
295. The *Billboard*. June 13, 1942. Legitimate. From Out Front. P. 10.
296. Ibid
297. Ibid
298. Ibid
299. The *New York Herald Tribune*. Circa 1945
300. Ibid.
301. Ibid.

and was met by a roomful of blonde hopefuls. They were all waiting to be considered for the George Kauffman play. "As my hair is black, my chances didn't look good."[302] However, she did see the producers taking notice. They eventually found a part for her in the production, and rehearsals began, as predicted, that November.

On December 30, 1942, *The Doughgirls* (1942) opened at the Lyceum Theatre. The play centered on three women (played by Virginia Field, Arleen Whelan, and Doris Nolan) living in Washington, DC during the Second World War. Added to the mix was comical Russian sniper, Natalia Chodorov, expertly played by Arlene. "I'm an Armenian playing a Russian,"[303] she said during an interview with the *Brooklyn Eagle*. She mastered the foreign accent and, by several accounts, was a standout among players. In fact, the entire reception for *The Doughgirls* (1942) was favorable. Arlene had a hit play at long last!

The show's 671 performances were eventful. During the successful run, Arlene met actress Mary Cooper, who had a small part in the play. The two would become close friends and share the stage several times throughout the ensuing decades. But *The Doughgirls* (1942) was important to Arlene. It became something of an escape from the inner turmoil she felt at the time. In the years since her marriage to Neil, she had accepted the fact that she wasn't in love with him. Her growing feelings for Martin only magnified that reality, and would eventually force her to find the inner strength to make a change.

Courage came slowly, and she painstakingly prolonged asking Neil for a divorce. She couldn't bring herself to hurt him, and making waves was contrary to her nature. Besides, Neil had given her no cause for the doubt she felt from the beginning. "We had some wonderful times together, she recalled, and though I wasn't in love with him, he was certainly loveable, and I *was* tremendously fond of him–which in some ways made things even harder for me."[304] With the pressure mounting, Arlene's tortured emotions caught up with her physically, and prompted what she described

---

302. Ibid.

303. *The Brooklyn Eagle. Circa 1942*

304. *Arlene Francis: A Memoir* (1978). By Arlene Francis with Florence Rome. P.39

as a "mini-breakdown."[305] She was admitted to the LeRoy Hospital under one condition: she would still be allowed to perform in *The Doughgirls* (1942).

The doctors agreed to Arlene's stipulation. Even if they didn't understand her belief in the medicinal properties of hard work, there was no denying that she was an actress in demand. From an outward perspective, the weight loss, short-temperedness, and fatigue she experienced would be common in anyone who worked as hard as she did. "I had such a heavy schedule at this period in my life," she recalled, "that one would have thought I wouldn't have had time for a private life. Well, sir, one would have been dead wrong. It was so private that I didn't dare mention it to anyone in the world. I had fallen in love with Martin."[306]

Love was something of a theme in the summer of 1943, and Arlene was asked to host the new radio show, *Blind Date* (1943). It aired nightly at eight, debuting from NBC's studio 6A at Rockefeller Center. It was a game on a mission to find love matches for eligible servicemen. The show was a symbol of American patriotism combined with a lighthearted formula for fun. Women and men were divided by a partition, and could only communicate by telephone on either side. The presence of an orchestra, a live audience, and Arlene's bubbly interplay between the contestants added to the show's amusing ambiance. The spontaneity the show allowed sometimes proved consequential; especially for an unscripted Arlene, who was sometimes scolded for her perceived double entendre.

Nevertheless, audiences accepted nearly anything she had to say. The occasional risqué remark never challenged the respect she had already earned from the public. Presumably, it made them like her all the more. The candor, bloopers, and moments of unrestraint proved to the show's listeners that this sophisticated young woman was just like the rest of us. The show not only offered a 30-minute boost in morale during wartime, but it was also among a wave of cash-prize shows steadily taking over

---

305. *Arlene Francis A Memoir* (1978). By Arlene Francis with Florence Rome P. 55
306. *Arlene Francis; A Memoir* (1978). By Arlene Francis with Florence Rome P. 53-54

radio games in the 40s. The consolation prize was $15, and the winners and their dates were treated to dinner (chaperoned by Arlene) at the Stork Club, with an extra $5 tossed in for good measure. The show was a success during its three-year radio run and would do well during its eventual transition to ABC television in the 50s.

In the summer of 44, the game began the occasional stint of taking the show on the road. Arlene hosted *Blind Date* (1943) in her birthplace of Boston and was given a welcoming reception. A publicity campaign was organized, and local department stores and railway stations displayed advertisements. The Ritz-Carlton Hotel held parties for the winning couples, and a specially designed stage was built for the event. An article covering the Boston show, read in part: "The newspaper coverage was abundant . . . Arlene Francis was escorted from the train to the radio station in a jeep."[307] A reported 700 people attended the broadcast at the RKO Theatre.

While hundreds of contestants were hoping for a blind date, Arlene had already found her perfect match. Her feelings for Martin were definite, but he was increasingly uncomfortable with the situation, such as it was. "Martin kept urging me to make a clean break with Neil. He felt it would be more honorable and decent and all that, and he made the point that I was prolonging the agony by putting it off, and that there was no point in making three people unhappy."[308] Martin's words rang true, and Arlene began a process which would help her take the steps needed to move forward with her life. She began sessions with psychoanalyst, Dr. Herman Nunberg. With his counsel, she was finally able to garner the courage to take control of her future.

She wrote a letter to Neil and took a room at the Hampshire House. Eventually, she agreed to meet with him in person to talk things over. She explained as much as she could without causing him any further hurt. It was difficult, but Neil was more understanding than she had imagined him to be. For Arlene, the ending of her ten-year marriage also afforded an insightful lesson into the human psyche. "I thought it

307. *Motion Picture Herald.* August 12, 1944. P. 53
308. *Arlene Francis: A Memoir* (1978). By Arlene Francis with Florence Rome. P. 54

would be the end for Neil if I left him . . . what ridiculous egos we have, for that is what it really is no matter what we tell ourselves!"[309] A divorce was granted in Juarez, Mexico. At long last, she was living life on her own terms, and it was a life that included Martin Gabel. Arlene decided to take some time before getting married again, however. She enjoyed being an independent woman and the new luxuries it allowed, such as having her own apartment.

There was also work to be done. She appeared in the role of Elvira in the Noel Coward play, *Blithe Spirit* (1945), and landed another lead on Broadway in *The Overtons* (1945), where she starred opposite Jack Whiting. The Vincent Lawrence script was about a happily married couple unaware of a plot to break them up. The show opened at the Booth Theatre on February 6, 1945, and ran for 175 performances, but television commitments forced her to leave the production, and the role of Cora Overton was taken over by actress Judith Evelyn. Arlene had to withdraw early due to hosting duties. *Blind Date* (1943) was going back on the travel circuit and would be broadcast from Hollywood for six weeks.

Martin also made a brief trip to the West Coast to conduct his masterful V-E Day narration of Norman Corwin's *On a Note of Triumph* (1945). Seared into the memories of millions, Corwin himself would later proclaim that his work had found "eloquent expression through Martin."[310] The program was broadcast live on CBS (KNX) radio from Los Angeles. *Billboard* magazine called it "The single greatest–and we use greatest in its fullest meaning–radio program we have ever heard." The presentation was so well received that listeners demanded an encore, and a transcription of Corwin's celebrated epic was published in book form immediately following the broadcast.

Aside from his success and effectiveness as an actor, Martin continued to work behind the scenes, producing plays such as Irwin Shaw's *The Assassin* (1945). Shaw was a playwright with whom Martin would collaborate occasionally throughout the years. "Irwin and I became

---

309. Ibid.

310. *Norman Corwin's Letters* (1994). By Norman Corwin. Edited by A.J. Langguth

friends because we liked to operate the same way,"[311] he explained. "We were part of what you could call the black-tie set. We liked to work until 11:30 at night, and then we'd start the round of clubs."[312] It was *The Assassin* (1945) that brought together their professional efforts for the first time on stage. The historical drama was based on the assassination of Admiral Francois Darlan[313] and received mixed reviews from critics who questioned the accuracy of the script. However, at the same time, the play was called "Absorbing" and Martin's production skill garnered considerable praise. *Variety* boasted that "Martin Gabel has caught the spirit of this work faithfully,"[314] But despite early accolades, *The Assassin* (1945) closed after only 13 performances at the National Theatre.

Short runs did not deter Martin from a steady pursuit of his work, and much of his determination and resilience had to do with a realistic yet hopeful view of his chosen profession. Martin, who believed that serious actors must have a sense of "power within,"[315] maintained that such a sense is required if one is to survive in an unpredictable arena like show business. He described this internalized power as "a constant, which survives snubs, and neglect, and rude dismissal, and changing times."[316] He asserted that it "keep[s] the genuinely gifted person pressing on, determined to be heard . . . secure in the knowledge that talent will, must, ultimately carry the day, however long delayed."[317] As a young player in the 1940s, Martin was learning these lessons with each new project.

During the war years, he directed at least one play for *Stage for Action*,[318] a progressive organization that produced theatrical performances in

---

311. The Philadelphia Inquirer, Apr. 5, 1953. W. Phila. High's Gabel Directs Locust Comedy. By, Barbara L. Wilson.

312. Ibid

313. *Broadway Plays and Musicals* (2017). by, Thomas S. Hischak.

314. *Variety* October 1945

315. American Academy of Dramatic Arts. Eighty Sixth Graduation Ceremonies. Tuesday, March 31, 1970. Transcript p. 15

316. Ibid.

317. Ibid.

318. Supreme Court of the State of New York transcripts, p. 147

support of war efforts.[319] On April 19, 1944, the company staged Arthur Miller's purposeful piece, *That They May Win* (1944). The play, performed at the ballroom of the Henry Hudson Hotel,[320] had been written for the theater group, and highlighted the issues of poverty and price control facing the families of deployed soldiers.[321] Later, *Stage for Action* would be among the organizations listed in the 1950 accusatory *Red Channels*.[322] And Martin, along with numerous notables in the entertainment sector, were also named in the publication. The immediate aftermath of *Red Channels* created an industry ban among the named actors, including Joseph Julian, who had been cited for performing in a *Stage for Action* play under Martin's direction.[323] The influence of the Hollywood Blacklist would not be broken until the following decade, and despite the risk of scrutiny, Martin continued to lend his talents to important causes.

He served on an executive committee in support of the United Jewish Appeal,[324] and in the summer of '44, he took part in a dramatic stage production raising awareness of anti-Semitism.[325] The dramatization, based on Ben Hecht's forthright volume, *A Guide for the Bedeviled*, was held at Carnegie Hall and was produced in collaboration with the *Emergency Committee to Save the Jewish People of Europe*. Its purpose was not only to make a statement, but also a change, and petitions for an appeal to President Roosevelt were distributed. It was through events like these that Martin was able to use his creative efforts to cultivate a public platform. For example, in November of '45, he staged an event[326] in protest of bigotry expressed by Rep. John E. Rankin and his Committee on Un-American Activities. The gathering, supported by the *Independent Citizens Committee of the Arts, Sciences, and Professions*, consisted of a

---

319. *WCFL Chicago's Voice of Labor* (1978). By Nathan Godfried.
320. Stage for Action U.S. Social Activist Theatre in the 1940s. 2016 by Chrystyna Dail
321. *Critical Companion to Arthur Miller: A Literary Reference to His Life and Work.* 2007. By, Susan C.W, Abbotson
322. Supreme Court of the State of New York transcripts, p, 146
323. Supreme Court of the State of New York transcripts, p. 147
324. *Radio Daily.* May 2, 1945. P. 2
325. *Variety.* June 21, 1944. P. 47
326. *Radio Daily.* November 23, 1945. P. 7

dramatization and a keynote speech delivered by Congressman Emanuel Celler.

However, the post-war era would offer a change of pace for Martin and Arlene. In 1946, Hollywood came calling, and asked Martin to co-produce (along with Walter Wanger) a forthcoming Susan Hayward picture, *Smash Up: The Story of a Woman* (1947). The opportunity meant that he would be living on the West Coast for a while, and this new reality was disconcerting to Arlene, who was worried that a long-distance arrangement could pose a potential threat to their relationship. When Martin briefly returned to New York on business, she decided that then would be the right time to get married. She recalled the moment: "When he returned months later, he found me pathetically thin with deep, dark circles under my eyes. When he asked me the nature of my distress, I said 'Martin, without you, I'm nothing. With you, I'm half of everything.'"[327]

They celebrated their official engagement with two gatherings. First, a group of Arlene's friends gave her a wedding shower at her apartment on Central Park South. The atmosphere was filled with fun and an ensemble of gifts and good wishes. A news article[328] noted guests Kitty Carlisle, Susan Hayward, and Marianne Stewart, wife of Martin's friend Louis Calhern. The event was described as "a pink champagne party." Afterward, the group gathered at the *Stork Club*, where they were met by Martin's friends. While there, they caught the attention of columnist Walter Winchell. He was famous for frequenting the *Stork*, where he broadcast his radio show from Table 50. Upon learning of their impending nuptials, he quickly joined the party. And because Arlene and Martin hadn't set a date, Winchell arranged a ceremony for the very next day.

Arlene's divorce had taken place in Mexico, and therefore was not acknowledged by the state of New York. But Winchell knew a judge in Patterson, New Jersey, and on May 14, 1946, Arlene and Martin were married. They were accompanied by two of Martin's closest friends, actor Lou Calhern and sportswriter Jimmy Cannon. During the ceremony,

---

327. *The Morning Call.* (Allentown, Pennsylvania) Old Hand Arlene Francis Offers Man-Snaring Tips. By, Phyllis Battle, May 3, 1962

328. *Iowa City Press Citizen.* May, 1946. Broadway A Pink Evening, by Jack O'Brien

officiated by judge Alexander MacLeod, the bride wore an aqua-colored bengaline dress with a matching Lily Daché hat.[329] Although the plans were sudden, news of the nuptials reached the press. Arlene spoke to a reporter for the *Patterson News* that day. "Everything is hearts and flowers with us,"[330] she said, referring to her spring bouquet and exquisite bridal set. Her rings were described as a large heart-shaped aquamarine with five cabochon rubies on each side set in gold, complete with a platinum wedding band of small diamond hearts.[331]

Following the wedding, Arlene, Martin, and the groomsman piled into the limousine for the ride back to New York. Humorous in hindsight, the drive home was a little less romantic than the new bride had envisioned. "Guess who got ignored as the groom and his two attendants rehashed a big prize fight of the previous week?" she recalled. Yes Indeed. The conversation, as I remember it, on my wedding day mind you, consisted largely of 'If he'd a give him his right to the jaw, it 'a been all over! and more in that vein."[332] So much for riding off into the sunset! Nevertheless, the Gabels were certain of their love from the start, and time proved them right. Upon appraisal, Martin once said, "Except in my marriage, I've had no instinct for success in my life."[333]

Actually, in 1946, success was waiting out west. Martin was due back on the set of *Smash Up* (1947), and there would be no time for Hollywood house-hunting. Fortunately, Arlene's friend and *Overtons* (1945) co-performer, Glenda Farrell, offered the temporary use of her vacant home. Martin flew back to Los Angeles immediately, and before Arlene could join her new husband, she had to wrap up several of her own work engagements. This was new territory for the fiercely driven actress, but Arlene willingly left Broadway behind—at least for the time being.

---

329. *The News Patterson* (New Jersey). May 15, 1946. Arlene Francis Weds Hollywood Notable
330. Ibid.
331. Ibid.
332. *Arlene Francis: A Memoir* (1978). By Arlene Francis with Florence Rome. P 64
333. Martin Gabel on *What's My Line?* June 18, 1961

# Chapter 4

"Back to Hollywood, Martin!"[334]

– Arlene Francis on What's My Line?

In the Summer of 1946, Los Angeles was a motion picture epicenter. Film noir was the order of the day, and producers like Martin Gabel were making magic behind the scenes. His current picture, *Smash Up: The Story of a Woman* (1947), was coming along at a steady pace, and life was full. Newly married, Arlene and Martin were in the process of settling into life in The Valley. Their temporary home was Glenda Farrell's borrowed house, and they were both excited about what lay ahead, but Arlene doubted whether she could make it in Movieland. "I wasn't Hollywood's notion of a big star."[335] Despite her uncertainty, she was ambitious and determined to find work. It simply wasn't in her nature to do otherwise. For now, domestic duties took center stage, and this time around, married life meant happiness and raising a family. The Gabels were ready to take on the world together, but they still had a few things to accomplish first—like unpacking the furniture.

"Is there anything I can do for you, darling?"[336] asked Martin as Arlene pulled the last of their luggage trunks into the living room. The crates had finally arrived from New York, carrying all of their worldly belongings. What should have been a warm and cozy scene became the setting for their first marital quarrel. Arlene remembered the event with good humor. When the trunks arrived, "Martin was sitting out on the terrace with Lou

---

334. *What's My Line?* May 24, 1964
335. *Arlene Francis: A Memoir* (1978). By Arlene Francis With Florence Rome. P. 72
336. *Arlene Francis: A Memoir* (1978). By Arlene Francis With Florence Rome p. 73

Calhern, laughing and scratching while I lugged suitcases and packing crates into the house, panting every step of the way."[337] Adjusting to their new life in Hollywood presented certain challenges. Firstly, Arlene wasn't used to housework as a primary occupation, and when Martin wasn't busy on the *Universal* set, he enjoyed playing a game of pool at the bar or frequenting the horse races. Although they had known each other for years before tying the knot, living together as husband and wife presented a different set of dynamics. "Domestic bliss to Marty meant that everything was blissful as long as I was the domestic,"[338] but their first spat as a married couple was short-lived. "We must have made up because shortly after that, I discovered I was pregnant."[339]

Martin was "ecstatic at the news,"[340] and his sensitive side surfaced immediately. He became very attentive and protective and was constantly concerned with his wife's wellbeing. She recalled some examples: ". . . Stuffing pillows behind my back when I sat down, shielding me from being jostled in a crowd."[341] His tenderness was touching, but after a while, Martin's constant nurturing began to wear on her nerves. "[He was] treating me generally as though I were recovering from a major heart attack. I finally had to tell him that pregnancy isn't a disease . . . and would he please buzz off and stop saying, 'Hadn't you better sit down, darling'?"[342]

Considering Martin's concerns, it is far from likely that he was pleased by her decision to take a stage role that summer, not to mention one that required considerable travel. Though she was nearly 40 years old, Arlene felt well and able to work during her pregnancy. Besides, her condition was not obvious in August of 1946. So, she joined actor Bert Lahr in a revival of *Burlesque* (1946)[343] at the Greenwich Playhouse in Connecticut for a week's run. She was cast as Bonny, a part originally

---

337. Ibid.
338. *Arlene Francis: A Memoir* (1978). By Arlene Francis with Florence Rome. P. 73
339. Ibid.
340. *Arlene Francis A Memoir* (1978). By Arlene Francis with Florence Rome. P. 74
341. Ibid.
342. *Arlene Francis: A Memoir* (1978). By Arlene Francis with Florence Rome. P. 74
343. *Bronxville Reporter*. August 8, 1946. P. 7

played by Barbara Stanwyck in the 1920s and later by Jean Parker on Broadway. The summer tryout was a success, and one special dress rehearsal was recorded as a 45-minute WNYC radio feature titled *Straw Hat Documentary (1946)*.[344] Following the final curtain, Arlene took on one more job before returning to Hollywood. She stepped in for panel moderator Paula Stone, and served as guest hostess of the radio show *Leave it to the Girls* (circa 1940).[345] The format consisted of a revolving panel of famous females answering advice questions from listeners.[346] The program focused on women's issues and ran the gamut from the serious to the silly.[347] Popular panelists included Lucille Ball, Sylvia Sidney, and Dorothy Kilgallen.[348] *Leave it to the Girls* (circa 1940) was known for its spontaneity and wit,[349] making Arlene the perfect complement to the lively atmosphere.

Once back in Los Angeles, there were other matters to attend to. The Gabel's moved from their borrowed house and settled into a bungalow at *The Garden of Allah* on the Sunset Strip. The sprawling Spanish-style property was once the home of silent film star Alla Nazimova. In the 1920s, it opened as a hotel and apartment complex. By the time Arlene and Martin arrived, it had already housed a number of notables, such as John Barrymore, F. Scott Fitzgerald, and even Albert Einstein, apocryphally. However, for the Gabels, the Garden of Allah was simply a place to call home while they awaited the birth of their baby, and typical of Arlene's ambitious nature, she was not content to wait without working.

In the fall of '46, her agent, Marty Goodman, contacted her about starring in a new radio drama called *The Affairs of Ann Scotland* (1946), for ABC. The 30-minute show was broadcast from Hollywood on Wednesday evenings. Arlene starred as Ann, the detective with the sultry voice, who travels the world chasing adventure and capturing male

---

344. *Daily News*. New York, August 21, 1946. Listening In.
345. *The Times Dispatch*, August 24, 1946 p. 9
346. *On the Air: The Encyclopedia of Old-Time Radio* (1998). By, John Dunning.
347. Ibid
348. Ibid
349. Ibid

prey with her seductive charms. The series premiere, titled "Too Many Husbands Spell Murder," was broadcast the day before Halloween. It told the shocking tale of an actress who discovers a corpse in her apartment.[350] The script's clever dialogue was enhanced by Arlene's enticing elocution and director Helen Mack's skillful insight.[351] The *Ann Scotland* (1946) set was indeed under the influence of the female. "I was *very* pregnant"[352] recalled Arlene, but "So what if I had to waddle into and out of the studio, if I had to stand sideways at the microphone? I was back in action and delighted about it."[353]

Martin's career in Hollywood was also flourishing at that time. Production on the Susan Hayward picture *Smash Up* (1945) wrapped in September, and by January, he was set to direct another Hayward vehicle, *The Washington Flyer* (1946). But before shooting began, Walter Wanger made a change and swapped the script for *The Lost Moment* (1947). This new film, based on the Henry James novel, *The Aspern Papers* (1888), would become Martin's sole credit as a motion picture director. The challenge of the task was intensified by conflict with the picture's leading lady. By several accounts, Susan Hayward and Martin consistently clashed on the set, and the movie wasn't a box office hit, but later critics would take note of Martin's skill behind the camera. In his book, *Memorable Films of the Forties* (1987), John Reid called his artistic direction "deft"[354] and described the film as "an atmospheric masterpiece."[355] Arlene was proud of Martin's success, but she was worried that it might signal a longer than anticipated stay in Hollywood.

A stage actress at heart, she feared being forgotten by the New York Theater scene. But her radio show, *Ann Scotland* (1946), was thriving,

---

350. The *Akron Beacon Journal.* (Akron Ohio). October 30, 1946. Special Spots.

351. *Radio Life.* January 26, 1947.

352. *Arlene Francis: A Memoir* (1978). By Arlene Francis with Florence Rome. P. 24

353. *Arlene Francis: A Memoir* (1978). By Arlene Francis with Florence Rome. P. 76

354. *Memorable Films of the Forties* (1987). By John Reid. P. 126. Retrieved from Google Books.

355. *Ibid*

and there was talk about the possibility of turning it into a movie with Arlene as its star[356]. Martin even made small appearances in the drama, and in January, *Radio Life* magazine columnist, Shirley Gordon, interviewed Arlene on the set. Naturally, she discussed her excitement about the impending arrival of the new baby. The article[357] noted how she "beamed" while talking about it. "It doesn't matter which it is," she said, "but if it's a girl, we have her name picked out. It'll be Kitty."[358] One of the reasons was that she and Martin were good friends with actress Kitty Carlisle, and Martin thought the name Kitty Gabel would fit nicely on a marquee. At the time, he was convinced that any child of theirs would be an actor. He was also sure that Arlene was carrying a boy. She recalled becoming a bit exasperated by his certainty, especially when he proudly referred to the baby as their son. "'Our *son*,'" I screamed. "Who gave you an inside track on what we're going to have?"[359]

They would soon find out for sure, but first, Arlene would finish the *Ann Scotland* (1946) series. She once said that she worked on that show "right up to time to go to the hospital."[360] Her exaggeration wasn't very far off. The baby was due February 1,[361] and the last episode aired on January 22. Newspaper listings that evening printed the following series synopsis: "Tonight at 8, the lady detective will set out to find the killer of a night club owner whose will provides $10,000 for the capture of his murderer."[362] The article also mused that the stork was arriving soon, and tonight's episode could be the last. Due to her delicate condition, the mother-to-be was escorted to and from the studio by a hired hand to guard her welfare.[363] "It was a funny situation now that I think about

---

356. *Ogdensburg Journal*. December 4, 1946
357. *Radio Life*. January 26, 1947.
358. Ibid.
359. *Arlene Francis: A Memoir* (1978). By Arlene Francis with Florence Rome. P. 81
360. *TV Radio Mirror*. July-December. 1955
361. *Radio Life*. January 26, 1947.
362. *The Indianapolis News*. January 22, 1947. Indianapolis On the Air. By Martha McHatton.
363. The Waco Tribune Jan, 4, 1947. New York: This and That.

it,"[364] Arlene reflected. "Here I was great with child, and acting as a private eyelash, dashing around having all sorts of wild adventures."[365] After one last escapade for *Ann Scotland* (1946), it was time to take it easy back at the Garden of Allah.

But part of the mystique of living there was the exciting nightlife located just across the street. It was tempting to enjoy dinner on the town or attend a party at one of the nearby supper clubs. So, with a few days left before she was to give birth, the vital and energetic Arlene gave a dinner party at The Player's restaurant. The Gabel's guest of honor was their friend, Aldous Huxley, whom Martin called "one of the greatest writers and philosophers of our time."[366] Arlene later referred to the event as "the dinner I remember best,"[367] and the reasons for that were about to become obvious. During the party, Huxley entertained the Gabel's with amusing stories about his practice of yoga. When one took an inadvertently humorous turn, Arlene forcibly tried to repress her laughter. "I'm sure it was that which brought on my labor pains,"[368] she recalled, and so, it was a note of humor that set the entire scene into motion. Looking back, she wasn't too surprised that laughter prompted the delivery of her son. "He's always hated to miss a joke."[369]

On that January evening, the Gabels were at the beginning of a life-changing experience. Arlene tried to remain calm as she told Martin what was happening. They promptly left the restaurant and returned to their bungalow. From there, the scene became what Arlene described as a "Keystone comedy sequence."[370] "There is no way to say it eloquently. The water broke, and we scurried all over the Garden of Allah, gathering

364. *Radio TV Mirror*. Jul – Dec 1955. The Gift of Happiness. As Daughter, Wife, Mother – and Beloved Star – Arlene Francis has earned and thoroughly enjoys The Gift of Happiness. By Helen Bolstad. PP. 58, 89. 90,91.
365. Ibid
366. Aldous Huxley's niece Sue Huxley appeared as a contestant on *What's My Line?* January 23, 1965. Her line was: Grooms and feeds prize cattle.
367. Arlene Francis: A Memoir (1978). By Arlene Francis with Florence Rome. P. 77
368. Arlene Francis A Memoir (1978). By Arlene Francis with Florence Rome. P. 78
369. Ibid.
370. Ibid.

up spare towels and wrapping me up in them."[371] Next, the inexperienced parents-to-be embarked on a wild ride to the hospital. Martin's anxiety took a toll on his driving skills, and in between her contractions and their LaSalle touring car swerving between lanes, Arlene struggled to direct Martin through the LA traffic. "I let out piercing shrieks of pain, alternating with terror."[372]

When they reached the hospital, the nervous couple had to part ways in the maternity ward. As was customary in those days, husbands and wives did not experience birth together. But while Arlene labored with her first and only child, Martin was likely undergoing his own form of distress. Not much attention was given to the plight of waiting fathers in those days, and many of them expressed their feelings of worry and elation in journals known as "Father's Books." These shared diaries of sorts were provided by hospitals and were standard in maternity waiting rooms back then. We will never know whether Martin made an entry in such a book, but he did write a special notation about the birth of his son in the margins of his copy of Oswald Spangler's *Decline of the West*. Martin wrote: "PETER BORN THIS MORNING, 5 AM, JAN 28 1947, 8 LBS 12 OUNCES.[373] "Suddenly the world was perfect,"[374] Arlene said of the moment she held her son in her arms for the first time, and "Martin!" she recalled, "Martin was not to be contained for the joy of having a son!!!"[375] Exuberant, he "woke up a florist"[376] and ordered three dozen Talisman roses to be delivered to her hospital room.

New motherhood was a special time for Arlene, and she became happily immersed in every experience. She lovingly tended to Peter and sat at his crib reading letters aloud from Lou Calhern, whom she and Martin had asked to be their son's godfather. "We were very sentimental

---

371. Ibid.
372. Ibid.
373. *Status Magazine*. A Duet for Two Stars. 1970. P. 37
374. *Arlene Francis: A Memoir* (1978) By Arlene Francis with Florence Rome. P. 78
375. Ibid.
376. Ibid.

in our feelings about Lou,"[377] said Arlene. He was a dear friend, and their decision had nothing to do with his ability to provide religious guidance, but rather, she explained, "to weld him even more into our family than he already was."[378] When Lou and his wife Marianne went back east for a play, he sent many letters addressed to an infant Peter. They were a thoughtful assortment of current events, peppered with humor and insights about manhood. Arlene later reflected on his place of importance in their lives. "The part that touches me was that it was obvious that the godfather-godson relationship meant something more to Lou than just an honorary status . . . How glad I am that we were able to let him share Peter with us. I know it enriched his life, as he has enriched ours."[379]

Martin also savored sweet moments with his newborn son. "Instead of crooning "Rock a Bye Baby" as any civilian (non-theatrical) father would have done [he began] whispering in his ear, "'All the world's a stage. . . .'"[380] Actually, the stage was something Arlene hadn't thought about since Peter's birth. The natural ease that came with being a mother brought a new sense of fulfillment. "I was amazed at how much pleasure I could derive from the sound of a burp, and for a while, I even stopped thinking about working."[381] Long before becoming a mother, Arlene had established a personal pursuit that satisfied her desire to work. She loved being an actress, but she attributed her ambitious nature, in part, to her own father's work ethic.[382] Constant work meant a steady stream of income – and she had a family of her own to think of now.

In time, Arlene got back into the rhythm of work. That May, she returned to radio in an afternoon drama called *The Best Things in Life* (1947).[383] The series starred her opposite Sam Wanamaker and was part of a new trend in post-war programming. Highlighting union activism, it

---

377. *Arlene Francis: A Memoir* (1978). By Arlene Francis with Florence Rome. P. 79

378. *Arlene Francis: A Memoir* (1978). By Arlene Francis with Florence Rome. P. 79

379. *Arlene Francis: A Memoir* (1978). By Arlene Francis with Florence Rome. P. 81

380. *Arlene Francis: A Memoir* (1978). By Arlene Francis with Florence Rome. P. 82

381. Ibid.

382. *Radio TV Mirror*. July-December. 1955.

383. The *Salt Lake City Tribune*. May 9, 1947

gave voice to the labor issues facing American workers.[384] The series struck a chord with listeners[385] and was sponsored by the American Federation of Labor.[386] It also brought Arlene back to the airwaves and prepped her for the next acting venture.

In July of '47, she made a brief trip east to star in the play *Candlelight* (1947)[387] at the County Theatre in Suffern, New York. The script was something of a silly, lighthearted love triangle, but it proved that Arlene could still headline a show. Although an advertisement in a local New York newspaper announced her soft comeback, its content did not exactly present Arlene as a seasoned stage actress. The piece referred to her as a "radio star"[388] and a "comparatively newcomer to the theatre."[389] While "newcomer" was not quite an accurate description, the article did mention that she had been in "constant demand"[390] following *The Doughgirls* (1945).

When Candlelight completed its week's run, Arlene returned to Hollywood, and was offered a role in the film adaptation of Arthur Miller's Pulitzer Prize-winning play *All My Sons* (1948).[391] In the film, released by *Universal*, Arlene played the role of Sue Bayliss. The part was small, but she would be in the company of actors such as Burt Lancaster and Edward G. Robinson. *All My Sons* (1948) was filmed on location in Santa Rosa, California and premiered that spring. It also gave Arlene her first credentials as a Hollywood film actress since *Murders in the Rue*

---

384. *Waves of Opposition: Labor and the Struggle for Democratic Radio* (2006). By, Elizabeth Fones-Wolf.

385. Ibid

386. The *Salt Lake City Tribune*. May 9, 1947

387. *Ramapo Valley Independent*. July 2, 1947

388. Ibid.

389. Ibid.

390. Ibid.

391. NOTE: In a 1961 article from the Miami (Oklahoma) Daily News-Record, Arlene stated: "When I was pregnant, somebody lined up a tiny part in 'All My Sons', just to keep me busy. I played that famous cliché, the girl next door. In her 1978 memoir, she places the film after the birth of her son. And production on the film did not begin until September of 1947.

*Morgue* (1932). Her career was broadening, and her next role would put her back on Broadway.

Elisabeth Bergner, who had produced *The Overtons*, asked her to appear in *Cup of Trembling* (1948). The story, based upon the Louis Paul novel, *Breakdown* (1941), was about women struggling with alcoholism. Ms. Bergner had the lead role, and Arlene was to co-star as Sheila Vane, a former alcoholic. When the offer was first presented to her, she was elated but struggled with the decision. The role would require her to travel east again, and the engagement would be longer than the seven-day run in *Candlelight* (1947). Martin urged her to go and calmed her conscience by reminding her that Peter would be in the good care of his father and nurse. She accepted the part.

*Cup of Trembling* (1948) opened on April 5, 1948 at the Colonial Theater in Boston, followed by a run at the Music Box in New York. The show closed in just over a month, and reviews were critical, but Arlene's performance garnered substantial praise. A write-up in *Billboard* called opening night "a grueling evening," while at the same time noted that "Miss Francis is stunningly attractive and pointedly effective."[392] Not a bad notice for a 40-year-old new mother re-entering the workforce! More importantly, the best thing to come from *Cup of Trembling* (1948) was the family reunion it prompted. Instead of Arlene returning to Hollywood after the close of the play, Martin and Peter would join her in New York. Martin was ready to get back to Broadway himself, and it was time to make the long-awaited return. Arlene recalled being reunited with her little family at the airport. At the time, her primary concern was whether her husband could handle the task of traveling with a toddler. Years later, Arlene would make a public apology to Martin, in her memoir, for doubting him. He not only handled the entire trip without incident, but the sight of Peter taking his first unsteady steps brought Arlene to tears. "Martin looked smug and happy, and I was a laughing, crying wreck."[393]

---

392. The *Billboard*. April 14, 1948. By Riley, B. Out of Town Opening. The Cup of Trembling. pp 41.

393. *Arlene Francis: A Memoir* (1978). By Arlene Francis with Florence Rome. P. 84

The couple had spent two eventful years in Hollywood. They had left the east coast as newlyweds and returned as a family of three— richer, stronger, and more determined than ever. Watch out, New York! The Gabels were home at last.

# Chapter Five

"My mother had a unique ability to transmit love across a television screen"[394]

– Peter Gabel

*What's My Line?* (1950) aired on television for the first time in February of 1950. The evolving medium of TV presented a new era in entertainment and brought Arlene Francis into the homes of viewers nationwide. The popular CBS game show challenged a panel of four notables to guess the occupations of contestants. Aside from its fun and simple format, the game was also an exceptional showcase for Arlene's quick wit and trademark charm. Television took notice of her, and she soon became a favorite fixture in the homes of American viewers. Typical of her ambitious nature, Arlene assumed a full schedule and welcomed new opportunities with enthusiasm. But in the pre-dawn of 1950, Arlene and Martin were returning to the rhythm of life in New York City. They were parents now, as well as actors, and the amount of work they took on had to be carefully considered. For Arlene, television offered a steady income and a secure place in the hearts of American viewers. However, it was not exclusively fulfilling. The Broadway stage still beckoned her, and when granted a spare moment, she answered its call.

The play, *Figure of a Girl* (1949), opened at New Haven's Shubert Theatre in January of 1949. Its future on the Great White Way depended on the success of the tryout. Based on a French play by Jean-Pierre Aumont, the two-act comedic drama was produced by *The Theatre Guild*.

---

394. News article. *Gentle Pioneers* (Circa 2001).

Arlene was cast in the role of Madeline Benoit-Benoit, a complicated character and the wife of a French financier. She inevitably falls in love with the wrong man, and the rest, as they say, is theatrical history. But despite the predictable undertones, *Figure of a Girl* (1949) made it to Broadway in February. It debuted, however, with a new title: *My Name is Aquilon* (1949). Reviews for the 31-show production were mixed. While one critic scolded the play's "talentless direction,"[395] Arlene received noteworthy recognition. The New York Theatre Critic's Review boasted: "The ever-reliable Arlene Francis is excellent as usual."[396] and *Billboard* praised her for "a truly great interpretation to a part that could easily have gotten out of hand."[397]

Martin was also back at work in the theatre. In the late 40s, he co-produced and directed *The Survivors* (1948). The script was written by Irwin Shaw and Peter Viertel, but at least one source credits Martin as a co-writer.[398] The western-themed production was set in a ranch town after the Civil War and featured Louis Calhern and Hume Cronyn. It opened to meager attendance at the Playhouse Theatre in January of 1948 and closed after only 8 performances. The response from critics was not as discouraging. *Variety* noted that Martin directed "with authority"[399] but suggested that the play would fare better as a Hollywood film. This latest effort marked Martin's second time as producer of an Irwin Shaw play since *The Assassin (1945)*. His collaborations with Shaw did not always result in professional success, but Martin explained that success was not the chief reason for the work. "When people ask me why I did Irwin Shaw's plays, I always recall an answer a Hollywood producer gave to a similar question. He said that he produced movies for many reasons— to

---

395. *The Collected Works of Harold Clurman* (1994). Edited by Marjorie Loggia and Glenn Young. P. 190

396. *The New York theatre Critic's Review* (1949). P. 365

397. The Billboard. January 15, 1949. The Billboard. Legitimate Out-of-Town Openings. PP 46-47

398. The Survivors Production Staff. IBDB Broadway Internet Database. https://www. ibdb.com

399. *Variety*. January 21, 1948. Legitimate. Plays on Broadway. P. 53

make money, and so on— but he was always hoping to find a movie to produce that he really loved."[400]

As working stage actors, Martin and Arlene were consistently striving for professional fulfillment. Broadway offered a platform for both talent and expression, and in recent years, several of Martin's productions had carried meaningful social messages. His role as Cassius in Welles's anti-fascist adaptation of Julius Caesar (1937) was of particular significance, and in the forties, his participation with Stage for Action and the Federal Theatre resulted in powerful stage dramas that challenged the status quo. His production of *The Medicine Show* (1940) served as a prime example. The play's director, Jules Dassin, recalled Martin asking him to stage the show around the time of the "tragic pink-slip days when people were being fired."[401] The message of *The Medicine Show* (1940) called attention to the unequal access to medical care in America,[402] and was among the socially progressive works cited as "living newspapers."[403]

As the 1950s approached, Martin was feeling the sting of the blacklist. The onset of McCarthyism had taken hold, and the fact that Martin had been named in *Red Channels* likely affected his employability. Arlene was incensed by the actions of Senator Joseph McCarthy, and the consequences suffered by blacklisted actors. She spoke sparingly but sharply on the subject, remarking that "The headlines McCarthy sought had often been achieved at the expense of the lives and careers of some of our dearest friends."[404]

Asserting her opinion was not typical of Arlene's public personality. She admitted, "I find it terribly hard to speak up or behave in a way that will arouse anger against me."[405] But Martin would often encourage

---

400. *The Philadelphia Inquirer*. Apr. 5, 1953. W. Phila. High's Gabel Directs Locust Comedy. By, Barbara L. Wilson.

401. *Voices from the Federal Theatre*. Edited by Bonnie Nelson Schwartz and the Educational Film Center. P. 19

402. Ibid.

403. *Voices from the Federal Theatre*. Edited by Bonnie Nelson Schwartz and the Educational Film Center. P. 18

404. Arlene Francis: A Memoir (1978). By Arlene Francis with Florence Rome. P. 29

405. Ibid

her to speak her mind. And she sometimes did, especially if she was passionate about a subject. She recalled being at a party when she was compelled to remark on her feelings about McCarthy. Martin overheard this rare triumph, and was quite pleased that she had heeded his advice: "You must learn to speak out!"[406] he would tell her. When she did, it was a proud moment for both of them. "I do remember Martin's face,"[407] she said, of his reaction to her uncharacteristic boldness. "His jaw dropped . . . he didn't say 'By George, she's got it,' but clearly, he was absolutely delighted with me."[408]

While the McCarthy era raged on, television was becoming a popular fixture in American entertainment. This would provide new opportunities for Arlene, who had been asked to reprise her duties as mistress of ceremonies for *Blind Date* (1949). The ABC TV version of the patriotic match-making show turned Arlene into a recognizable public figure. "I had my picture in the paper hundreds of times," she explained, "but I could go almost anywhere with only the stray theater-goer recognizing me in a public place."[409] That all changed with television, and Arlene became a familiar face to people all over the country.

*Blind Date's* (1949) TV success rivaled its radio fame, and Arlene's spunky presence kept pace with the young contestants. *TV Radio Mirror* noted that "Arlene, an attractive brunette, reminds [the dating hopefuls] that she's not only one of the old married chaperones for the evening but also the mother of a two-year old boy."[410] She was most definitely a proud mother (mentioning Peter on the air when she got the chance), but she was not quite "old" as the piece suggested. At forty-two, Arlene could have easily been taken for a woman of thirty. Her youthful vitality and versatility made her a top choice for a returning hostess. A review in *Variety* noted that "Arlene Francis again demonstrated her ability to turn

---

406. Ibid
407. Arlene Francis: A Memoir (1978). By Arlene Francis with Florence Rome. P 30
408. Ibid
409. Arlene Francis: A Memoir (1978). By Arlene Francis with Florence Rome
410. *TV Radio Mirror,* July -Dec. 1949

a witty phrase quickly."[411] The article also complimented her "femcee chores"[412] as "charming and natural"[413] but gently criticized her occasional "overdone gabbing" with contestants.

One particularly amusing *Blind Date* (1949) guest was Bonzo, the famous monkey. "He took one look at me and zing went the strings of his heart"[414] recalled Arlene. The two engaged in humorous interplay for a while, and the audience howled with laughter as the monkey held tightly to Arlene, refusing to be separated from her. Bonzo ignored a few friendly attempts to part ways, and as a result, Arlene's voice took on a more serious tone. The otherwise docile animal became upset and promptly bit her on the finger. The handlers intervened, and Bonzo was escorted from the stage. In the spirit of the show must go on, Arlene waited until the end of the program to receive medical treatment. Fortunately, there happened to be a doctor in the audience that night. After the show, he bandaged Arlene's bleeding finger before she proceeded to the hospital for a tetanus shot. However, Bonzo met with a terrible fate the next day, succumbing to smoke inhalation during a fire in the building where he was caged.

Regardless of the occasional mishap, *Blind Date* (1949) had made a successful transition from radio to television, and Arlene followed suit. Nevertheless, she refused to abandon the theatre in the process. In December of 1949, she appeared on Broadway as Carolyn Hopewell in the play *Metropole* (1949) at the Lyceum Theatre. The show's reception was lackluster, and it closed after only two performances. However, Ward Morehouse of the *New York Theatre Critic's Review*[415] called Arlene "incisive" and credited her for enlivening the play during her first scene. The fact that Arlene was consistently named a stand-out presence in the opinion of critics propelled her career forward; and although she would have preferred another role on Broadway,

---

411. *Variety.* October 1950 Television Reviews
412. Ibid.
413. Ibid.
414. *Arlene Francis: A Memoir* (1978). By Arlene Francis with Florence Rome. P. 88
415. *New York's Theatre Critic's Review.* December 7, 1949. P. 202

her next job offer would cement her status as a television game show icon.

*What's My Line?* (1950) didn't sound particularly exciting to Arlene at first. Unlike other games of the era, there were no antics or large prizes. The show, created by Mark Goodson and Bill Todman, would simply consist of a panel of four who would try to guess the occupations of contestants. To excite viewers, the game included a "Mystery Guest" segment. A celebrity would appear on each show and do their best to stump the now blindfolded panel. The program was moderated by John Daly, and the panel initially consisted of Dorothy Kilgallen, Dr. Richard H. Hoffman, Louis Untermeyer, and Arlene Francis.

The first show was broadcast live from New York on February 2, 1950. It was originally aired every other Tuesday on CBS TV. That summer, it began airing Sunday evenings at 10:30 pm and would assume that timeslot for the next seventeen years. Interestingly, Arlene was absent from the debut broadcast. "I don't honestly remember why I missed it, but I didn't think anything earth-shattering was going to result from this modest little show."[416] Back then, there was no way of knowing that *What's My line?* (1950) would eventually prove itself to be one of the longest-running game shows on television.

During the program's early period, a few adjustments would be made to the panel. Dr. Hoffman was replaced by comedy writer Hal Block, and Bennet Cerf permanently replaced Louis Untermeyer. The expulsion of Untermeyer reflected the influence of the McCarthy era. "Those were the days of the intimidation of networks and sponsors,"[417] Arlene recalled, "And Louis was suspected of having friends on the left side of the political spectrum. He was replaced...under circumstances which we were all pretty ashamed of, but which we could do nothing about... nobody felt strong enough to fight the tide of reaction which had overtaken the country."[418] Producer Mark Goodson expressed his own

---

416. *Arlene Francis: A Memoir* (1978). By Arlene Francis with Florence Rome. P. 92
417. *Arlene Francis: A Memoir* (1978). By Arlene Francis with Florence Rome. P. 93
418. *Ibid*

regret in a 1991 op-ed published in the New York Times. "I can't help but feeling that if I'd shown more courage . . . .if more of us would have been willing to take the heat, we could have brought that disgraceful era to a more rapid close."[419]

For the time being, *What's My Line?* (1950) offered audiences a chance to escape into a world of wit, style, and sophistication. By 1951, nearly 12 million American households had a television set,[420] and many of them were tuned to *What's My Line?* (1950) The program's initial format allowed viewers the chance to play along. According to the show's first review in *Variety,* this added a factor of fun. "The program has a strong element of viewer participation... About halfway in each segment, however, the audience is let in on the guest's trade, at which point the panel's fumbling to hit it provides laughs."[421] Humor did become an inadvertent part of the program. And, as Arlene noted, "The ad-libs were genuine, and, of course, unpredictable."[422] The spontaneous personality of Hal Block, for example, garnered mixed responses. "He got a little too cute at times, but it added to the fun,"[423] wrote an early reviewer. Apparently, CBS had concerns, and Hal Block was later replaced by comedian Fred Allen. Going forward, the regular panel lineup would remain unchanged until the untimely deaths of Allen in 1956 and Dorothy Kilgallen in 1965. The two were irreplaceable, and their seats would be filled with a series of revolving guest panelists throughout the years.

From the beginning, Arlene, Bennet, Fred, and Dorothy were the perfect complements to each other. John Daly expertly led the troop, bringing with him a large dose of competency and class. In addition to being a moderator, he had a successful career in broadcast journalism,

---

419. *If I Stood Up Earlier* (1991). By Mark Goodson. The New York Times http://www. nytimes.com
420. *History of Television* article by, Michael Stephens. New York University. https://www.nyc.edu
421. Variety. Wednesday. February 22, 1950 p. 31
422. *Arlene Francis: A Memoir* (1978). By Arlene Francis with Florence Rome P 94
423. *Variety.* Wednesday August 16, 1950 p. 31

even serving as a White House news correspondent. However, his association with *What's My Line?* (1950) endeared him to viewers. The special ingredient that made the show so entertaining has often been pondered. Arlene offered at least one explanation: "I think the ad-lib quality was one of the show's greatest assets. The tension and excitement were terrific for all of us."[424]

Each panelist brought something unique to the table. Dorothy Kilgallen was an accomplished journalist, and writer of the popular column, *The Voice of Broadway*. Her sharp mind and competitive nature kept viewers on the edge of their seat. Bennet Cerf, publisher and founder of *Random House*, clearly loved guessing occupations. Fred Allen kept everyone laughing, and Arlene left everyone wanting more. She declared that *What's My Line?* (1950) was "some of the greatest fun I've ever had," and beginning in the 1950s, it would become "not so much a show for me, but a way of life."[425]

The success of the program inevitably forced Arlene to make a decision regarding her career focus. *What's My Line?* (1950) offered no signs of slowing down, and in light of that reality, it became "Utterly impossible for me to regard the theatre as my major aim, for I could never be too far from where [the show] was broadcasting."[426] Nevertheless, Arlene Francis, the panelist, was by no means an adequate substitute for Arlene Francis, the actress. She wanted the best of both worlds, and although that might be impossible to obtain, she was ambitious enough to try.

In June of 1950, Arlene appeared in the film *With These Hands* (1950). The documentary-style picture, produced by the International Ladies Garment Workers Union, dramatized the events of the Triangle Shirtwaist Factory Fire in Manhattan in 1911. Arlene had a solid role in the film, playing Jenny, the mother of a small child and the wife of a cloak-maker, portrayed by Sam Levine. The movie was well-received. Reviews praised the film for being "professional and high grade,"[427] and Arlene's

---

424. *Arlene Francis: A Memoir* (1978). By Arlene Francis with Florence Rome. P. 94
425. *Arlene Francis: A Memoir* (1978). By Arlene Francis with Florence Rome.
426. *Arlene Francis: A Memoir* (1978). By Arlene Francis with Florence Rome. P. 93
427. *Variety*. Film Reviews. June 1950

performance was called "sure and appealing."[428] *With These Hands* (1950) was recognized at the 1951 Academy Awards with a nomination for Best Documentary Feature film.[429]

As the fifties moved forward, Arlene was juggling regular stints on both *What's My Line?* (1950) and *Blind Date (1949)*. In addition, she signed on to yet another television program, *Prize Performance* (1950) on CBS. The show was a short-lived summer series and a forerunner to televised talent competitions. Hosted by broadcaster Cedric Adams, with actor Peter Donald and Arlene as judges, the show featured children demonstrating a variety of talents. A winner was chosen each week, and at the end of five weeks, they would compete for a $500 scholarship. *Prize Performance* was aired live on Mondays and Tuesdays until September of 1950.[430] By this time, her work on television was a constant, but she had by no means forgotten the theatre.

In April of 1950, she starred opposite Melvyn Douglas in the Edmund Wilson play, *The Little Blue Light* (1950). Martin had a role in the production as well, and it would mark the first time they appeared on the same stage since *Danton's Death (1938)*. This new play offered an unusual plot. The script placed an assortment of characters in a futuristic setting. Arlene portrayed Judith, the wife of a liberal newspaper writer. Martin was cast as a gardener, whose identity was later revealed to be Ahasuerus, the "Wandering Jew." Each character is tangled in a mysterious unfolding of ultimate destruction. The story was described as "a weird mishmash of politics, religion, philosophy . . . [and] dire prophecy."[431] According to one review, Martin gave a "provocative"[432] performance while Arlene "appeared constrained and "ill-at-ease."[433] *The Little Blue Light* (1950) was a peculiar play, and perhaps best described by

---

428. Ibid.
429. Winners and Nominees Documentary Feature 1951. https://www.oscars.org
430. *The Complete Directory of Prime-Time Network and Cable TV Shows 1946 -present* 9th ed. (2007). By Tim Brooks and Earle Marsh
431. *The Brooklyn Eagle.* April 30, 1950. Curtain Time by, Louis Schaffer
432. Ibid.
433. Ibid.

critic Louis Schaffer as "a conversation piece." It ran for 16 performances at the ANTA Theatre.

On Sunday nights, Arlene was on the panel of *What's My Line?* (1950) In September of 1951, she appeared sporting an eye patch emblazoned with a CBS logo. It was a symbol of the first in a series of eye incidents that would befall her in the years to come. This particular injury occurred in the most unlikely of ways. She explained, "Peter was sitting on my lap watching a Disney cartoon."[434] "Something in the movie scared him. He turned to bury his head in my shoulder, at the same time lifting his hand."[435] The result was a scratched cornea and a few weeks of wearing a protective cover. Arlene took it in stride, however, and in her effortless way, turned the eye patch into a fashion statement.

In addition to *What's My Line?* (1950) she became part of a new NBC-TV game called *Answer Yes or No* (1950), hosted by Moss Hart. The show was presented in a discussion-style format in response to current topics. The contestants were husband and wife teams who would compete against the show's regular panelists: Kitty Carlisle, Quentin Reynolds, and Arlene Francis. An early news article advertising the show, named Arlene and the other panelists as "co-partners in the package" [who] will cut in on the profits on a percentage basis."[436] *Answer Yes or No* (1950) aired for just three months. Arlene was the only one to remain on the panel until the program's finale in July of 1950.[437]

As her popularity on television grew, she became more than just a game show favorite. Arlene's sense of style made her a model for millions of American women. This was due in part to her Sunday night appearances on *What's My Line?* (1950) "Dressing in evening clothes gave our show a look of casual elegance," she explained. "When the walk-in entrance was cancelled to save more time for the playing of the game,

---

434. *Arlene Francis: A Memoir* (1978). By Arlene Francis with Florence Rome P. 105
435. Ibid
436. *Variety*. April. 1950. Husband, Wives Let Arguments Pay off. P. 2
437. *The Complete Directory to Prime-Time Network and Cable TV Shows 1946 – Present.* Tim Brooks and Earle Marsh. P. 70

people called in irritation because they wanted the fashion show!"[438] Female viewers resonated with Arlene's versatile sense of style. Even while dressed to the nines, she was unafraid to playfully adjust the shoulder straps of her dress or toss her head back with explosive laughter. There was a realness about her, and she proved that a woman could be both regal and relaxed. Looking glamourous didn't have to mean appearing stoic and uncomfortable. Arlene made beauty attainable, and her fashion personality might well have been described as elegance having fun.

Viewers wanted more. Arlene was asked to host a weekly TV program called *Fashion Magic* (1951). As its title reveals, the show offered beauty tips and wardrobe advice for women. It aired Tuesday afternoons at 3:30 pm on CBS and was noted for being a weekly viewing highlight. It was dubbed "a show not to be missed"[439] by *Radio Television Mirror* and Arlene was named "one of America's best dressed women."[440] Around that time, her signature diamond heart pendant also became an influential fashion statement. Millions of American women wanted an "Arlene Francis heart necklace" of their own, and replicas were made and sold at department stores. As beautiful as the pendant was, Arlene wore it out of sentimentality. Martin presented it to her as a gift on their first wedding anniversary, and she never took it off, except to have it cleaned or repaired. Aside from being a public-appointed fashion connoisseur, Arlene's position as a friendly, intelligent, and capable personality made her a favorite with viewers and networks. But she was still a stage actress, and neither she nor Martin strayed very far from Broadway.

In December 1950, *King Lear* (1606) opened at the National Theatre. Martin appeared as the Earl of Kent, with Louis Calhern cast in the title role. Arlene was not in the play, but one particular performance would become something of a family affair. It was decided that their young son, Peter, should attend the performance. "He was only about three years old,

---

438. *Arlene Francis: A Memoir* (1978). By Arlene Francis with Florence Rome. P. 94
439. *Radio Television Mirror*. Jul. – Dec. 1951. Program Highlights in Television Viewing P. 73
440. *Radio Television Mirror*. Jul. – Dec. 1951. Program Highlights in Television Viewing

but I didn't care,"[441] Arlene explained. She thought it was important that he see his father and godfather, Louis Calhern, on the stage. It was no doubt a proud moment for Martin, who, from his son's infancy, had tried to impart a Shakespearean education. This particular evening, however, would take a humorous turn. Arlene recalled the event: "Peter had been sitting quietly as an angel"[442] as the play unfolded, but the volatile scene between King Lear and the Earl of Kent disturbed him. "I felt his little body tense up, and finally, unable to contain himself any longer, he piped out, 'Uncle Lou shouldn't talk to Daddy like that!' He broke up the entire audience, and the cast had a hard time keeping its composure too."[443] Peter made his last appearance in the audience, and King Lear ran for 48 performances.

The following year, Martin began working briefly on television. He served as Master of Ceremonies for the game show *With This Ring* (1951), a question-and-answer program for engaged couples.[444] Originally titled *Happily Ever After* (1951), the show presented contestants with a set of what-would-you-do questions followed by insightful evaluations from celebrity judges. While the program was initially hosted by Bill Slater, it was Martin who presided over the last two episodes in March of 1951. The show's demise came just 60 days after its debut. In an age of emerging entertainment, it provided Martin with a limited opportunity to join the televised game show ranks for the first time. *With This Ring* (1951) became no more than a passing casualty of early programming, but Martin's next professional appearance would create a lasting impression.

In March of 1951, he made his film acting debut in the motion picture, *M* (1951). The one-letter title stood for murder, and the film noir cast Martin as Charlie Marshall, the boss of a crime syndicate who sets out in search of a child-murderer. The movie was a remake of

---

441. *Arlene Francis: A Memoir* (1978). By Arlene Francis with Florence Rome. P. 86
442. Ibid.
443. Ibid.
444. *The Complete Directory to Prime-Time Network and Cable TV Shows 1946 – Present* (2009). By Tim Brooks and Earle F. Marsh. P. 1531

the acclaimed 1931 German picture of the same name, starring actor Peter Lorre and directed by Fritz Lang. Twenty years later, the updated version featured David Wayne, Howard Da Silva, and Luther Adler. *M* (1951) was well-received by *Variety* and Martin's performance was called "outstanding," but its future on the big screen was threatened by censorship and the blacklist. Because the film's director, Joseph Losey, was under investigation by the House Committee on Un-American Activities, and because *M* featured blacklisted actors, some screenings were boycotted.[445] In addition, the state of Ohio also banned the film, citing its potential for dangerous influence.[446] The ban was overturned by the Supreme Court in 1954[447]

The controversy surrounding *M* (1951) had no apparent ill effect on Martin's career, and he was cast in *Fourteen Hours* for 20th Century Fox. The movie was loosely based[448] on an article in the *New Yorker* covering the 1938 suicide of John William Warde. Directed by Henry Hathaway, the noir-style drama starred Richard Basehart, Grace Kelley, and Agnes Moorehead. Martin played the part of Dr. Strauss, a psychiatrist who attempts to coach a distraught man from the ledge of a high-rise building. Martin's crisp diction and sensitive inflections made him an excellent fit for the role. *Fourteen Hours* (1951) was nominated for an Academy Award for Best Art Direction, and was named among the top 10 pictures of 1951.[449]

One of the many consistencies in Martin's career was his participation in projects that were skillfully made and purposefully driven. For example, he narrated the 1950 V-E Day anniversary documentary, *Pursuit of Peace (Fear Itself)* (1950), co-produced by Norman Corwin. The program, written by Allan Sloane, aired on Mutual Radio and recounted the events

---

445. Muller, Eddie (April 28, 2019) Intro to the Turner Classic Movies presentation of *M*

446. *Dirty Words and Filthy Pictures: Film and the First Amendment.* (2016). By, Jeremy Geltzer p. 145

447. *Hollywood and the Law* (2017) by, Paul McDonald Emily Carman, Eric Hoyt. P.140

448. *Photoplay* Jan – Jun 1951

449. National Board of Review of Motion Pictures, 1951

of Victory Day.[450] Reviews for the piece were substantial, with *Variety* calling it a "searching and eloquent statement" and declaring Martin's narration to be "informed and trenchant."[451] The dramatic work was his second collaboration with Corwin and led to his subsequent narration of the educational film *Day of Deliverance* (1951).

The Deliverance project chronicled the aftermath of the Holocaust, and focused on "the relief, reconstruction, and resettlement operations for Jews in Europe, Africa, and the near east."[452] It was written by Raphael Levy and sponsored by the Jewish humanitarian organization, *The Joint Committee*. The documentary-style feature also provided a Yiddish translation, narrated by Norman Gilmovsky.[453] A review called the effort "fair" but noted the "effectiveness of the narration."[454] Regardless of its reception, the piece covered a subject close to Martin's heart. He felt a connection to the plight and pride of his ancestors and was "given to speaking of 'My People' with great emotion"[455] noted Arlene.

In addition to an internalized sensitivity, Martin also had the ability to evoke deep feelings through his work. His distinctive voice was a highly affective instrument that stirred more than the auditory senses. Recognition of this rare ability to capture the attention of listeners resulted in numerous projects requiring expert elocution. Such was his narration in the 1952 televised mini-series, *Mr. Lincoln: The End and the Beginning* (1952).[456] The program aired on CBS in five bi-weekly installments and starred actor Royal Dano as Abraham Lincoln. Martin's narration readied the viewing audience for the progressing scenes, and his delivery of Walt Whitman's poem, "When Lilacs Last in the Dooryard Bloom'd," provided a dramatic soundtrack. Though his great success was

---

450. *Variety.* May 1950 Radio Reviews
451. Ibid
452. *Educational Film Guide.* (1951). P. 276
453. *The Jewish Audio-Visual Review.* Volumes 9-16. 1959
454. Ibid
455. Arlene Francis: A Memoir (1978). By Arlene Francis with Florence Rome. P. 61
456. Abraham Lincoln on Screen: Fictional and Documentary. By Mark S. Reinhart

undeniably fueled by the power of the spoken word, Martin's next project required a far different approach.

In the fall of 52, he appeared in the spy-noir thriller, *The Thief* (1952) starring Ray Milland. Interestingly, neither Martin, who played an "enemy agent" nor any of the other actors in the film used their voices. The movie's unique method of storytelling contained no spoken dialogue. This was compensated for, however, by an Oscar-nominated score. *The Thief* (1952) was an initial success, and Jonathan Kilbourne of *Modern Screen* noted that "Martin Gabel is superb as the Communist contact man."[457] His versatility as an actor was a great strength for his durability on screen and stage. Continually noted for his superior efforts, critics came to expect greatness from Martin Gabel. And he did not disappoint.

Cast as a racketeer in *Deadline USA* (1952), Martin turned in a skillful performance. The crime-noir starred Humphrey Bogart and told the tale of a newspaper editor who risks failure for freedom of the press. Although it broke no records at the box office,[458] the film became a solid piece of the 1950's motion picture cannon. Martin expertly navigated the character of Tomas Rienzi and once again proved his ability to make the most of a supporting role. His performance was also a memorable one in the Gabel family, with Peter calling it "one of my favorites of my father's roles."[459]

While Martin's projects tackled heavy subjects, Arlene's work leaned predominately toward the lighter side. During the fifties, she was asked to co-host two CBS radio shows with Bill Cullen. The first was called *It Happens Every Day* (1952), and featured five-minute humorous news stories. The entertaining sound bite was a hit with listeners. It was picked up by ABC radio, and its air time was expanded from one day a week to six.[460] In addition to the show's positive reception, Arlene and Bill also teamed up on *Fun for All* (1952), a male vs. female quiz game.[461] The

---

457. *Movie Reviews. Modern Screen.* Dec. 1952 -Nov. 1953
458. *Tough as Nails: The Life and Films of Richard Brooks* (2011). By Douglass K. Daniel
459. Email communication with Peter Gabel August 20, 2020
460. *Sponsor.* March 1950 p. 16
461. *Quizmaster. The Life and Times and Fun and Games of Bill Cullen.* (2013). By, Adam Nedeff.

weekend show aired on ABC and CBS,[462] proving that radio programming was holding its own during the onset of television.

TV was steadily taking over. Its early evolution was one of the primary reasons why *What's My Line?* (1950) was so successful. Airing on only one of three major TV networks at the time, the show created a collective viewership. This not only provided Arlene with maximum exposure to American audiences (further exemplified by her presence on all three networks in the ensuing years), but it also formed a nationwide community of viewers, brought together every Sunday at 10:30 pm. Peter later attributed the show's early network presence to its overall impact. "When you were watching *What's My Line?* (1950) you knew the whole country was watching it with you."[463] This element, combined with the show's unique brand of charm, created a bond with TV audiences. Ratings spoke volumes, and not all shows could survive.

*Blind Date* (1949) was cancelled in 1952 after three years on ABC TV. Viewers would miss the lively program, but for TV's favorite "femcee," a potentially comparable replacement was on the horizon. That summer, Arlene began moderating the televised game show, *That Reminds Me* (1952). It aired Wednesday nights on NBC, but its reception was meager at best. An early review called it a "watered-down variation of *What's My Line?*"[464] The show did offer a similar premise. A panel (including Nina Foch, Robert Coote, and Bill Cullen) was challenged to guess the identity of a mystery celebrity after being given a set of clues. The program was later re-packaged under the name "*Who's There?*" (1952).[465] but inevitably experienced a brief broadcast run. Regardless of critical reception or cancellations, game shows were an amusing diversion for television audiences. TV had more to offer, and Arlene was ready and willing to grow with the medium.

In the summer of '52, she was asked to host the pilot of a film series called *Visit* (1952). It would showcase 15-minute interview

---

462. Ibid
463. Email communication with Peter Gabel August 20, 2020
464. *Variety.* March 5,1950. Television Reviews
465. *Billboard.* July 5 1952. P. 4

profiles of notable personalities, including Eleanor Roosevelt and David Rockefeller.[466] The series would place Arlene in one of her first positions as an interviewer. She had a natural curiosity about people and expressed a genuine interest that made guests instantly comfortable. *Visit* (1952) would provide a viable platform for those attributes. It was also filmed on location in the guests' homes, resulting in a personal and intimate atmosphere. An interview platform like *Visit* (1952) was clearly something she believed in. A news article noted that "Miss Francis is part owner of the package."[467] In the years to follow, Jack Paar would declare Arlene to be "the best interviewer in the business,"[468] and by the early 1950s, she was already on her way to earning the title.

---

466. *Variety.* August 1952 p. 27
467. Ibid.
468. *The Index -Journal* (Greenwood South Carolina) June 18, 1983

# Chapter Six

"On my left is a winsome little lady who's always ready, willing, and Gabel."[469]

— Bennet Cerf introducing Arlene on *What's My Line?*

*Variety* magazine dubbed Arlene the Queen of TV in 1952.[470] Just two years later, her growing popularity would lead to a position as hostess of the NBC TV daytime show, Home. Breaking new ground, it challenged the standard for women's programming and influenced future shows of its kind. By the mid-1950s, Arlene was named the third most famous woman in America, and she would appear in programs on all three major networks at the same time. Her bubbly personality and genuine appeal as "America's Sweetheart" made her a magnet for ratings and loyal viewership. Dominating television during the 50s, she became a symbol of the attractive and intelligent woman. This attribute of feminine capability inadvertently changed the status quo for women in media, and at the same time, made Arlene all the more loveable. Irrespective of the accolades, she was consistently driven by a personal desire to be her best. and this surfaced in the early days of *What's My Line?* (1950)

"Learn to listen louder."[471] That was the advice Martin gave Arlene at the show's outset. She had initially expressed her frustration to him about being unable to find the right line of questioning. Martin suggested she hone in on questions asked by the other panelists rather than prepare for her cross-examination.[472] This improved the way Arlene approached

---

469. What's My Line? episode. December 2, 1951
470. *Variety.* January 1952
471. *Guideposts Classics.* March 13, 1984 https://www.guideposts.org
472. Ibid.

her job as a panelist, but most importantly, it made her a more receptive listener— a skill that would become increasingly important in her evolving career. For years to come, that career would frequently include her favored medium, the theatre. By her own admission, it was the "caviar of the entertainment world," and she and Martin took pride in every performance.

By 1953, both Gabels had their sights set on the stage. That spring, Martin co-produced Richard Condon's play *Men of Distinction* (1953). The plot[473] was said to be reflective of the 1953 case[474] involving accused playboy Minot F. "Mickey" Jelke. But when queried about the connection, Martin told the *Philadelphia Inquirer* that the play was not based on the trial, and asserted that it was simply a story about a public relations man – a subject that he had contemplated writing about for some time. "Public-relations men and the part they play in society have always interested me. I discussed the possibility of writing a farce on the subject with Richard Condon a couple of years ago . . . I didn't write it myself because I can't sit still that long."[475]

The play did materialize at the hand of Condon, featuring Chandler Cowles, Robert Preston, and Orson Bean. Martin was originally slated for the Preston role, but decided to devote his energy to behind-the-scenes production.[476] "Directing and producing is enough to keep me busy," he said before the play's opening at Philadelphia's Locust Theatre, "We had three auditions to raise money, and I read all the parts myself."[477] Despite best efforts, the play was not well-received on Broadway and experienced only a brief four-performance run at the 48th Street Theatre. In showbusiness, outcomes were never certain. But for determined performers, the risk was often worth the chance.

473. *American Theatre: A Chronicle of Comedy and Drama, 1930 -1969 (1996).* By, Gerald Boardman p. 314

474. *National Affairs: The Guilty Student.* March 9, 1953 Time.com

475. The *Philadelphia Inquirer.* Apr. 5, 1953. W. Phila. High's Gabel Directs Locust Comedy. By, Barbara L. Wilson.

476. *Billboard.* March 14, 1953. Legit Line by, Bob Francis.

477. The Philadelphia Inquirer. Apr. 5, 1953. W. Phila. High's Gabel Directs Locust Comedy. By, Barbara L. Wilson.

Martin was vocal about his belief in taking creative chances. "Bravery, in conceiving a part, seems to me of immense importance,"[478] he said. "The fear of making oneself ridiculous is present in all of us, and when approaching a role, there is always the inclination to play it safe – to do what one has succeeded with before. I think that to be a grave error."[479] He praised actors such as Lawrence Olivier for taking creative liberties in performances of Shakespeare's Henry V and Othello[480], but, in the broader sense, Martin, himself, exhibited a certain boldness. Since the beginning of his career, he had moved effortlessly between the roles of actor, producer, director and narrator. Whether behind the scenes or before an audience, he was unafraid to stretch creatively and ultimately rise to the next occasion.

Arlene took a hopeful leap in July of 53 and appeared in an off-Broadway production of *Road to Rome* (1953). The play was set during the Second Punic War and dramatized Hannibal's failed attempt to capture the city of Rome. Arlene starred opposite John Baragray, and performed in a limited run at the outdoor *Playhouse in the Park,* in Philadelphia. Due to her commitments on *What's My Line?* she had to be strategic about the parts she could accept. However, "When the Road to Rome (1953) idea came up, I jumped on it,"[481] she said. Her reception to the project was wise. *Variety* noted that her "drawing power" was responsible for the highest attendance of the season.[482] A spectator described the impact of her entrance: "Arlene Francis swept onto the stage in a red robe partially covering a flowing Roman gown, voluminous, concealing, and yet seductive."[483] Arlene's response to the engagement was just as riveting. "I've enjoyed every rehearsal and reveled in every performance."[484]

---

478. Transcript from the commencement ceremonies for the American Academy of the Dramatic Arts (1974).

479. Ibid

480. Ibid

481. *Variety*. July 1954

482. Ibid

483. *Summer Stock.* Stars Go Trouping and How They Love it – Rehearsals, heat and all. 1953

484. Ibid.

However, television demanded her presence, and soon, she began hosting *Talent Patrol* (1953) on ABC TV. Sponsored by the Army, the program gave enlisted soldiers a chance to present their hidden talents. Its premise was similar to that of the radio program, *Stars in Khaki 'n Blue* (1953), on which Arlene also served as hostess. When she joined *Talent Patrol* in 1953, she replaced previous emcees Steve Allen and Bud Collyer, and the show's title was eventually changed to *Soldier Parade* (1953). Airing live from the Elysee Theatre for two years, its lively and fun format was due in part to the amusing talent and celebrity guests as well as Arlene's ebullient personality. An article advertising for *Soldier Parade* (1953) noted her natural flair: "With amazing zest, she bounces all over the stage, laughing, talking, and kidding with the young performers, and the warmth of her smile never grows cold."[485]

In addition to regular TV commitments, Arlene landed another role on Broadway. She was cast as Constance Warburton in *Late Love* (1953). The play's tepid out-of-town reviews offered ill-fated predictions, but the production opened at the National Theatre in October of 1953. After a month's engagement, it ran at the Forrest Theatre until January, for a total of 95 performances. Arlene hadn't performed on Broadway since *The Little Blue Light* (1950), and an article advertising *Late Love* (1953) noted her return to the legitimate theatre after "a long absence."[486] Arlene missed the stage as much as it missed her, but lengthy intervals between plays were becoming common in light of her TV commitments.

In early 1954, she was asked to replace George Jessel[487] on *The Comeback Story* (1954) for ABC. It was an interview program featuring guests who had conquered extraordinary hardships.[488] Although it was billed as "America's most talked about new show,"[489] by the time Arlene took over as host, the program was nearing the end of it run. She led the

---

485. *Life of the Soldier and the Airman.* Army's TV Gal. January 1955
486. *Variety.* Wednesday September 30, 1953. Plays Out of Town.
487. *The Complete Dictionary to Prime-Time Network and Cable Shows TV Shows 1946 – Present* (2009). Tim Brooks and Earle Marsh p. 161
488. *The Complete Dictionary to Prime-Time Network and Cable Shows TV Shows 1946 – Present* (2009). Tim Brooks and Earle Marsh. P. 70
489. *Laugh! Cry! Thrill!* News clipping Ad for The Comeback Story circa 1954

series for just over 30 days, but brevity notwithstanding, *The Comeback Story* helped bring the art of conversation to television, and once again proved Arlene to be more than a game show personality.

In March of 1954, she ventured into the world of daytime TV, introducing herself to a new group of viewers: American housewives. Broadcasting executive Sylvester Pat Weaver created the show *Home* (1954) as a complement to the already popular *Today Show* (1952) on NBC. With the eventual inception of *The Tonight Show* (1952), all three programs were marketed together. But *Home* (1954) was special. Produced by Richard Linkreum, the program was formatted as a magazine in motion and brought to life the features commonly found in women's publications of the era. There were the expected cooking demonstrations and sewing segments. There was also an intellectual aspect to *Home* (1954), and the program kept viewers informed of current news events. In addition, there were segments addressing family and marriage issues.[490] Importantly, *Home's* (1954) content was guided by behind-the-scenes experts in food, fashion, and psychology.[491] Everything about the show was innovative and first-rate. The Norman Paris Trio composed live music, and a ground-breaking circular set featured machines that could produce snow, fog, or an on-set rain shower. The special effects were only part of what made *Home (1954)* unique. Arguably, the show's greatest strength was its selling power. Countless brand name appliances were demonstrated on-air, and *Home's* (1954) top saleswoman was none other than its charming hostess.

After auditioning 200 women,[492] NBC executives chose Arlene to be *Home's* (1954) Editor-in-Chief. But she had been on their radar from the beginning. During the show's creation process, NBC approached Arlene about leading one of the "magazine" departments. At the time, she declined due to an already full schedule. A year later, as the show

---

490. *Television: Critical Concepts in Media and Cultural Studies* (2003). By Toby Miller. 2003
491. Ibid.
492. Ibid.

neared its premiere, the timing was right.[493] "They suddenly offered me the overall position, and it sounded terrific."[494] She accepted the job after talking it over with Martin.[495] Hugh Downs, who described Arlene as "one of the easiest people to work with you could imagine,"[496] was chosen as an assistant and the show's announcer. Ultimately, NBC had settled on an excellent choice to lead the domestic program. Arlene was a working woman, but she also had a family. With her position on *Home*, she became the personification of her own core beliefs about women's roles. "I am all for marriage and a career,"[497] she said. While she took great pride in her work, she explained that her "most important jobs"[498] were being a wife and mother: "To run a good house, to keep her family well fed, happy, healthy, and comfortable is the basic job of every woman in the world".[499]

Arlene's active career was satisfying, but her family was her greatest love. "Their big apartment is a real home,"[500] noted one visiting journalist, and at the center of the Gabel's home and hearts was their son, Peter. Arlene said that her son was her "favorite subject."[501] "He's such a wonderful boy and I'm so proud of him,"[502] she told *Radio TV Mirror's* Marie Haller. Arlene related that on most mornings, she and Peter would have breakfast together. "This always starts the day off just perfectly."[503] Martin's absence from the morning meal was a result of his keeping "theatre hours," she explained.

In the fall of 1954, Martin was working nights on Broadway, co-producing the Harry Kurnitz play, *Reclining Figure* (1954). He performed

---

493. *The Daily Times* (New Philadelphia, Ohio) February 10, 1954
494. Ibid.
495. Ibid.
496. *Radio TV Mirror* Jan -Jun 1956
497. *Radio TV Mirror* Jul-Dec 1957.
498. Ibid.
499. Ibid.
500. *Wifely Pleasures* (n.d). By, Richard Plum
501. *Radio TV Mirror* (1957)
502. Ibid.
503. Ibid.

in the comedy as Jonas Astorg, and the role called for a costume consisting of a gray wig and a moustache. One observer wrote: "Martin Gabel is hardly recognizable,"[504] but it was more importantly noted that "he steals the play."[505] *Reclining Figure* experienced successful engagements at the Lyceum and Holiday theatres, running for 116 performances.

The mid-50s were an extremely busy time for the Gabels. Monday through Friday, Arlene hosted the *Home* (1954) show on NBC. She was mistress of ceremonies for *Soldier Parade* (1953) on Saturday nights on ABC, and she appeared on the panel of *What's My Line?* (1950) Sunday evenings on CBS. Her work schedule was full, but so was her off-screen life, and she endeavored to maintain a proper balance. "I have a modern life based on a terribly old-fashioned idea."[506] While Arlene believed in a woman making use of her talents, her values were also rooted in domesticity.[507] "I'm almost an anti-feminist,"[508] she admitted to journalist Helen Bolstad in 1955. Yet, at the same time, she was leading a daytime show, the first of its kind and breaking new ground for women in media. Arlene's own views were reflective of a woman who worked professionally and lived domestically, who labored and loved and reaped the benefits of both.

Maintaining strong familial bonds was important to her, and she kept a close relationship with her parents. They lived nearby, and their loving presence was a constant. Although the Kazanjians had initial doubts about their daughter's decision to pursue show business, they were both certain and proud of the woman she had become. "She is my daughter; nothing has ever changed that,"[509] her mother Leah told *RedBook* magazine in the 1950s. "The inner person remains the same. I am prouder of the friends she has made and kept than of her material success."[510]

---

504. *Modern Screen* Dec. 1954-1955
505. Ibid.
506. *Radio TV Mirror* July – Dec 1955
507. Ibid
508. Ibid
509. *RedBook* magazine, October 1956. A Happy Woman. Michael Drury.
510. Ibid

Success was steady. *Home* was preparing to become an afternoon sensation if NBC could increase ratings.[511] It was decided that the show would focus less on products and more on people.[512] As a result, an interview element was incorporated, which gave Arlene a chance to use her gift for communication. Among those who appeared on the program were then-senator John F. Kennedy, future first lady Jaqueline Kennedy, Pearl S. Buck,[513] Norman Vincent Peale,[514] and many others. But one of the most memorable guests on *Home* (1954) was Helen Keller. The program dedicated a full hour to her story, and her appearance marked her first on television.[515]

The conversation took place with the help of an interpreter, who translated Arlene's words by tapping into Helen Keller's hand. It was a moving experience for Arlene, and she felt compelled to communicate her sincere admiration. An article covering the broadcast noted a special moment near the show's conclusion: "Arlene knew that her guest could also read lips with her fingertips, so at the end of the interview she took Miss Keller's hand and placed it on her mouth."[516] Arlene also recalled the moving exchange: "I was so overwhelmed by the realization of what this woman had accomplished that I said, 'God bless you,' kissed her and – well, I wept."[517]

The on-set interviews were only one portion of *Home* (1954). As the program progressed, Arlene began conducting remotes, traveling with the show to locations around the world. Due to this change in her routine, she was occasionally absent from the *What's My Line?* (1950) panel. However, Arlene was more concerned about being away from her family. She candidly admitted, "I was on a rugged schedule . . . and part

---

511. *Television: Critical Concepts in Media and Cultural Studies* (2003). By Toby Miller.
512. Ibid.
513. *What Women Watched: Daytime Television in the 1950s* (2009). By Marsha F. Cassidy
514. Ibid.
515. *RedBook* magazine. October 1956 A Happy Woman. Michael Drury.
516. Ibid.
517. Ibid.

of the time I was too busy to run my *own* home."[518] Arlene and Martin both worked consistently, but they strove to be discerning, especially where their son was concerned. "We have tried to give him the security of independence backed up by our love for him,"[519] Arlene explained. When the *Home* (1954) show was broadcast from Japan, it meant being away for longer than usual. She recalled saying goodbye to an eight-year-old Peter just before leaving for the airport. "He gave me a rather casual kiss, and I said, 'Hey, I'm going all the way to Japan. Is that all the kiss I get?'"[520] "He looked at me puzzled, and said, 'But mom, you'll be right back.'"[521]

Peter was an extremely bright child and attended Hunter College Elementary, a school for advanced students. One of Arlene's favorite things to do was help him with his homework. "I like to be at the apartment when Peter gets home from school,"[522] she explained. "He likes to have me around when he's doing his homework, and I love it. I really do find it exciting when he can do fractions in his head and arrive at the correct answers long before I can figure them out on paper."[523] These moments between mother and son were precious and important. "For all the times I didn't pick Peter up from school and take him to the park, because I couldn't, we would have a special adventure of our own: a baseball game, an afternoon at the movies, a heart-to-heart talk at bedtime."[524]

By 1955, Arlene had already reached extraordinary milestones. During an interview with the *Post Standard News*, she was asked if there were any more goals she hoped to accomplish. Her responses were thoughtful and reflected her greatest personal desires. "I do hope to live to see my son Peter graduate from college,"[525] she said. Although he was only eight at the time, Arlene was already thinking about the distant future. "I want to see

---

518. *Arlene Francis: A Memoir* (1978). By Arlene Francis with Florence Rome. P. 113
519. *RedBook* Magazine. October 1956 A Happy Woman. Michael Drury
520. Ibid
521. Ibid.
522. *Radio TV Mirror* Jul – Dec 1957
523. Ibid.
524. Ibid.
525. Ibid.

him grow into a happy, intelligent, well-balanced man."[526] She also stated her wish to have a hit play on Broadway, produced by Martin, of course.

The solidity of the Gabel's marriage also withstood the challenges of their demanding careers. The success of their relationship was due in part to their willingness to make it succeed. "Martin and I still make dates to see each other," she said, "we appreciate the time we have together."[527] Part of their durability was the care they put into the details. For example, Martin was a very well-read intellectual. Arlene thought that increasing her knowledge of world politics could enhance the quality of their conversations, and so, with a schedule already bursting at the seams, she took an evening course in international affairs at Hunter College in New York City.[528]

Martin surmised that her growing interest and concern for global conditions surpassed a conversational interest. He related that "Her politics are grounded in a deep abhorrence of man's inhumanity to man."[529] "She crosses party lines, always voting for the candidate whose allegiance to social justice she believes most genuine."[530] Martin also offered another reason for Arlene's increasing interest in acquiring world knowledge. "Part of this is due to the fact that we have one son, and [Arlene] has a persistent anxiety about the nature of the world he will find himself in."[531]

This type of insight into his wife's innermost feelings contributed to his sensitivity as a husband. And in his own way, Martin also took time for meaningful gestures. One such occasion began with a tiny new addition to the *What's My Line?* (1950) panel. Dorothy Kilgallen was expecting her third child in the spring of 1954, and in a "semi-kidding sort of way,"[532] Arlene envied her condition. The possibility of having a second

---

526. Ibid.
527. *Radio TV Mirror* Jul – Dec 1955
528. *Wifely Pleasures* (n.d.). Magazine feature. By, Roger Plum.
529. *Encore magazine.* Circa 1960s. A Duet for Two Stars.
530. Ibid.
531. Ibid.
532. *Wifely Pleasures.* (n.d). Magazine feature. By, Roger Plum.

child at this stage in Arlene's life would have been less than feasible, but she was a woman and a mother above all, and her maternal inclinations were only natural. Her notion became something of a lighthearted point of amusement between her and Martin for a while.[533] Of course, a baby wasn't in their future, but Martin thought of another new addition for his wife, and he bought her a petite diamond[534] to be set in the center of the heart pendant he had given her on their first anniversary.

Interestingly, the center diamond made its debut on the *What's My Line?* (1950) episode coinciding with the birth of Dorothy's son, Kerry Kollmar. When Bennet Cerf announced Arlene on the panel that evening, he said: "This is a big night for *What's My Line?*"[535] "As you know, Dorothy Kilgallen had a little boy the other day, and it looks as though the beautiful lady on my right has been giving birth too because if you look closely, Miss Francis has that diamond heart around her neck, and it's given birth to a little diamond inside of it."[536] Arlene laughed, gave Bennett's arm a light squeeze, and replied, "I was nervous there for a moment!"[537]

Bennett Cerf and his wife Phyllis were good friends of the Gabels, and they became neighbors during the early years of *What's My Line?* (1950) Arlene and Martin had a house built adjacent to the Cerf's estate in Mount Kisco, New York. It served as a weekend family retreat, and when *What's My Line?* (1950) was on hiatus, the Gabels could vacation there. It was a simple and cozy house, built for a close and loving family. "There's nothing elegant about our summer home"[538] Arlene said. "It's small but is situated on top of a hill from which there is a breathtaking view."[539] She explained that the primary reason for building it was so that "Peter could enjoy suburban living."[540] Beyond the confines of the city, life moved

---

533. Ibid.
534. Ibid.
535. *What's My Line?* March 21, 1954
536. Ibid.
537. Ibid.
538. *Radio TV Mirror* Jan – Jun 1957
539. Ibid.
540. Ibid.

at a slower pace. The house in Mount Kisco provided opportunities for swimming, and bike-riding and weekend guests. Peter also became good friends with the Cerf's children, Jonathan and Christopher.

During the time the house was being built, Arlene was hosting *Home*, and the show had commissioned an architect to expertly design it and equip it with the modern appliances featured on the show. Interior decorations, however, were something Arlene liked to manage on her own. When a segment on *Home* (1954) demonstrated a do-it-yourself carpet installation using a square-by-square method, Arlene decided to give it a try, and she asked Phyllis Cerf to lend a hand. Together, the two of them carpeted the living room of the Mount Kisco house. The results were successful, but the experience was not without a humorous moment. "I don't remember whether we were in dungarees or just what exactly our work clothes were, Arlene related. Obviously, however, we looked pretty seedy."[541] Known for being fashion-forward, it was a rare moment to see Arlene in such attire. She certainly wasn't anticipating visitors during her carpet project when, unexpectedly, the doorbell rang. "Trying to protect me, Phyllis offered to answer it while I tried to hide under the carpet squares."[542] Standing at the door was a woman who had come to welcome Arlene to the neighborhood. Given the circumstances, this might have caused an awkward scene, but there would be no need to save face. The woman didn't recognize Arlene in her unsavory ensemble. "She took one last look around, gasped, and explained that she hadn't realized the charladies were still working!"[543]

When they weren't spending weekends in Mount Kisco, the family resumed life in the city. In March of 1955, Arlene, Martin, and Peter appeared on *Person to Person* (1953). The program was hosted by Edward R. Murrow and featured live interviews from the homes of notable personalities. During the broadcast, the Gabel's talked about their current projects, Arlene gave a brief tour of their apartment, and Peter played the

---

541. *Radio TV Mirror* Jan -Jun 1957
542. Ibid.
543. Ibid.

violin for the viewing audience, but becoming an entertainer was not something that particularly interested him. When Mr. Murrow asked an eight-year-old Peter if he had any plans to be an actor, he replied, "No, I don't think so."[544] "I'm not sure what I want to be. A baseball player maybe."[545] Having led Mount Kisco's little league team with a .426 batting average, a career in sports was then a viable consideration for the youngest Gabel.

One of Martin's projects discussed on *Person to Person* was *Serenade* (1955),[546] a musical he was planning to produce based upon the James M. Cain novel. He had petitioned Arthur Laurents to write the play and wanted Stephen Sondheim to compose the score.[547] Still, despite urging from Jerome Robbins and Leonard Bernstein to join them on a different project, Laurents agreed to take on *Serenade*.[548] His loyalty was perhaps rooted in a fortuitous piece of advice he once received from Martin. "He told me during the war that if I didn't stay home from parties, I would never write a play."[549] The result of Martin's counsel was *Home of the Brave* (1946). However, the future was not as promising for *Serenade* (1955). Creative conflicts led to the project's cancellation,[550] and Laurents and Sondheim later joined forces with Robbins and Bernstein, creating *West Side Story*. Interestingly, Martin once owned the rights to the musical prior to its production,[551] but by the latter half of the 1950s, he went to work on other projects for the big screen and the Broadway stage.

In 1955, he was seen in the George Axelrod play, *Will Success Spoil Rock Hunter?* (1955) Martin had replaced actor Henry Morgan,[552] and

---

544. *Arlene Francis: A Memoir* (1978) By Arlene Francis with Florence Rome. P. 88
545. Ibid.
546. Person to Person March 25, 1955 [summary] The Paley Center for Media https://www.paleycenter.org
547. *Original Story: A Memoir of Broadway and Hollywood* (2001). By, Arthur Laurents.
548. Ibid.
549. Ibid.
550. Ibid.
551. Email Communication with Peter Gabel August 20, 2020
552. *Modern Screen* Jan -Nov 1956

had appeared as Irving Lasalle in the comedy about a magazine writer who sells his soul for fame. The cast starred Jayne Mansfield and Walter Matthau, and ran for 444 performances at the Belasco and Shubert Theatres. Martin did not appear in the subsequent motion picture based on the play. Instead, he co-produced the stage production, *The Hidden River* (1957), with Henry Margolis. The three-act drama, based on the novel by Storm Jameson, experienced a steady engagement at the Playhouse Theatre, closing after 61 performances.

While Martin's theatre credits accumulated, he was featured in another film before the decade's end. The MGM motion picture *Tip on a Dead Jockey* (1957) premiered in 1957 and was based on a story by Irwin Shaw. The film starred Robert Taylor and featured Martin as Bert Smith, a mysterious deal-maker with a destructive plan. His performance was impressive, prompting one critic to note that Martin played the heavy with "considerable skill."[553] His appearance in *Tip on a Dead Jockey* (1957) almost made for another collaboration with Orson Welles. Originally set to direct the picture,[554] Welles was replaced by Richard Thorpe due to prior commitments.[555] Unanticipated adjustments were common in film and on television, but some changes were more difficult to accept than others.

The *Home* (1954) show was cancelled in the summer of 57. Arlene received the news while on location in Silver Springs, Florida, and was greatly saddened. The program had afforded memorable moments and exciting opportunities. During her tenure as *Home's* (1954) editor-in-chief, Arlene traveled the globe, interviewed locals and notables alike, and even became the first woman to open the New York Stock Exchange. She also endured a few accidents. An underwater adventure went awry during a remote at Catalina Island. In what was intended to be an uncomplicated segment, Arlene descended to the bottom of the Pacific Ocean in a diving bell. Unbeknownst to her, something went wrong with the air pressure, and the chamber was abruptly

553. *Motion Picture Daily* Jul -Sept 1957
554. *Orson Welles: A Biography.* 2005 by Barbara Leaming
555. *Films and Filming* (1957). Vol. 3, Issues 5-12 p. 28

propelled to the surface. Emerging unharmed and in good spirits, she declared: "Wow, now I know what it feels like to be a champagne cork!"[556]

Another incident happened while Arlene was leading viewers on a tour through Steeplechase Park. It was a popular amusement site on Coney Island at the time, boasting the latest in extravagant attractions. Viewers had begun to anticipate Arlene's venturesome frolics during remotes for *Home*, and a *TV Guide* listing for the show that day announced: "Arlene Francis parachute jumps at Steeplechase Park."[557] However, it was during her demonstration of the moving sidewalk that a mishap occurred. The platform was set into motion before she could secure her position, and in a split second, "I was thrown over the rail," she explained, ". . . sirens blaring, ambulance lights flashing."[558] Her leg had been severely broken, but she returned to preside over *Home* (1954) without missing a beat.

Arlene certainly experienced her share of hits and misses on live television, and she deservedly received recognition for her efforts on *Home* (1954). She was one of the first people to win the Stella Award for television achievement,[559] and she was nominated for Emmys for Best Contribution to Daytime Programming[560] and Best Female Personality.[561] *Home* was also chosen by *TV Radio Guide* Magazine as the Favorite TV Women's Program. But the attention wasn't enough to spare the show's cut. Many considerations have surfaced as to exactly why *Home* was cancelled. The general consensus is that it was simply too expensive and high-end. The initial awe of its modern appeal eventually failed to resonate with the average American housewife.[562] The show's focus precariously vacillated between representing women as both consumers

---

556. *Los Angeles Times* (2001). Arlene Francis; Bubbly Wit of Early TV.
557. *TV Guide*. Circa 1950s
558. *Arlene Francis: A Memoir* (1978). By Arlene Francis with Florence Rome.
559. *Sponsor Magazine* (1956)
560. 9th Annual Emmy Awards Nominees and Winners (1956-1957) https://www.emmys.com
561. Ibid
562. *Television: Critical Concepts in Media and Cultural Studies* (2003). By Toby Miller

of products and consumers of knowledge.[563] This dichotomy was perhaps detrimental to the loyal establishment of viewer interest. At the same time, it was a bold step toward the redefinition of feminine roles.

On the future of women on television, Arlene had this to say: "The time may come when a woman hosts a talk show that isn't focused on home, food, and fashion."[564] This statement illustrated Arlene's changing attitude toward feminism in the post *Home* (1954) years, and she wasn't alone in her ambivalence. According to media scholar Marsha F. Cassidy, *Home* (1954) itself presented a rather contradictory view of modern femininity in the 1950's. While intended to be reflective of the average American family, the program modeled a new-age version of domesticity, and in so doing, inadvertently opened the door for women to think beyond the confines of a kitchen.[565] Arlene also noted the show's dualistic approach. "We operated on the assumption that the American woman is intellectually curious about the world she has helped to build, as well as about the ingredients of Vichyssoise,"[566] she said. "*Home* was a four-year college education for me and I regret that I couldn't go on to get my Ph.D."[567]

The final edition of *Home* (1954) aired on NBC on August 9, 1957, after three and a half years on television. It was an emotional experience for Arlene, who, prior to the finale, had been instructed to maintain her composure.[568] That was a curious admonishment considering her steadfast presence in a male-dominated arena. For a rare moment, there was concern that the capable editor-in-chief would exhibit a stereotypically female trait. "Well, I don't want to weep,"[569] she said

---

563. *What Women Watched: Daytime Television in the 1950s* (2009). By, Marsha F. Cassidy

564. *Journal Herald.* March 21, 1980

565. *What Women Watched: Daytime Television in the 1950s* (2009). By, Marsha F. Cassidy

566. *Herald and Review.* Decatur, Illinois. Tuesday August 16, 1960. Marie Torre Reports. Arlene Francis Replies.

567. Ibid.

568. *Television Talk. A History of the Television TV Show* (2002). By Bernard M. Timberg

569. Ibid.

during the closing moments of *Home's* (1954) last show, "but this is a big family and everyone has gotten very attached."[570] Arlene ended *Home* on a note of inspiration and recited the Prayer of St. Francis of Assisi:[571] ". . . Where there is hatred, let me sow love, where there is injury, pardon; where there is doubt, faith . . . and where there is sadness, joy. . . ."[572]

When *Home* went off the air, NBC executive David Tebet offered Arlene a very lucrative position as hostess of *The Today Show* (1952). She knew her way around the program, having substituted for Dave Garroway several times over the years. On one occasion, she interviewed survivors from the shipwreck of the Andrea Doria on the set of *Today* (1952).[573] Incidentally, she would later become the first woman to guest-host *The Tonight Show* (1952).[574] But in 1957, it was *Today* (1952) that NBC wished to offer her on a permanent basis. To the network's probable surprise, Arlene flatly declined. There was a good reason for her decision. Hosting *Today* (1952) meant rising before dawn and keeping a schedule that would make it next to impossible to spend quality time with Martin and Peter. "My child was still very young,"[575] "and I thought about Martin being on his own most evenings. What sort of life would that be for him?"[576] Her rejection of *Today (1952)* also afforded Arlene a moment of insight. "Even if I hadn't had such overwhelming personal reasons for not wanting to accept the position on *Today* (1952), I would have certainly balked at the idea of a co-host!"[577] NBC had planned to pair Arlene with Hugh Downs again. "I loved [him] and we had worked well together on

---

570. Ibid.

571. Ibid.

572. Ibid.

573. *Alive! On the Andrea Doria. The Greatest Sea Rescue in History* (2006). By, Pierette Dominica Simpson.

574. Q&A Arlene Francis First female to guest-host The Tonight Show in 1962. MGHS Hour

575. Interview with Arlene Herson DVD. 1987

576. *Arlene Francis: A Memoir* (1978). By Arlene Francis with Florence Rome. P. 161

577. Ibid.

*Home,*"[578] she explained, but "My ego was a touch out of hand,"[579] "I was in that period in my life when I felt I deserved to be top banana."[580]

As it turned out, Barbara Walters successfully anchored the *Today* (1952) show, and Arlene didn't grieve over her decision to decline. "I've never regretted it, except for one time when Barbara took the show to China. I was so jealous!"[581] Arlene was complimentary of Ms. Walters' competency and took no credit for inadvertently launching her highly successful career. She was later asked where she thought Barbara Walters would be if circumstances had been different. "She'd be somewhere," Arlene replied. "Don't worry about that girl; she knows how to run a parade."[582]

Arlene was a wonder-woman herself. The work she had accomplished thus far would have left anyone pondering an early retirement, but as 1958 approached, she had only begun to scratch the surface of a career that would span the next three decades. Arlene's tenacity remained steadfast despite the unpredictable nature of success. She once divulged that her formula for perseverance was the result of being fully present. "I don't think too much about the future,"[583] she said. "Living life to its fullest every moment—that means happiness to me. Do that, and you can't lose."[584]

---

578. Ibid.
579. Ibid.
580. Ibid.
581. Interview with Arlene Herson DVD. 1987
582. Ibid.
583. *TV Radio Mirror* Jan – Jun 1957
584. *TV Radio Mirror* Jan -Jun 1958

Arlene Francis at 15 years old (1922). Photo from the collection of Peter Gabel.

Arlene Francis with her mother, Leah Kazanjian (circa 1920s). Photo from the collection of Peter Gabel.

Arlene Francis: An emerging actress (circa late 1920s). Photo from the collection of Peter Gabel.

Arlene Francis: A young star (circa 1930s). Photo from the collection of Peter Gabel.

A publicity shot for the play All That Glitters (1938). The photo was taken by her father Aram Kazanjian. Photo from the collection of Neil Feria.

Showing her skills as a comedic actress with Allyn Joslyn in the play *All That Glitters* (1938). Photo from the collection of Peter Gabel.

Arlene Francis with Ed Wynn in publicity for the radio show *Blind Date* (1943) on the Blue Network. Photo from the collection of Neil Feria.

Arlene Francis in the play *The Road to Rome* (1952). Photo from the collection of Peter Gabel.

Arlene and Martin's son Peter Gabel at about two years old. (Circa 1949). Photo from the collection of Peter Gabel.

Peter Gabel's third birthday party (1950). Peter looks toward the camera as his parents smile proudly. Grandfather Aram Kazanjian stands at right. Photo from the collection of Peter Gabel.

The Gabels at home in New York with their son Peter. (Circa 1953). Photo from the collection of Peter Gabel.

The Gabels play a game of cards with their young son Peter. (Circa 1957). Photo from the collection of Neil Feria.

Hosting *Talent Patrol* aka *Soldier Parade* (Circa 1953). Photographer: Tony DeVito. Photo from the collection of Neil Feria.

Arlene Francis as hostess of *Home* (Circa 1954). Photo from the collection of Neil Feria.

Arlene Francis on *Home* (Circa 1954) with her son Peter Gabel, co-host Hugh Downs and unidentified child. Photo from the collection of Peter Gabel.

A study in elegance. Arlene Francis (circa 1955). Photographer: Tony DeVito. Photo from the collection of Neil Feria.

Arlene Francis wearing her trademark heart-shaped necklace (she never took it off). (Circa 1950s). Photo from the collection of Neil Feria.

Arlene Francis with the Stella Award for excellence in television (1956). Conant & Company Publications Council Incorporated. Photo from the collection of Neil Feria.

Arlene with a bouquet of "Arlene Francis" roses, a variety that was named after her in the 1950s. (Circa 1957). Photo from the collection of Neil Feria.

A casual pose. Arlene Francis (Circa 1961). Possibly taken at the Gabel's summer house in Mt. Kisco, New York. Photo from the collection of Peter Gabel.

Arlene as a panelist on *What's My Line?* (1961) with co-panelist Dorothy Kilgallen and guest Jerry Lewis. (a position she held for 25 years). Photo from the collection of Neil Feria.

Arlene Francis in publicity for the play *Once More with Feeling* (1958). Photo from the collection of Peter Gabel.

Arlene Francis wearing an Arnold Scaasi gown at the March of Dimes fashion show (1959). New York Journal American staff photo. Photographer: Robbins. Photo from the collection of Neil Feria.

Arlene Francis with Robert Forster in *Mrs. Dally* (1965). Photo from the collection of Peter Gabel.

Arlene Francis with Robert Forster in *Mrs. Dally* (1965). Photo from the collection of Peter Gabel.

Arlene Francis and Martin Gabel with their son Peter Gabel (circa mid-1970s). Photo from the collection of Peter Gabel.

Arlene Francis with friend Frank Sinatra at their induction into the Broadcaster's Hall of Fame (1982). World Press International New York. Photo from the collection of Neil Feria.

Always Smiling. Arlene Francis (Circa 1970s). Photo from the collection of Peter Gabel.

An ageless beauty. Arlene Francis (circa 1980). Photo from the collection of Neil Feria.

# Chapter Seven

"Nothing brings more pleasure to a performer or a poker player than a full house"[585]

– Arlene Francis

During the late 1950s, Arlene Francis entered a new era of achievement. Following the cancellation of the *Home* (1954) show, she began exploring other opportunities. *What's My Line?* (1950) was entering its eighth year on network television by this time, and Arlene's work on radio was about to make a significant comeback. She still frequented the medium on a regular basis, appearing on NBC's Monitor and hosting the program *Family Living* (1959). However, that was just a precursor to the WOR radio interview show she would host for the better half of the next twenty-five years. In keeping with her love for acting, she also made time to star in several plays, including the highly successful *Once More with Feeling* (1958). It would mark her longest run since the *Doughgirls* (1942) and provide a notable collaboration between her and Martin. Together, they reaped the rewards of success and celebrated the milestones of individual achievements. The unpredictable sixties were fast approaching, but in the summer of 1957, Arlene was busy preparing for the debut of a new TV variety program, aptly titled, *The Arlene Francis Show* (1957).

Viewers tuned in weekday mornings at 10:00am for a 30-minute dose of charm. Backed by six advertisers,[586] including Owens-Corning Fiberglass Corporation and The House of Westmore, *The Arlene Francis Show* (1957) made its first appearance on NBC TV on August 12, 1957.

---

585. News article covering a lecture by Ms. Francis (Circa 1980s)
586. *Motion Picture Daily.* Jul – Sept 1957. Six Signs Francis

Its early timeslot was somewhat unusual for a variety program. Similar offerings typically aired in the evenings, but Arlene's show provided a breath of fresh entertainment to the mid-morning lineup. It was a whimsical mix of fun and amusement, led by a very welcoming hostess. Arlene provided a self-described version of her position: "I would preside as mistress of ceremonies, making funnies, ad-libbing with the rest of the talent, sort of a Bob Hope with curls."[587]

Her disarming humor no doubt eased the tension of her first day on set. She was still recovering from a leg injury, and hosted the show from the confines of a wheelchair. "And to think I planned to do a trampoline act on my opening program,"[588] she told the viewing audience. Hugh Downs assisted as the show's announcer (even carrying Arlene across the threshold),[589] and the friendly chemistry they shared on *Home* (1954) was ever present, but the new program was very much built around Arlene's public appeal. "She's the whole show"[590] boasted an early notice, "even to the program's visual motif.[591] The heart-shaped diamond pendant which has become Ms. Francis's trademark on television frames the show's opening and closing shots."[592] However, the content in between initially struggled to hit its stride.

Part of the program included spontaneous audience participation, and a play-along cross-word game called Cross My Heart. On the first show, live music was provided by a quartet, and during a storytelling segment, Arlene recited the fable *An Alarm Clock Named Eunice*, which one observer noted as being "more cute than funny."[593] Arlene had her own ideas for what she hoped the show would become. For starters, she wanted to focus on an interview component and perhaps even travel with

---

587. *Arlene Francis: A Memoir* (1978). By Arlene Francis with Florence Rome.
588. Arlene Francis news clipping August 1957
589. *Kingsport Times*. Arlene Francis Possess Unusual Talent in Presenting TV Show. August 13 1957. By Jack O'Brian
590. *Broadcasting Telecasting* August 1957
591. Ibid
592. Ibid
593. Arlene Francis news clipping August 1957

the show as she did with *Home* (1954).[594] Despite a debut that was called "quite dull," the program did carry a note of promise. "It has one very winning ingredient remarked a reviewer, and that, as John Daly puts it on *What's My Line?* is Miss Arlene."[595]

Few television shows could compare to *What's My Line?* (1950) The magic that happened between the panel was a large contributor to its enduring popularity. When Martin began appearing frequently as a guest panelist, it made for even more memorable and humorous moments. The couple often had the opportunity to introduce each other, and Arlene, in her typically playful manner, once presented her husband by saying: "And now, a gentleman who is wearing a bachelor button as a boutonniere which doesn't fool me for one minute."[596] The Gabels were indeed a winning combination. They worked well as a team, as spouses, parents, panelists, or actors. In the late 1950s, they would begin rehearsals for one of their greatest collaborations on Broadway.

Martin was preparing to produce the Harry Kurnitz play, *Once More, With Feeling* (1959). Arlene was impressed by the comedic script and dearly wanted to play the female lead, but her potential future in the production was not guaranteed. Being the producer's wife did not automatically qualify her as right for the part,[597] even though she'd had her eye on the role for a while. The prospect of the play was under consideration when she was working on *Home*,[598] and now, occupied with her new variety program, Martin was concerned about her becoming overworked. "Sometimes, in the evening, when I look a little tired under the eyes, Martin stares at me and repeatedly asks if I really think I can tackle the play along with my other activities."[599] Arlene was certain,

---

594. *Radio TV Mirror* Jan - Jun 1957 Arlene Francis Who Does it all Herself. Marie Haller
595. Arlene Francis news clipping August 1957
596. What's My Line? (Cira 1958).
597. *Arlene Francis: A Memoir* (1978). By Arlene Francis with Florence Rome. P. 163
598. *Oakland Tribune.* August 7, 1956. Arlene Francis Loves her Work. Marie Torre.
599. Ibid

but she still had to win the approval of Harry Kurnitz. He was a good friend of the Gabel's and a very discerning playwright. Naturally, Arlene was thrilled and flattered when she was offered the role of Dolly Fabian. Martin casually gave her the good news over breakfast. "I leapt across the table and gave him a terrific hug,"[600] she recalled. With that, it was official.

Arlene wasn't the only one who coveted a role in the play. Actor Bill Macy, best known for appearing on the 70s sitcom *Maude* (1972), was struggling to break into the acting business in the 1950s and had taken a job as a cab driver in New York City. Martin had been a passenger of his and accidently left the script for *Once More, With Feeling* (1958) in the backseat of Macy's cab. Upon returning the script to Martin, he inquired if there might be a part for him in the play.[601] As it turned out, Bill Macy understudied Walter Matthau in the comedy and received his first introduction to a colorful cast of theatrical characters.

Arlene would star opposite Joseph Cotten as the charming harpist and wife of a tyrannical orchestra conductor. She and Joe Cotten had previously worked together in the Mercury Theatre and the Gabels were well acquainted with many in the production, including director George Axelrod. This camaraderie gave the play "a cozy aura"[602] Arlene explained. Added to the mix was her friend, clothing designer, Arnold Scaasi, whom she approached about designing her wardrobe for the play. Arlene was one of his earliest clients, and related going to his showroom when the couturier was just getting started. "He had one sewing machine and me."[603] "She walked up three flights of stairs and bought the first made-to-order clothes I ever did, said Scaasi, "That's how it all started."[604] Since then, his career had advanced steadily, and the prestige of his association

---

600. Ibid
601. *Observer-Reporter* Sept, 22, 1980. Bill Macy Blends In
602. *Arlene Francis: A Memoir* (1978). By Arlene Francis with Florence Rome. P. 163
603. *Palm Beach Daily News*. February 23, 1983. Rain Didn't Hamper Turnout for Scaasi Show p. 10
604. *Daily News*. Apr. 9, 1984. New York. Arlene Francis gets big Sign-off.

with *Once More with Feeling*, (1958) added to his impressively growing reputation.

The gowns he designed for the production largely contributed to the perception of the character Dolly Fabian. When Arlene initially consulted with Scaasi about the costumes, she explained that they should reflect the no-frills wardrobe of a music teacher.[605] The innovative designer had a different vision, and suggested a style befitting of a harp instructor that was both wealthy and glamourous.[606] This cultivated persona would likely resonate better with audiences who were accustomed to seeing Arlene dressed in high fashion. Harry Kurnitz agreed[607] to the wardrobe angle, and Scaasi set about creating some of the most iconic designs of his career to date. Arlene would be dressed in a regal collection of fur, silk, chiffon, and brocade. The most memorable of the designs appeared in the play's final act. "I went all out in the last scene, Scaasi explained, putting Arlene in a floor-length off-the-shoulder red satin evening cloak over a glistening silver . . . long evening dress, tied in red satin at the waist."[608]

While the play was readying for Broadway success, *The Arlene Francis Show* (1957) was floundering despite best efforts. Since its TV debut, the program featured interviews with notable guests such as Carole Burnett, Anne Bancroft, and comedian Sam Levenson.[609] Arlene also provided entertainment, even performing a parodied version of Marlene Dietrich's rendition of The Boys in the Backroom. Interacting with the audience remained a format staple, and during a segment titled Talk Your Way Out of It, she chose a random gentleman from the audience to act with her in an impromptu skit about a wife catching her husband on a date with another woman.[610] A reviewer called the segment "a little strained

---

605. *The Women I Have Dressed (And Undressed!)* (2004). By Arnold Scaasi.

606. Ibid

607. Ibid

608. Ibid

609. TV: Arlene Francis She is Hostess of New Daytime Program of Music, Interviews, and Games J.F. Shanley

610. Arlene Francis Possesses Unusual Talent in Presenting TV Show (1958). Jack O' Brian

and empty,"[611] and noted that the routine seemed a bit out-of-place for morning television.

The inability of the show's content to complement its timeslot could have contributed to a decline in ratings. Arlene noted this potential problem while reflecting on the demise of *Home* (1954). The program had been one of the first to travel and feature roving reports from around the world.[612] "People used to say our *Home* (1954) documentaries should have been done in the evening so they could have been seen more widely."[613] However, *Home* had been canceled with or without good reason, and her new NBC variety show also came to an abrupt end in June of 1958, before ever reaching its full potential. As a result, Arlene Francis regrettably disappeared from daytime television. However, true to her indomitable spirit, the curtain would soon rise on her next adventure.

*Once More, With Feeling* (1958) opened at The National Theatre on October 21, 1958, the day after Arlene's 51st birthday. The premiere was attracted a who's who of Broadway, and the entire production was received favorably. Arlene's performance was called "luminous and winning,"[614] and her "dazzling costumes"[615] were acknowledged by the *New York Theatre Critics Review*. The play, which ran for 263 stellar performances, was later made into a 1960 motion picture starring Yul Brynner and Kay Kendell. However, Arlene's shining moments were on the stage. She had added another hit play to her credit, and fondly placed the production among her happiest theater experiences.

She was not only in top form as an actress, but she looked as divine as ever. While age was never a subject Arlene cared to discuss publicly, she seemed virtually untouched by the passing years, despite the gradual lightening of her naturally dark hair. Described as "the color of peanut butter" in the mid-1950s, it eventually reached a stunning pale blonde in

---

611. Ibid
612. *Detroit Free Press*. Nov. 28, 1960. After Three Years off TV Arlene Longs for Home. By, Bettelou Peterson
613. Ibid
614. *The Women I Have Dressed (And Undressed!)* (2004). By Arnold Scaasi.
615. *New York Theatre Critics' Reviews* (1958) vol 19 -21 p. 77

the 1960s. Most of the changes had to be deciphered in black & white by the television viewing audiences, and it was a perceivably golden-haired Arlene who introduced Martin on the February 15, 1959 episode of *What's My Line?* (1950) He was appearing in a new play at the time, and Arlene proudly took a moment to acknowledge her husband's recent achievements by remarking that his "reviews in the new Broadway hit *The Rivalry* were so brilliant that I have to devote the rest of my life putting these reviews to music."[616]

Martin was cast as Stephen Douglas in Norman Corwin's *The Rivalry* (1959). The play dramatized the historical Lincoln-Douglas debates and featured Richard Boone as Abraham Lincoln. After a lengthy tour throughout the U.S. and Canada,[617] the play made it to Broadway in February of 1959 for an 81-show run. In a part originally offered to actor Brian Donlevy,[618] Martin assumed the role of Douglas, and maintained it amidst changes to the primary performers. Raymond Massey had portrayed Lincoln in the touring production and Nancy Kelley replaced Agnes Moorehead in the role of Adele Douglas.[619] In addition to a solid cast, the play's Broadway score was composed by David Amram, who fondly recalled Martin both on and off the stage. "I admired his spirit . . . he was peppery and lively and a terrific actor with a lot of power, style, and a great sense of humor."[620]

The next project on the busy actor's schedule was a new evening discussion show. In March of 1959, he debuted as host of *Martin Gabel's Roundtable* (1959) on WNTA TV channel 13.[621] The half-hour program filled the 11:30 pm time slot and featured a mix of conversation, complete with musical intermissions by pianist Joe Buskin. Arlene sometimes joined Martin on the program, including the occasion of its

---

616. *What's My Line?* episode 1959
617. *Agnes Moorehead on Radio, Stage and Television.* (2017). By Axel Nissen
618. Ibid
619. *I Love the Illusion: The Life and Career of Agnes Moorehead* (2007). By, Charles Tranberg
620. *Vibrations: A Memoir* (2015) by David Amram p. 316
621. Martin Gabel's Roundtable show listing

premiere with actor James Garner. Subsequent guests included George Axelrod, Martha Wright, and Anne Bancroft. The scarcity of information regarding the show's history lends to the assumption that it was a short-lived experiment in the litany of late-night talk.

Indeed, one of the signatures of showbusiness is its unpredictability. Arlene knew this all too well, and the back-to-back cancelations of *Home* (1954) and her variety show gave her increased pause. "Busy though I was, there was a nagging suspicion in my mind that the success train I'd been riding for so long had begun to slow down."[622] *Once More with Feeling* (1958) had been an exciting and profitable distraction, but after the closing curtain, her next job wasn't guaranteed. For Arlene, that prospect was disheartening. "I would get depressed if I weren't working every minute."[623] Her reaction toward inactivity was perhaps as much a product of her adverse attitude toward retirement as it was of the sincere pleasure she took in her endeavors. "Idleness is the dangerous thing in this world, not work,"[624] she said. "I do what I enjoy doing. I don't think I'm motivated by ambition alone."[625]

In 1960, Arlene continued to follow her bliss and appeared in Noel Coward's series of plays, *Tonight at 8:30* (1960). She performed in two of the productions at the Coconut Grove Playhouse in Florida. In the first drama, *Still Life* (1960), Arlene portrayed a married woman engaged in a love affair with a physician. According to one review, she navigated the role with "too much restraint" and "could have let quite a bit more of her own radiance shine through."[626] However, she demonstrated less inhibition in the second play, the British musical satire, *Red Peppers.* For this role, Arlene shined opposite James Mitchell as one half of a Mr.

---

622. *Arlene Francis: A Memoir (1978). By Arlene Francis with Florence Rome.* P. 164

623. *Arlene Francis: A Memoir (1978) By Arlene Francis with Florence Rome.* P. 165

624. *The Lima Citizen.* Lima, Ohio Feb. 1, 1958 Idleness, Not Work, Dangerous, Says Arlene. By, Anthony La Camera

625. *Sunday News.* Lancaster, Pennsylvania. Mar. 19, 1972. Arlene Francis Declares: Life is the Only Party. By, Margaret McManus

626. *Fort Lauderdale News.* Jan. 1960. By Dick Hoekstra. Arlene Francis in two Plays Hardly Enough to Fill an Evening. P. 22

& Mrs. song and dance team. "Arlene Francis shows a deft shoe as a hoofer and comes off quite well with a real heavy cockney accent. [She] and Mr. Mitchell deliver a delightful version of Noel Coward's song strolling through Piccadilly."[627] Both plays garnered mixed reception, and one review asserted that even the Noel Coward-Arlene Francis combination could not make for an entirely enjoyable production.

At this point in her career, Arlene took less-than-favorable reviews in stride. In June of 1960, she starred in her next stage production, *Amphitryon 38* (1960). Directed by Martin, it provided a modern take on a tale of Greek mythology. Both Arlene's "captivating"[628] performance and Martin's ability to make ancient Greece "as fresh and urban as last night's Jack Paar show,"[629] were praised. However, when the show opened in Westport, production was cut short by tragedy. The Gabels had been staying at their Mount Kisco house during the play's summer run, and in the interim, their Ritz Tower apartment was undergoing renovations. In the process, the air conditioning unit in their bedroom was temporarily removed, creating a large opening. A worker in the apartment covered the gaping space with a towel, held in place by two dumbbells used for exercise. During a cleaning, one of the dumbbells dislodged and plummeted eight stories down, fatally striking a man below. The man was with his family at the time, exiting the Le Pavilion restaurant during a vacation to New York City.

Arlene was devastated by what had happened. Although she wasn't anywhere near the vicinity of the accident, she harbored deep, self-inflicted guilt. "I couldn't help feeling that, however inadvertently, I had been responsible for somebody's death."[630] She wrote a letter to the widow of the man who was killed, expressing her feelings and condolences. "I told her I would do anything in my power to help her, although I was

627. Ibid

628. The News (Patterson, New Jersey). June 28, 1960. Arlene Francis Captivating at Paper Mill.

629. The Central New Jersey Home News. (New Brunswick, New Jersey) Jun 28. 1960. It Happened Last Night. Earl Wilson

630. Arlene Francis: A Memoir. (1978). By Arlene Francis with Florence Rome. P. 109

sure that nothing I could do would compensate for her loss."[631] Insurance would provide the financial settlement, but the emotional pain of the incident lingered. Peter remembers being in Mount Kisco shortly after they got the news, standing near his mother's bedroom door, hearing the sound of her sobbing.[632]

Some of that sadness was allayed by a response she received to her letter. The niece of the ill-fated man had replied, asking to meet with her.[633] It was during their meeting that the young woman conveyed the rest of the story. As it turned out, the family had traveled to Manhattan to consult with a doctor. The woman had received a terminal diagnosis but had learned during their visit that she was perfectly well.[634] "So, she explained to Arlene, I wanted you to know that while one life was taken on that trip, another was given back."[635] The enormity of the moment left Arlene overcome. "I absolutely went to pieces,"[636] she said upon reflection. "I cannot remember a more emotionally charged moment in my life, and I will cherish it forever."[637]

In the aftermath of personal misfortune, Arlene's public never stopped believing in her. She was approached by Julian Messner Inc. book publishers to pen a volume on the subject of charm. At first, she dismissed the proposal, asserting that writing a how-to book on charm was far too pretentious.[638] After consultation with her publisher about taking a different approach, she agreed to write *That Certain Something: The Magic of Charm* (1960). The result was a book focused on the characteristics of charm in action as opposed to an instruction manual. Peppered with humor, heart, and quotations from notables like Eleanor Roosevelt and Sir James Barrie, the book quickly became a 1960s bestseller. Her steadfast presence as a panelist on *What's My Line?*

---

631. Ibid

632. Peter Gabel interview with Gary Wetstein (2018).

633. *Arlene Francis: A Memoir* (1978). By Arlene Francis with Florence Rome. P. 106

634. *Arlene Francis: A Memoir* (1978). By Arlene Francis with Florence Rome. P. 107

635. Ibid

636. Ibid

637. Ibid

638. *Arlene Francis: A Memoir* (1978) By Arlene Francis with Florence Rome P. 158

(1950) no doubt contributed to the book's public appeal. Martin even sat in for her on the panel one Sunday night while she pressed toward the publisher's deadline. Even without the added publicity, Arlene could still have succeeded. *What's My Line?* (1950) was simply an additional platform and showcase for her admirable assets. She was somebody that everyone was rooting for, whether performing in a play, writing a book or appearing on a game show.

Her natural consideration for others made her all the more charming, and that quality would sometimes become evident when certain guest panelists made wildly notable appearances. When Groucho Marx visited the *What's My Line?* (1950) panel in 1959,[639] he tested patience and capacity for laughter all at the same time. Seated next to Arlene, he had the entire theater in stitches as he chomped at the bit to repeatedly ask the futile question: "Is it found in the kitchen?"[640] This of course made his routine all the more hysterical—or exasperating! Arlene took this in a fun stride, graciously responding to Groucho's attempts to over-talk her by gently grasping his arm in a hold-your-tongue-for-a-moment gesture. She even paid homage to his antics by telling the next contestant: "Groucho wants to know if your product is found in the kitchen."[641]

As entertaining as that episode was, it could not match the chemistry between Arlene and one other memorable guest panelist, Jerry Mahoney, the famous ventriloquist dummy voiced by Paul Winchell. The life-like puppet's on-screen flirtations with Arlene made for some of the show's funniest ad-lib moments: "Did you bring Paul Winchell with you?"[642] Arlene asked. "Yeah, he's over there,"[643] Jerry replied with a tinge of jealousy, "but what you see in him I'll never know!"[644] Sometimes, when his sweet talk carried on, Arlene considerately silenced him by saying: "You be quiet now while we play the game, alright dear? Just hold

---

639. *What's My Line?* Episode September 20, 1959
640. Ibid
641. Ibid
642. *What's My Line?* Episode June 3, 1956
643. Ibid
644. Ibid

beautiful thoughts."[645] Even an overzealous puppet was the recipient of her kindness.

From guest panelists to colleagues, nearly everyone who worked with Arlene was impressed by her good nature and sincerity. Garth Dietrick, former director of *Home* (1954) had this to say about the magnanimous Miss Francis. "I worked with a lot of people, but never anyone so selfless, so considerate. Arlene is the most. She is willing to inconvenience herself so that a guest or other people on the show can be seen to better advantage."[646] Nearly every affirmative adjective has been used to describe her, and there is perhaps no other public figure who has earned their reputation so genuinely. Although Arlene was largely just being herself on camera, she did not take for granted television's ability to project the true essence of a performer. "Television is a personal thing, she explained, not remote like movies where people are just playing characters."[647] Audiences did feel a personal connection with Arlene, and that was due in part to the strength of her natural personality on programs like *Home* (1954) and *What's My Line?* (1950) as opposed to any stage or film role.

Radio was also an ideal medium for expressive communication. In the early 60s, Arlene began a live afternoon interview program on WOR. The show was initially broadcast from Sardi's restaurant in New York City and was later aired from WOR headquarters in Manhattan. Produced by Jean Bach, wife of *What's My Line?* (1950) production coordinator Bob Bach, *The Arlene Francis Show* aired on the east coast and quickly became a favorite with listeners. As a predominately talk-radio station, WOR was already one of the most enduring on the dial. It had gained steady popularity since its premiere broadcast in 1922 and was eventually dubbed The Voice of New York. Arlene could have easily held that same title. In addition to her numerous acting credits on radio and a plethora of emcee positions on a variety of networks, she was recognized with the 1959 Peabody Award for the syndicated radio program *Family Living*.

---

645. *What's My Line?* Circa 1956
646. *Pittsburgh Sun -Telegraph.* Dec. 30, 1956. Video's First Lady. P. 11
647. *The Tampa Tribune.* Jan. 19, 1956. TV Star Fell in Love Under a Broadway Stage. P. 31

However, her new live show would propel her career in broadcast even further.

*The Arlene Francis Show* (1957) received consistent acclaim. It featured interviews with some of the biggest names in the entertainment industry, including Arlene's very first guest, Rock Hudson. The program also welcomed an array of notables including Dr. Martin Luther King Jr.,[648] former president Jimmy Carter, and UN Ambassador Adlai Stevenson, an occasion she called "one of my happiest moments."[649] Arlene conscientiously prepared for her guests. She would read their latest book and take time to educate herself about the person with whom she would be communicating. This effort made her increasingly well-versed in public and world affairs, and Martin once explained how his wife's broadening savviness changed preconceived ideas about their balance of intellect. "Our relationship, in the beginning, had as a tacit assumption that I was the bookish and educated one. It is simply no longer true and it has to be faced."[650] The radio show not only provided Arlene with a continuing education, but it also became one of the highest rated and most respected programs on WOR.

For Martin, television was a prime medium during the 60s. He made several guest appearances on dramatic programs such as the series *Cain's Hundred* (1961) and the TV movie *The Power and the Glory* (1961), opposite Lawrence Olivier. Martin related the motivations behind his involvement in the Graham Greene adaptation. "I was interested in doing *The Power and the Glory* (1961) for two reasons. First, there was an impressive lineup of performers. Second, there was important money involved."[651] As a great and well-respected actor, Martin was a highly sought-after presence. Despite his frequent credits on television, he conveyed that it was not his preferred platform. "I've never wanted

648. *Dr. Martin Luther King, Jr. Dreaming of Equality* (2005). By, Ann S. Manheimer. Interview date: June 19, 1967.
649. Interview with Arlene Herson 1987 DVD
650. *Status Magazine.* Circa 1969. A Duet of Two Stars.
651. Call-Chronicle Allentown, PA. Oct. 29, 1961. Cynthia Lowry

a regular job on television,"[652] he told a writer for the *Associated Press* in 1961, citing TV's limitations for the cultivated art of performance. "Acting is a craft, he explained, "and one of the most important factors in being good at it is time—time to reflect on a character, to practice, polish, and tone down. You don't have time on television and you don't have time in motion pictures."[653] Clearly, Martin shared Arlene's sentiments about the stage. "The theatre has always been my first interest,"[654] he said.

That interest was the focus of Martin's next project – one that would mark his greatest Broadway success as an actor. In March of 1961, he was featured as the eccentric publisher Basil Smythe in the Hugh Wheeler play, *Big Fish Little Fish* (1961). The story centered on a cast of characters led by Jason Robards, Hume Cronyn, George Grizzard, and Martin Gabel. It tackled heavy subject matter, detailing the aftermath of a university professor's scandalous dismissal. The script was critically praised for its treatment of the lead character's (portrayed by Jason Robards) concealed homosexuality.[655] As one of the first creative works to address the theme, it was dealt with lightly according to most sources. Hume Cronyn chronicled the day-day events on set in a later-published diary, noting how he pored over the script with Wheeler during pre-production discussions, debating over how to best address the subject. "We begin to eliminate certain lines . . . These attempts to prejudice audience or critical reception are always tricky. You may end up safe but regretful."[656]

Director John Gielgud called *Big Fish Little Fish* (1961) "A most rewarding piece of work."[657] The play opened on Broadway at the ANTA playhouse on March 15, 1961 and ran for 105 performances. *The New*

---

652. Ibid

653. Ibid

654. Ibid

655. *Theatre Journal.* May 1961. Broadway in Review. Vol 13 (2) John Gassner.

656. *Theatre Arts on Acting* (2013). By Laurence Senelick p. 76 Excerpt from Dear Diary by Hume Cronyn. Taylor & Francis. Format e book. Retrieved from Google Books.

657. *An Actor and His Time* (1997). By George Gielgud. P. 153

*York Times Theatre Review* noted that Martin Gabel "communicates a sense of rich individuality"[658] to a an otherwise "somewhat equivocal character."[659] The success of the production was rewarded with four nominations and two wins at the fifteenth annual Tony Awards. Gielgud won for Best Director and Martin took home the honor for Best Featured Actor. Before thanking Hugh Wheeler for "writing such a brilliant part," Martin declared: "I would like to say that this is the first prize I've won since Arlene Francis consented to be my wife."[660]

Arlene came close to starring in a Tony-winning play herself in the 1960s. She was offered the role of Martha in *Who's Afraid of Virginia Wolf?* (1962) The prospect was thrilling and came along with an enticing salary of $5,000 a week for six weeks.[661] Nevertheless, Arlene's mother was repulsed by the idea of her daughter appearing in a production that could be considered profane. Eager to accept the role, this created a dilemma for Arlene. Ultimately, she placed her own desires aside and turned down the offer. In retrospect, she regretted her decision. "I'm not proud of that story"[662] she admitted, and pointed out that "it illustrates what I think is an essential flaw in my character."[663] Arlene found it extremely difficult to be opposing, and in the case of Virginia Woolf, it resulted in her giving up on something she truly wanted. "It's hard to believe that even at that point, when I was a married woman with a child, I still couldn't consider doing something my mother didn't want me to do."[664]

Work was never as important as earning the love and respect of her family. They were the source of her history, and at the same time a great influence on her present and future. Her father's strong work ethic had obviously influenced his ambitious daughter, and when Mr. Kazanjian

---

658. *New York Times Theatre Reviews* (1960)
659. Ibid
660. The 1961 Tony Awards telecast. YouTube
661. *Arlene Francis: A Memoir* (1978). By Arlene Francis with Florence Rome. P. 28
662. Ibid
663. Ibid
664. Ibid

retired from the photography business after many years, he had great difficulty adjusting to the absence of constant activity. "He had never learned how to cope with leisure— not in large doses,"[665] Arlene explained. As time went on, he began exhibiting troubling symptoms, which could no longer be attributed to the depression of a regretful retirement. His memory was failing at an alarming rate and "He had begun to have fantasies about living in another period of his life . . ."[666] The symptoms were characteristic of Alzheimer's disease.[667] After consultation with doctors, it was recommended that he enter a skilled living facility where he could receive professional care.

Arlene and her mother struggled to make such a difficult decision. "We were just about destroyed by our conflicts."[668] Still, the best interest of her father's health was paramount, and they eventually found a competent nursing home nearby. One decision Arlene wished she had made differently was requesting that her father have a private room. Upon reflection, she noted that "It would have been far better for him to have a companion; a roommate with whom he could have had some kind of human relationship."[669] She visited her father daily, and held onto brief and rare instances when the veil of his illness lifted. She shared a touching moment that occurred between them. During one visit, ". . . He looked up at me with twinkling eyes and winked. I lived on the memory of that wink for weeks."[670] After he passed away, Martin and Arlene decided it best for her mother to take an apartment in the Ritz Tower where they lived. The closeness of family was important to them, and they could depend on the support of each other. "Martin was pure gold through all of those dreadful years, and he was wonderfully gentle with my mother."[671]

---

665. *Arlene Francis: A Memoir* (1978). By Arlene Francis with Florence Rome. P. 166
666. Ibid
667. National Institute on Aging. http://www.nia.nih.gov
668. *Arlene Francis: A Memoir* (1978). By Arlene Francis with Florence Rome. P. 167
669. Ibid
670. Ibid
671. *Arlene Francis A Memoir* (1978) By Arlene Francis with Florence Rome. P. 168

The strength that the Gabels found in each other remained constant despite life's unpredictability. By this time, Arlene's visibility on television and Martin's success on the stage kept them in the limelight during the ensuing decade. However, the accolades were never guaranteed. While Martin's Tony Award solidified his position as a Broadway mainstay, the cancelation of Arlene's daytime variety program reinforced the fickle nature of show business. The Gabels were named Husband and Wife Team of the Year by the National Father's Day Committee in 1961, and the couple's public esteem remained as strong as their private devotion. Together, they moved forward into an eventful future.

# Chapter Eight

"Arlene Francis has finally become a movie star."[672]

— Newsday


As the 1960s unfolded, Arlene appeared in two motion pictures. In 1961, she played opposite James Cagney as the wife of a soft drink executive in Billy Wilder's *One, Two, Three* (1961). Legend has it that she got the part because Wilder was looking for an "Arlene Francis type."[673] Aside from the documentary film *With These Hands* (1951), Arlene hadn't appeared in a motion picture since *All My Sons* (1948). She was widely recognizable from her position on *What's My Line?* (1950) but this new role would give her a chance to grace the big screen for a change and demonstrate her skill as a comedic actress. Seeing her in a comedy was perhaps no stretch of the imagination for those accustomed to watching her game show appearances. Arlene's natural sense of humor was famous, but her ability to perform well in a film showed that she could deliver lines as well as she could ad-lib, and, it gave her a chance to live out one of her earliest career fantasies.

"I'd always wanted to be in movies,"[674] she told journalist Mary Pangalos in 1961. "That's how it all started."[675] A span of nearly 30 years had elapsed between then and her first role in *Murders in the Rue Morgue* (1932). Arlene called her work in *One, Two, Three* (1961) "my

---

672. *Newsday*. Cira 1961.

673. *Some Like it Wilder. The Life and Controversial Films of Billy Wilder* 2010 by. Gene Phillips p. 251

674. Newsday (Suffolk Edition) (Melville, New York) Dec. 21, 1961. Arlene Francis Finally Gets into The Movies. By Mary Pangalos.

675. Ibid

first real part,"[676] and she credited director Billy Wilder for being the reason she agreed to take it. "He was the most marvelous director," and, his confidence in her help calm her nerves. "He treated me as if I were the biggest pro in town."[677] The public also believed she could pull off her first real movie role. Her current popularity on television made her an instant sensation. In fact, her association with *What's My Line?* (1950) was so prominent at the time that the picture paid the show a small tribute. During one scene in the film, Arlene, in character, calls out "conference!" before huddling together with her children for a discussion. Loyal TV viewers no doubt recognized this signature move often conducted by the panel on *What's My Line?* (1950)

Arlene had to take leave from the show in order to film on location in Munich, Germany. She was interviewed on set, and discussed, among other things, the ample amount of luggage she brought with her. "I'm going to be here ten weeks, she explained, and I'm furnishing my own wardrobe for the picture."[678] Arlene also warned audiences that her trademark heart necklace would not be seen in the film, but she added that "for good luck," she will still be wearing it on a long chain concealed from the cameras. "I'll be wearing my diamond heart down where my heart really is."[679]

During production, Arlene enjoyed the lively presence of James Cagney, who tap danced during every lunchtime.[680] "Jimmy was no youngster, she said, but he certainly looked it. . . he was a lovely man, a pro, a dedicated tireless worker."[681] Peter recalled being off-camera watching Cagney play a scene. "I was there in Munich when it took 104 takes, I think, for him to correctly recite his long monologue on the phone when Paul Ford's character is about to arrive to see his daughter who is

676. Newsday (Suffolk Edition) (Melville, New York) Dec. 21, 1961. Arlene Francis Finally Gets into The Movies. By Mary Pangalos
677. Ibid
678. TV's Arlene Francis A Film Fraulein in Munich Now. It Happened Last Night. 1961 By, Earl Wilson
679. Ibid
680. Email communication with Peter Gabel January 27, 2021
681. Arlene Francis: A Memoir (1978). By Arlene Francis with Florence Rome.

pregnant by the Horst Buchholz Marxist character. That was amazing to watch, with everyone on the set being so tense after twenty-five or fifty takes."[682] Despite a mixed bag of reviews, *One, Two, Three* (1961) was generally regarded as a success and gave Arlene a much-needed boost in morale. Her role as Phyllis MacNamara was memorable, and the fast-paced comedy garnered 1962 Oscar and Golden Globe nominations for Best Picture and Best Cinematography.

"I'm not a motion picture performer,"[683] Arlene later asserted, but her lack of identification as a film actress by no means prevented the acceptance of selected offers; neither did it dissuade the interest of the movie-going audiences. In 1963, she appeared in *The Thrill of it All* (1963). With a script co-written by Carl Reiner, Arlene was a featured actress in the Doris Day-James Garner romantic comedy. She played the supporting role of Mrs. Fraleigh, a middle-aged woman gleefully expecting her first child. Although herself about fifty-five years old at the time, she portrayed the role convincingly. Her character's storyline runs alongside that of the picture's leading actors and intersects in meaningful and humorous ways throughout the film. Garner is incidentally Mrs. Fraleigh's obstetrician whose wife (Doris Day) becomes briefly famous with the help of the Fraleigh family. Arlene received ample camera time, from gracing the film's opening scene to giving birth in the backseat of a Rolls Royce at the picture's end. Critic Bosley Crowther of the *New York Times* wrote favorably of the film but would not go so far as to call it great.[684] He did, however, refer to Arlene as "extremely funny."[685] The movie was a box-office success and the actress added another hit film to her credit.

Scenes for *The Thrill of it All* (1963) had been shot in Hollywood, and because Arlene was playing an expectant mother in the picture, one news article humorously predicted that she would take "maternity leave"[686]

---

682. Email communication with Peter Gabel January 27, 2021

683. 1966 Interview with George Douth. 1966 Arlene Francis Radio Interview. May 30, 2019. YouTube

684. The New York Times. Aug. 2, 1963. Screen: The Thrill of it All Opens at Music Hall: Doris Day Stars in Carl Reiner Comedy. https://www.nytimes.com

685. Ibid

686. News clipping. 1963

from *What's My Line?* (1950) As it turned out, there would be no need for an absence. Her schedule was arranged so that she could fly back to New York on weekends to appear on the panel. Martin introduced her on the November 25, 1962 episode as "A woman who's been commuting so much between New York and California that the only time I get to spend a half hour with her is on this program."[687] His appearances as a guest panelist on the show increased steadily throughout the mid-sixties, and in a few special broadcasts, he even attempted to fool his wife during the mystery guest segment. Even so, after speaking just a few sentences in a disguised voice, his identity was soon discovered by Arlene who famously declared: "There comes a time when a man talks too much!"[688]

In between regular game show appearances and her WOR radio program, Arlene still made time for the theatre. In 1963, she starred in the Carolyn Greene comedy, *Janus*, and received a special honor for breaking attendance records[689] at the Playhouse on the Mall in Paramus, New Jersey. News coverage attributed the play's success to Arlene's "personal appeal."[690] Yet she was more than just a likeable presence, she was a capable actress. While her personality might well have attracted audiences, she also possessed the talent to hold their attention. Such accolades were recognized by Broadway, and Arlene was asked to step in for Margaret Leighton as star of the Tony-nominated *Tchin-Tchin* (1963) during its final month at the Ethel Barrymore Theatre.

She was cast opposite Jack Klugman in the play by French novelist Francois Billetdoux. Reviews for the overall production were excellent, albeit most notices only mention Leighton's performance. However, the fact that Arlene was chosen to assume the coveted role even for a short period speaks volumes of her credibility and versatility. "I'm thankful to the director, Warner LeRoy, she said. I've wanted all my life to play an emotional role. Nobody's ever thought of me as being serious. Now

---

687. What's My Line? November 25, 1960
688. What's My Line? December 25, 1960
689. *The Record* (Hackensack, New Jersey. March 11, 1963. Theatre Record Set by Arlene Francis
690. Ibid

I've got the opportunity."[691] The role definitely had its moments of levity complete with comedic scenes between her and Klugman. Most importantly, it was personally satisfying for the ever-ambitious actress. Looking back, she placed it among her fondest theatre experiences, saying: "I think that the happiest five weeks of my professional career were when I took over the Broadway lead of "Tchin-Tchin (1963)."[692]

Soon after the play closed, Arlene visited friends on Long Island's south shore. She arrived on a Saturday night and left the following drizzly afternoon. She was scheduled to appear for the live taping of *What's My Line?* (1950) that Sunday evening and allowed herself plenty of time to make the trip back into the city. While driving on the Northern State Parkway, Arlene was involved in a severe traffic accident. According to reports, she was driving in the second lane, nearest the divider, when the car in front of her suddenly skidded on the slippery road. She stepped on the brake, sending her car over the divider and into the oncoming lane of traffic, resulting in a horrific collision.[693]

She lost consciousness on impact, and an ambulance transported her to the hospital with a broken collar bone, cracked ribs, and a concussion. Once stabilized, she began asking about the condition of the passengers in the other car. It was Martin who gently conveyed the heartbreaking news[694] that a woman had been killed in the accident. Arlene was beside herself. In light of the dumbbell fatality just a few years prior, matters were compounded. "Mentally and emotionally, I was just about ready for an institution."[695] She was released from the hospital two weeks later and faced a lawsuit.[696] An eyewitness at the scene testified in Arlene's defense,

691. *Delaware County Daily Times* (Chester, Pennsylvania) May 18, 1963. Arlene Francis' Formula: Don't Waste Time in Anger p. 25

692. *Toledo Blade.* Jul 5 1964 Arlene Francis: A Study in Energy. Cynthia Lowry

693. Records & Briefs. New York State Appellate Division. Transcript. https://www. google.com/books/edition/Records_Briefs_New_York_State_Appellate/i8AzJLohPXI C?hl=en&gbpv=1&dq=arlene+francis+gabel&pg=PA256&printsec=frontcover

694. *Orlando Sentinel.* Sept. 1, 1963. TV's Unlucky Star. Arlene Francis is Carefree on Camera but Tragedy Pursues Her Private Life. By Christina Kirk.

695. *Arlene Francis: A Memoir* (1978). By Arlene Francis with Florence Rome. P. 107

696. Ibid

but a settlement was reached ahead of a jury's verdict,[697] and even though she knew it wasn't so, she couldn't help but feel that settling was in some way an inferred admission of guilt.[698] While physically on the mend, she descended into a deep depression.

The period following the tragedy was an introspective one for Arlene, and she took some time before returning to *What's My Line?* (1950) and to her daily radio program. It also afforded an opportunity for soul searching. "I'm not a religious person in any formal sense, she said during one of her first interviews following the accident, but I believe the ways of The Almighty are more mysterious than I can understand."[699] She credited the outpouring of love she received from the public in helping her heal, explaining that along with the "tremendous support"[700] of Martin and Peter, she was overwhelmed by the unexpected reinforcement from the public. "The thousands of prayer cards and letters from people of all faiths which told me they were praying for me. I believe with all my heart that those vibrations got through to me. And to God. I *have* to believe in the healing quality of that kind of positive love . . . it brought me from the very depths of despair, from a depression I didn't think I could get out of, to being myself again."[701]

While Arlene found her bearings, Martin worked steadily. In the spring of 63, he appeared in Irwin Shaw's *Children from Their Games* (1963). He starred as Melvin Peabody in the play about a suicidal and ailing cynic.[702] Despite a competent cast including Gene Hackman, Brenda Vaccaro, and Peggy Cass, the production only ran for 4 performances at the Morosco Theatre. Its meager reception did not

---

697. Records & Briefs. New York State Appellate Division. Transcript. https://www.google.com/books/edition/Records_Briefs_New_York_State_Appellate/i8AzJLohPXI C?hl=en&gbpv=1&dq=arlene+francis+gabel&pg=PA256&printsec=frontcover
698. *Arlene Francis: A Memoir* (1978). By Arlene Francis with Florence Rome P. 107
699. *Orlando Sentinel.* Sept. 1, 1963. TV's Unlucky Star. Arlene Francis is Carefree on Camera but Tragedy Pursues Her Private Life. Christina Kirk.
700. *Arlene Francis A Memoir.* (1978). By Arlene Francis with Florence Rome P. 109
701. Ibid
702. *Broadway Plays and Musicals: Descriptions and Essential Facts of More Than 14,000 shows through 2007.* (2009). By Thomas S. Hischak

forestall acting offers. The following year, Alfred Hitchcock petitioned Martin[703] to play Sydney Strutt in the film, *Marnie* (1964), starring Tippi Hedren and Sean Connery. Martin's performance was called "impressive,"[704] and the film has since become a controversial classic. His frequent appearances in popular pictures illustrated careful forethought about the roles he would accept. Even from the beginning, when Arlene was seeking out parts in movies, Martin gave her sound guidance: "The only small roles you can play are cameos in prestige pictures."[705] Through the years, his featured and supporting roles in top-rated films such as the Oscar-nominated *Divorce American Style* (1967), reflected the wisdom of his own advice.

The Gabel's both strove toward similar goals. But they were neither competitive nor envious of the other's success. "There's no competition, said Martin. Arlene's far better known to the public. I've been introduced a couple of times in my life as Mr. Francis. That's never bothered me. Being respected by my fellow theatre people is the uppermost level of my aspirations."[706] Martin was certainly acknowledged as a first-rate actor on Broadway, and Arlene's regular position as a television personality placed her before audiences far and wide. Martin took great pride in her success, once declaring on *What's My Line?* (1950) that he was "proud to be known the world over as Arlene Francis's husband."[707] "She's much wittier than I am, said Martin, she's a lighter, amusing personality."[708] The appeal of television was a vehicle for Arlene's popularity, but at the same time, she felt it a hindrance to her primary career interest. "The panel show is fun, she said, but people forget you're an actress."[709]

Arlene did her best to remind them. In 1964, she starred in Samuel Taylor's *Beekman Place* (1964). In a role previously offered to Vivian

703. *Hitchcock and the Making of Marnie.* (2013). By, Tony Lee Moral

704. *The Films of Alfred Hitchcock* (1989). By Neil Sinyard

705. *Arlene Francis: A Memoir* (1978) By Arlene Francis with Florence Rome. P. 82

706. The High Point Enterprise. May 18, 1969

707. What's My Line episode circa 1960s

708. *Philadelphia Daily News.* Jan. 5, 1970. Critics? Bah! Says Actor in Sheep. By Charles Petzold.

709. *The Journal New York.* Don Olsen

Vance,[710] Arlene portrayed the character, Pamela Piper. The play opened at the Morosco Theatre in October and closed after 29 performances. *The New York Theatre Critics' Review* had harsh words for Taylor's characters, referring to them as puppets on strings,[711] but noted that "Arlene Francis brings so much personal animation to the role of Pamela that she becomes occasionally amusing if not credible."[712] Typically acknowledged by critics, Arlene received one of her most favorable reviews for an off-Broadway production of *Kind Sir* (1964). Her performance at the Ivanhoe Theatre in Chicago was covered by Roger Dettmer of the *Chicago American*. He wrote: "When I think of all the wasted years, knowing Arlene Francis only as a Sunday night detective on television, when in fact her line is acting, and doing so with a vivacity, poise, concentration, and discipline unbettered that I am aware of by any other American leading lady of her generation."[713] Those words were likely gratifying to an actress who feared being forgotten.

Arlene made a lasting impact wherever she went, and plenty of memorable moments were seen on television. On the July 5, 1964 episode of *What's My Line?* (1950) Peter appeared as a mystery guest for the first time. A recent graduate of Deerfield Academy in Massachusetts, his occupation was a guide at The World's Fair, where he had taken a summer job before entering Harvard College in the fall. He expertly stumped the panel including his mother who shouted in disbelief when she removed her blindfold. Arlene once told the humorous story of seeing Peter before she left to do the show that evening. He was carrying a blue suit over his shoulder and casually mentioned that he was taking it to the dry cleaners.[714] Of course, he was actually headed to *What's My Line?* (1950) "If that is any model of your deception in the future, I'm in a lot of trouble!"[715] Arlene said laughingly from the panel. Years later, she still

---

710. *Lucille Ball F&Q: Everything Left to Know About America's Favorite Redhead.* (2011). Barry Monush.
711. *The New York Theatre Critics' Reviews* volumes 25-26 p. 199
712. Ibid
713. The *Chicago American.* 1964
714. Interview with Arlene Herson 1987. DVD
715. What's My Line? July 5, 1964

recalled the joy she felt at her son's appearance on the show. "Oh, it was such a pleasure to see him in that blue suit."[716]

By early 1965, the patriarch of the Gabel family was in the spotlight. Martin was cast as Professor Moriarty in the Sherlock Holmes-inspired musical, *Baker Street* (1965). He got the chance to sing in the production, and Peter later reminisced about his father's preparation and praised his performance. "I remember [him] rehearsing around the house "I Shall Miss You Holmes," the one singing number of his life. He was only worried about hitting the first note. And his Irish accent was so good. His entrance in the show was also a great moment, his chair turning to face the audience with E=Mc squared in the background."[717] *The New York Critics' Theatre Review* also noted: "Martin Gabel's impressive organ of a voice had the perfect quality of menace for the sinister genius of crime."[718] The play ran for 311 performances at the Broadway and Martin Beck Theatres, and was awarded the 1965 Tony Award for Best Scenic Design.

During the run of the play, Martin made appearances on the panel of *What's My Line?* (1950). The musical received mentions from Arlene who once introduced her husband as "Professor Moriarty from Baker Street— A devil on stage, an angel at home."[719] The play also found its way into one of the Gabel's funniest exchanges.[720] The panel was trying to guess the product involved with a contestant's occupation. Arlene asked if she would ever wear the product and was given a "no" answer. When the next panelist received a "yes" to a similar question, Arlene interjected: "Why did I get a "no" then!?"[721] Before anyone else had the chance to answer, Martin replied: "Because dear, it costs less than $3,000!"[722] The audience went wild with laughter, and Arlene was rendered silent while

---

716. Ibid

717. Peter Gabel comment on photo in the WML (CBS) Facebook Group. May 29, 2020

718. *New York Critics' Theatre Reviews* Volume 26. P 367

719. *What's My Line?* Episode April 4, 1965

720. *What's My Line?* Episode Jan. 3, 1965

721. Ibid.

722. Ibid.

Martin smiled smugly. "Why do you think I'm working in *Baker Street?*" he continued. Never speechless for very long, Arlene quipped: "You may have to live in Baker Street after that remark!" The Gabel's were so obviously in love that their occasional on-screen "arguments" were all taken in fun. But just for good measure, they usually made up by the end of the show. "See ya later, professor,"[723] Arlene said, while Martin blushed.

The Gabel's next project was a joint effort. On September 22, 1965, *Mrs. Dally* (1965) opened at the John Golden Theatre in New York. The play originally caught the attention of Arlene when she attended an off-Broadway production of *Mrs. Dally Has a Lover,* starring actress Estelle Parsons.[724] Ms. Parsons had previously worked as a special projects' editor on *Home,* and would later be recognized as the memorable grandmother-matriarch on the television sitcom *Rosanne.* However, in the early 1960s, Parsons' stage role in a two-person intimate drama intrigued Arlene, who enthusiastically resolved to try her hand at a portrayal of Mrs. Dally. She approached the play's writer, William Hanley, with her aspirations.[725] The young playwright had achieved recent success with his production, for which he won the 1963 Drama Desk Award.[726] For Arlene's performance, Hanley decided to re-construct the play by merging it with his sequel of sorts titled: *Today is Independence Day* (1965). The entire dramatic piece would now be divided into two parts, and the new production was simply re-titled, *Mrs. Dally* (1965).

A summer tryout was arranged. The show was originally set to be presented by Hume Cronyn and Jerome Hellman, under the direction of Joseph Anthony.[727] However, due to prior commitments, Cronyn and

---

723. What's My Line" Dec, 6 1964

724. Foundation Interviews. YouTube (Aug. 29, 2018). Estelle Parsons on working on "The Home Show" with Arlene Francis.

725. Ibid

726. *The New York Times* (June 3, 2012). D. Hevesi. William Hanley, Playwright and TV Writer Dies at 80.

727. The New York Times. (Aug. 23, 1965). S. Zolotow. Season's Opener A Family Affair.

Hellman had to withdraw.[728] As a result, the show debuted on Broadway with a new sponsor and producer—Martin Gabel.[729] The play would feature a young Robert Forster who played Frankie (The Lover). The role marked Forster's first on Broadway, and would prove instrumental in launching a lengthy acting career in motion pictures.[730] Ralph Meeker appeared in the conclusive second half of the play, as Sam (Mr. Dally). The conclusion had never before been produced on stage,[731] making Arlene the first to perform the dramatic finale. She also surmounted another feat for *Mrs. Dally* (1965): Learning to play the trombone. The part called for her to master the jazzy Turner Layton and Harry Creamer piece, "After Your Gone," which she would perform in the play's first act. Prior to production, she took lessons with famed musician Lillian Briggs to prepare for the performance. Only those fortunate enough to watch the play live on stage would hear the polished Arlene Francis version.

If audiences hadn't thought of Arlene as a trombonist, they would be even more surprised to see her take on a character like Evalyn Dally. Playing the role of a married woman engaging in an affair with an eighteen-year-old neighbor would prove a considerable feat as an actress. Although the show ran for only 53 performances, it helped to showcase her versatility. Peter fondly remembered the production. "Mom gave a very good performance in a role contrary to her image. As I recall Bosley Crowther's review in the *New York Times*, he gave her a fine notice."[732] Comparatively, *The Saturday Review*[733] used adjectives like "convincing" and "honest" to describe her efforts. Drama critic Hobe Morrison boasted of her "depth"[734] and "disciplined emotional force."[735] He also noted her

728. Ibid

729. Ibid

730. CNN Cable News Network. Oct. 12,2019 Turner Broadcasting System

731. *Mrs. Dally Has a Lover and Other Plays* (1963). By William Hanley. The Dial Press New York.

732. Peter Gabel comment on WML CBS Facebook posting.

733. *The Saturday Review* 1965 Vol. 48

734. *The Record* Hackensack, New Jersey. Proves She's Fine Actress. Arlene Francis Surprises in Mrs. Dally Title Role

735. Ibid.

ability to remain entirely in character. "Never by the flicker of an eyelash does she fall back on the familiar mannerisms and charm so effective on the air."[736]

Even Arlene's fellow *What's My Line?* (1950) panelist Dorothy Kilgallen covered the play in her column, *The Voice of Broadway*. She wrote with honesty about her great esteem for *Mrs. Dally* (1965), making it clear that her favorable reaction had not to do with being Arlene's colleague.[737] As a columnist with a reputation for not mincing words, Kilgallen was careful in her review of the play. She went so far as to admit criticizing close friends for faux pas, but noted that if she had not liked Arlene's play, she would simply "refrain from mentioning it."[738] Yet, she did like it and wrote of it glowingly. "It's beautifully written, splendidly directed and perfectly cast,"[739] she gushed. "I saw tears come to the eyes of the opening night audience."[740] Amidst the recognition, Arlene took the most pride in the warm reception she received from actress Katherine Cornell, who went backstage to personally compliment her after a show. "It implied acceptance of me as a colleague, she explained, and was a greater accolade in my mind than even a good notice."[741] Despite the occasional criticism of Hanley's script, Arlene's performance was consistently praised.

In addition to appearing in productions like *Mrs. Dally* (1965), Arlene still frequented the off-Broadway circuit. She co-starred with her longtime friend Mary Cooper in summer stock revivals of John Van Druten's *Old Acquaintance* (1967). The play, which had been adapted for the screen in a 1943 film starring Bette Davis, was a perfect vehicle for Arlene. She played the role of Katherine Markham to excellent reviews, and much was made about the glamourous Scaasi gowns she wore in the play. It was even reported that the Playhouse on the Mall made insurance

---

736. Ibid.
737. *The Voice of Broadway.* Sep. 24, 1965. By Dorothy Kilgallen Ashbury Park Press.
738. Ibid
739. Ibid
740. Ibid
741. Arlene Francis: A Memoir (1978). By Arlene Francis with Florence Rome. P. 53

provisions for the costumes in the sum of $100,000.[742] Along with the fanfare, the production provided an opportunity for two real-life friends to work together again.

Arlene and Mary Cooper first met while appearing in *The Doughgirls* (1942). "She likes me to say it happened in 1958,"[743] said Miss Cooper jokingly during an interview the two did with columnist Norma Harrison. While reflecting on the intervening years, she related that Arlene had not changed but was "more poised now that her confidence has grown" "She always wanted to be loved, and she is. [Arlene] is one of the few people in show business one doesn't hear any gossip about."[744] That remark led to the telling of a humorous story. Mary related that she and Arlene spent the entire day together practicing their lines, even while under the hair dryer at the beauty parlor. Those around them did not realize they were reciting a script. "People acted strangely when I said lines like 'There never was a man you didn't have an affair with.' [They] wondered who was talking to Miss Francis that way."[745] *Old Acquaintance* (1967) offered its own brand of humor on stage and was noted for its honest take on the human condition. "We find ourselves laughing at ourselves, not the characters, noted a reviewer. That is comedy in the true sense."[746] The play ran for over a year, and Arlene was praised for exuding "pure professional finesse." *The Herald News* boasted that she had "long ago proven herself a star, and her performance as Katherine Markham further adds to her reputation."

Such recognition was among the chief reasons for her continual success on the stage. In 1966, Arlene joined the ensemble cast of *Dinner at Eight* (1966). She appeared as Carlotta Vance in the successful Broadway revival. The George Kauffman and Edna Ferber play was made famous in 1933 with an all-star screen adaptation by Metro Goldwyn Mayer. It was

---

742. *The Record.* Hackensack, New Jersey. June. 21, 1967. Arlene Parades Charm, Fashions at Mall. By, Ken Wallace.

743. *The Record* Hackensack, New Jersey. June. 1967. Its Takes a Bit of Doing to Be Arlene Francis, But She Does It Well. By, Norma Harrison. P 21

744. Ibid

745. Ibid

746. *The Herald News* Jun. 22, 1967. Old Acquaintance, starring Arlene Francis Opens at Mall. By Jim Kordell.

brought to life over thirty years later on the Broadway stage, opening at the Alvin Theatre, and running for a total of 127 performances. One review called the production "A pleasant example of our stage's historic vitality"[747] while another chastised it for being "too recent for vintage esteem and too dated for current entertainment taste."[748] The entire cast appeared in the mystery guest segment on the September 25, 1966 episode of *What's My Line?* (1950). Arlene failed to guess their identities that evening. She had also been stumped by Joe Cotton when he appeared as mystery guest during the run of *Once More with Feeling* (1958).[749] Perhaps, Arlene so separated the game show platform from her theatrical aspirations that she could not consciously bridge the two worlds concurrently.

In the summer of 1967, a small corner of the game show world evaporated. *What's My Line?* (1950) was cancelled after 17 years on CBS. Ratings had taken a significant fall despite winning three Emmys and a 1962 Golden Globe. The show's cut was the signal of a "fading era,"[750] according to journalist Richard K. Doan. Television in the late 60s was gravitating toward a new and younger generation.[751] Still, *What's My Line?* (1950) was a testament to style and class and an example of what can happen when a group of intelligent and witty individuals get together for half an hour. Arlene was greatly saddened by the show's cancellation. "It's almost like the loss of a loved one, "[752]she told TV critic Percy Shain. When the last episode aired on September 3, 1967, John Daly took the mystery guest seat. It had never occurred in the history of the show, as he was always the back-up plan in case the scheduled celebrity was late in arriving. John employed a humorously high-pitched voice during the segment, but the panel eventually recognized their moderator. "Are you going out of business like the rest of us?" Arlene asked.

---

747. *The New York Critic's Theatre Reviews* Vol. 27 page 290

748. *Fort Worth Star Telegram.* Sep. 28, 1966. Dinner at Eight at Awkward Stage —Both Too Old, Too New by William Glover p. 31.

749. *What's My Line?* Episode Jan 11, 1959

750. End of the Line. Why the Granddaddy of the TV Game Shows Finally is Finished. Richard K. Doan June 19, 1967

751. Ibid

752. *The Boston Globe.* Arlene Francis: Sad but Happy. By Percy Shain. Jun. 11, 1967

In actuality, her career was far from finished. If her track record for tenacity was any indicator of future possibilities, Arlene was well prepared for the next phase of her life. She had successfully transitioned from daytime television to afternoon talk radio in the 1960s, all the while starring in Broadway shows, appearing in feature films, and above all, enjoying her life as a wife and mother. During an interview with Mike Wallace, she asserted that her own role as a woman was not rooted in being dominant.[753] "I have no desire to do some great world's work, she said, except through my own family and my own peace, and to connect that back with the world."[754]

Regardless of humble ideals, she had carved for herself an uncommon place of prominence in the public sphere. Her position as "America's Sweetheart" combined with her leadership role in a man's world[755] continued to make her a trailblazer. This dichotomy only furthered her appeal and allowed her to resonate with women from all walks of life. It did not, however, reconcile her own ambivalent relationship to feminism. In consideration of her work in a male dominated profession, she once stated: "I've never had to ask myself why can't I do it if he's doing it?"[756] While speaking from a subjective standpoint, those remarks did not entirely limit her evolving views on feminism in general. "Women are absolutely on par with men, she said. I think that if a woman does the same job as a man, she should get paid the same."[757] Arlene's career to date reflected the respect of her peers and the perspective of the world in which she lived and worked. Her ability to adapt to changing times would be tested in the coming decade. But in typical fashion, she would not only endure— she would succeed.

---

753. *Television Talk: The History of the TV Talk Show* (2002) By Bernard M. Timberg. P. 43

754. Ibid & The Mike Wallace Interview with Arlene Francis. 1959. The Paley Center for Media https://www.paleycenter.org

755. Email communication with Peter Gabel. Jan, 27, 2021

756. *Green Bay Press-Gazette* Arlene is Back. June 20, 1978 by, Marion Christy

757. *Fort Worth Star Telegram.* Arlene Francis Offers Views. Feb 15, 1970. By Katie Brown. P 22

# Chapter Nine

"Arlene will always be twenty-two next October"[758]
— Gil Fates, executive producer of *What's My Line?* (1950)


The forever young Arlene Francis approached the 1970s with grace. She traveled to London after the *What's My Line?* (1950) finale to appear as Ann Treadwell in the televised movie *Laura* (1968). Despite the film's lackluster reception, Arlene's acting career might have finally taken precedence if not for a syndicated CBS revival. In the summer of 1968, a new version of *What's My Line?* (1950) would again place her before TV audiences on a regular basis. In addition to the show's eventual seven-year run, Arlene continued to make an impressive impact: penning her memoirs, appearing on film and taking roles both on and off Broadway. She and Martin would also work together again, co-starring in stage productions such as *The Lion in Winter* (1973). The Gabels reveled in professional success, but took even greater pride in personal pleasures, such as watching their son graduate Phi Beta Kappa from Harvard. During the years that followed, Arlene maintained a position of public prominence while relinquishing the status of being in demand. Always revered for her sense of style, she was appointed to the board of directors of the luxury department store Bonwit Teller. The brand would sponsor many of the ensembles she wore on the syndicated version of *What's My Line?* (1968) and by July of 68, the reincarnation of the series was about to debut with a new look, a new host, and an almost new panel.

---

758. *What's My Line? The Inside History of TV's Most Famous Panel Show.* By Gil Fates. January 1 (1978).

"I had very mixed feelings about it,"[759] Arlene said of the revamped *What's My Line?* (1968) The new series consisted of a semi-revolving panel of four. Arlene and comedian Soupy Sales held permanent positions while the other two seats were frequented by notables such as Alan Alda and Joanna Barnes. The syndicated version aired in color five days a week, and it was hosted by journalist Wally Bruner, who was later succeeded by actor Larry Blyden. Operating on a different schedule than the original series, a week's worth of episodes were taped in one day, with short breaks for wardrobe changes.[760] The syndicated show carried the potential to draw new audiences. It looked promising from the start, but one of the program's earliest silent critics was Arlene.

"At first, I desperately missed the good old days and my former colleagues,"[761] she recalled. Geared toward a younger generation, the show was different from the original series. Although the format remained largely similar, the contestant's occupations could be a bit more "with the times." Challengers ranged from a piano-playing chicken to the International Playboy Playmate of the Year to president Jimmy Carter, who the panel did not recognize as the then governor of Georgia. One new addition to the show was the frequent demonstration of a contestant's product or talent. Occasionally, the panel participated, performing tasks such as making an omelet or playing the tambourine. In one episode, the panel taste-tested caviar to determine which was the most expensive— a test Arlene passed with flying colors! The show certainly contributed its share of laughable fun, such as the time Larry Blyden introduced Arlene as "a woman who has always seen herself as a rich man's plaything."[762] Still, what was missing most was the undeniable spark of camaraderie that had been cultivated between the original panel. Arlene was glad to be a part of the new program, but it took some time to adjust.

---

759. *Arlene Francis: A Memoir* (1978). By Arlene Francis with Florence Rome. P. 193
760. *Intelligencer Journal.* May 27, 1975. What's My Line? Panelist Arlene Francis Has Special Charm.
761. *Arlene Francis: A Memoir* (1978). By Arlene Francis with Florence Rome. P. 194
762. What's My Line? (circa 1974). syndicated version.

Inadvertently, the updated *What's My Line?* (1968) prompted Arlene to evaluate her position as an entertainer working in a medium that was only getting younger. It also taught her an important lesson about letting go. "Gone in my opinion was the good taste of yesteryear,"[763] she said of her initial feelings about the new game show. "It came over me one day that I was getting to be a bit of yesteryear myself, and that if I didn't watch it, I'd be in a powdered wig and carrying a walking stick, shaking it at young whippersnappers."[764] This realization helped Arlene to ease into the changes and relinquish the futile attempt to slow the passing of years. In so doing, she eventually appreciated the differences that the new series brought to the table. "It was agonizing reappraisal time, she explained, but I came to a decision—get with it or get out of it."[765]

Arlene was determined to stay with it as long as possible. In addition to her place on the panel, she joined the off-Broadway cast of *Pal Joey* (1969) in August. She took singing lessons[766] to prepare for her performances of "The Lady is a Tramp" and "Bewitched, Bothered and Bewildered." The play, which opened to mixed reception, ran at several theaters during a summer tour. "Arlene misses the mark," noted a review[767] of her performance at the Poinciana Playhouse in Palm Beach, Florida. Subsequently called "too well-bred for the role,"[768] Arlene's perceived failure was certainly not the result of too little effort. This wasn't the first time she had met the challenge of preparing for a stage role with lessons in the fine arts. Whether it was learning to play the trombone for *Mrs. Dally* (1965) or singing in *Pal Joey* (1969), Arlene was an actress with enduring ambition, and a willingness to refine her craft.

In January, she performed in *Façade* (1971). The unique stage production presented the poetry of Edith Sitwell accompanied by the orchestral arrangements of William Walton. Arlene was a prime choice

763. Ibid
764. Ibid
765. Ibid
766. *Status Magazine.* Circa 1969. A Duet for Two Stars
767. The *Miami Herald.* Mar. 16 1971. Warmed-Over Joey Closes.by Veda Graves.
768. Ibid

for the recitations. She had previously performed a few poems with composer Skitch Henderson, and her speaking voice had nearly earned its own reputation as a golden instrument. This would be different than an acting role, but Arlene decided to take it. Part of her reason for accepting *Façade* (1971) was the fact that it was to be performed at Jordan Hall in Boston. "My son, who is at Harvard, is having a birthday at that time, so I thought 'why not?' it will be my chance to see my son for dinner."[769] Aside from personal satisfaction, Arlene found the twenty-one-poem production to be a trying experience. She especially struggled to keep time with the orchestra. "If you're not on the beat, you're lost. I'm not a musician and preparing for this has been harder than preparing for a play."[770]

Taking creative chances was also familiar territory to Martin. In the early 1970s, he appeared in Art Buchwald's first Broadway play, *Sheep on the Runway* (1970). He was cast in the role of a visiting journalist stirring up rumors of communism in a small Himalayan village.[771] Directed by Gene Saks, the satirical comedy opened to harsh reviews during an off-Broadway tryout at the New Locust Theatre in Philadelphia. During an interview at the Variety Club, Martin openly disagreed with the critics. "I think they made a big mistake. This play requires a sympathetic attitude, and I don't think we got that here."[772] He agreed there was room for the comedic development of his character, but fiercely defended the production. "Art Buchwald is a friend of mine. He's written a farce, a spoof on The Establishment, and I think [the notices] reflect a conservative point of view." Despite the early criticism, Martin had high hopes for the play's future. "Younger people should go for it, he said, and I think New York will go for it, assuming it's funny enough."[773]

---

769. *The Boston Globe.* Jan, 26, 1971. Arlene Francis Tries a New Line. by, Ellen Pfeifer.
770. Ibid
771. *Life* magazine March 27, 1970
772. *Philadelphia Daily News.* Critics? Jan. 05, 1970. Bah! Says Actor in "Sheep" by Charles Petzold.
773. Ibid

The play made it to Broadway in late January, and ran for 105 performances at the Helen Hayes Theatre. At this point in his career, Martin had already solidified a sterling reputation as an actor. And in his mind, every appearance could well be his last. "My plans are never to do anything again,"[774] he said after *Sheep on the Runway* (1970) closed. With an impressive body of work behind him, Martin admitted that he would now prefer to spend his time at the horse races rather than on the stage. His reasons for continuing to work were attributed to Arlene's encouragement. "She's driving me," he explained. "My wife thinks her career is just beginning and she thinks we both should be working."[775]

Arlene's attitude toward Martin's career had perhaps to do with her long-held belief in the detrimental consequences of retirement. "People fall apart when they retire."[776] Not only did she believe that work was an optimal contributor to viability, but she had witnessed firsthand her own father's decline after giving up the photography business. Steady work meant security, and inactivity posed a possible threat to the future. Through the years, however, Arlene explained that she did not just work for the sake of keeping busy. She had a great affinity for the theatre in addition to a genuine zest for life. "My biggest problem is that there aren't enough hours in a day! I'm interested in doing so many things."[777]

Several of Arlene's interests surpassed a direct relation to showbusiness. At the heart of her carefree and fun personality was a woman who felt deeply about the world around her. In March of 1971, she narrated *Silenced Majority*, the very first women's rights multimedia kit.[778] Consisting of a five-part program on filmstrip, record, and cassette, complete with discussion guides, promotional buttons, and posters, the kit was distributed to schools and community centers.[779] It featured

774. Ibid

775. Ibid

776. Interview with Eileen Prose. 1979. Arlene Francis. Eileen Prose. May 8, 2017. YouTube

777. *Deseret News*. Salt Lake City Utah. Her Special Charm. May 26, 1969. By Rose Mary Pedersen. P. 16

778. *The Cincinnati Enquirer*. Mar 14, 1971. Silenced Majority.

779. Ibid

topics including *Liberation NOW, Women Jobs and the Law,* and *Rapping with the Feminists,* a discussion with female leaders such as writer Kate Millet, advocate and attorney Florynce Kennedy, and playwright Megan Terry.[780] Although Arlene never considered herself a feminist,[781] she had undoubtedly held a female leadership position for decades.

"She was an important figure in the history of the women's movement," said her son Peter, because she increased the role of women, particularly with [her position] as editor-in-chief of the Home Show [in the 50s.]"[782] She was the first female host of a game show and the first woman to host *The Tonight Show* (1954). "When Jack Paar took a break, my mother replaced him, and that was very significant to women's power to play those roles that my mother was comfortable playing."[783] Arlene's own views were largely ambivalent. While remaining steadfast in her opinion that females need not lose their femininity in pursuit of achievement,[784] she blatantly expressed her belief in gender equality on a 1960 episode of *What's My Line?* (1950) declaring that "men are not a superior sex, but an equal sex." A decade later, she discussed the topic at a post-lecture press conference in Fort Worth, Texas. An article covering her appearance related the following: "Miss Francis said she is interested in women's rights but said she is not a member of the Women's Liberation Movement."[785] During the conference, she stated: "[Women] are entitled to voice their opinions and certainly should. But I still believe that the glorious difference between men and women is that we are feminine and they are masculine. We can have our rights and still be women."[786]

---

780. *Federal Women's Program Handbook.* (1977). United States: Department of Defense, Depts. of the Army and the Air Force, National Guard Bureau.

781. Peter Gabel interview with W. Gary Wetstein. 2018

782. Ibid

783. Ibid

784. *Television Talk: The History of the TV Talk Show* (2002) by Bernard M. Timberg. P. 43 & The Mike Wallace Interview with Arlene Francis. 1959. The Paley Center for Media https://www.paleycenter.org

785. *Fort Worth Star-Telegram* Feb. 15, 1970. Arlene Francis Offers Views. Tv Panelist Thinks Men Need Pill. By Katie Brown. P. 22

786. Ibid

Her participation in a project like *Silenced Majority* showed her interest in feminism without sacrificing her own feminine identity. Her lack of complete immersion in women's lib had partly to do with her rejection of aggression.[787] "[My mother] would never have associated herself with the anger of the movement,"[788] affirmed Peter. But in an era of debate, she did comment publicly on core issues permeating second-wave feminism. Reacting to the 1970 congressional hearings on the hazardous side-effects of the birth control pill, she voiced her concerns: "I do think they should find some oral contraceptive for men until they find out why [the pill] is killing some women."[789] Furthermore, she expounded on the issue of a woman's right to choose. "I think it's shocking that we can't have our abortion laws repealed, but I do think it's coming."[790] Her comments were made just two months before the state of New York legalized abortion,[791] and three years before the Supreme Court's ruling on *Roe v. Wade*.[792] Despite her generally agreeable nature, Arlene tended to be more outspoken in regard to societal matters.

"I'd like to see more women care—really care about politics, charity, and service work." she told a news journalist, adding that striving toward social change should be attained "in a sensible, non-violent way."[793] When asked what career she would have chosen if not for acting, she replied: "I guess I'd like to be a writer or something related to the arts . . . and I could be perfectly happy in some phase of child education. . . or perhaps even psychiatry."[794] From the beginning of her theatrical pursuits, Arlene

787. *Television Talk: The History of the TV Talk Show* (2002). By Bernard M. Timberg. P. 43 & The Mike Wallace Interview with Arlene Francis. 1959. The Paley Center for Media https://www.paleycenter.org
788. Peter Gabel Interview with W. Gary Wetstein. 2018
789. Ibid
790. *Fort Worth Star-Telegram* Feb. 15, 1970. Arlene Francis Offers Views. TV Panelist Thinks Men Need Pill. By Katie Brown. P. 22
791. The New York Times. Apr. 9, 2000. '70 Abortion Law: New York said Yes, [Apr. 1970] Stunning the Nation. Richard Perez-Pena https://www.nytimes.com
792. Roe v. Wade was decided by the Supreme Court on January 22, 1973
793. *The Miami Herald*. Aug, 8 1957 By Eleanor Darnton. TV's Darling Arlene Francis Says Stage is Her First Love. P. 30
794. Ibid

worked hard to establish a fulfilling stage career. She had achieved her goal, but that did not mean she was devoid of regrets. "In the larger sense, I would like to have had a deeper, more profound education, a more scholarly one with more emphasis on the cultural."[795]

Nevertheless, she had made an influential impact where education was concerned. The American College of Monaco offered the Arlene Francis Drama Scholarship[796] from 1968 until the institution closed in 1970, benefiting pupils with an "active interest in theatre and theatrical literature."[797] The 1969 recipient, Jill Dye, was interviewed by Arlene on WOR radio, where the young aspirant expressed her desire to work in international communications.[798] Adding to her association with higher learning, Arlene also served on the council board of the University of Utah, and was awarded two honorary doctorates in the humanities; one from American International College in Springfield, Massachusetts and the other from Keuka College in New York. Arlene spoke during the 1966 commencement ceremonies at Keuka. Addressing the female graduates she said: "Defining the role of women is about as simple as constructing the Gemini space capsule with paper clips, a hair roller, and some scotch tape."[799] Blending humor with a message of hope and empowerment, she lauded the trademark strength of women. "We can handle so well all the roles that we are destined to fill in our lifetime."[800]

Arlene filled more than her share of roles. Throughout the years, she acknowledged her accomplishments as an actress, but also expressed a

795. *The Miami Herald.* Aug, 8 1957 By Eleanor Darnton. TV's Darling Arlene Francis Says Stage is Her First Love. P. 30

796. *The Montclair Times.* (Montclair, New Jersey). Student Ambassadors. Oct. 1, 1970 p. 9

797. *The Montclair Times* (Montclair, New Jersey) Jill Dyes Earns Scholarship. Jun. 12. 1969 p. 36

798. *The Montclair Times.* (Montclair, New Jersey). Oct. 1, 1970. Student Ambassadors. p. 9

799. *The Central New Jersey Home News.* Jun.13, 1966. Arlene Francis Gives Advice to Graduates. & Arlene Francis Speaks at Keuka College. By Dick Eisenhart. *Democrat and Chronicle* (Rochester, New York) Jun 13, 1966

800. Ibid

longing to have made an impact on a different level. "What I would really like to have been able to do, she once explained, is to have applied some of the things I have learned are important— about tolerance, sympathy, responding to life. . . ."[801] In some instances, however, her professional contributions became a model for the values she held dear. In the early 1970s, she appeared among a chorus of over 100 notables in the televised public service announcement, *Love. It comes in all colors*, promoting racial unity. Sponsored by the *National Urban Coalition*, the commercial featured Ray Charles, Peggy Cass, Ed Sullivan, Ruby Dee, and many more, singing and swaying to the rousing "Let the Sunshine In." Interestingly, the song was from the popular Broadway musical, *Hair*, a show for which Arlene later expressed mixed feelings. "I didn't even go to see *Hair*,"[802] she wrote in her memoir, explaining that while she agreed with the play's anti-Vietnam War theme, she was at the same time critical of the show's use of nudity.[803]

The theatre was a creative platform during the 70s, an era when elements of nudity and profanity began to fall under the umbrella of self-expression. Inasmuch as Arlene stood by her viewpoints, she worried whether her personal standards of decorum could cause her to be labeled prudish or archaic.[804] "Miss Francis does not bridge the generation gap, asserted the *Chicago Tribune*, she belongs to the mature."[805] However, Arlene's opinions were perhaps rooted deeper in politics and virtue than they were in age. "As a liberal, I suffer from the dichotomy that commits me to freedom of the press and a firm stand against censorship on one hand, but makes me want to sweep all that filth into the gutter on the other hand."[806] Her contemplative interest in societal issues and active participation in charitable causes spoke to her awareness and fueled her open-hearted compassion.

---

801. The *Miami Herald*. Aug, 8 1957 By Eleanor Darnton. TV's Darling Arlene Francis Says Stage is Her First Love. P. 30

802. *Arlene Francis: A Memoir* (1978). By Arlene Francis with Florence Rome. P. 187

803. Ibid

804. *Arlene Francis: A Memoir* (1978). By Arlene Francis with Florence Rome. P. 197

805. *The Chicago Tribune*. Her Line? May 22, 1978. She's Arlene Francis. By, Karen Peterson. P. 44

806. *Arlene Francis: A Memoir* (1978) By Arlene Francis with Florence Rome. P. 197

Behind the scenes, she supported organizations such as the *American Foundation for the Blind*[807] and the *New York State Heart Fund*.[808] In turn, those efforts helped to keep her outlook on life in perspective. "I'll tell you something else, she said, when queried about her easy-going personality, "I'm on the board of the *United Cerebral Palsy Association*. When you see and work with people who really have trouble, things like whether a TV set is just so or the script is right are nothing."[809] Her love for people was genuine and inspiring, and she hoped that perhaps even a small portion of her popularity had to do with the public's recognition of a mutual admiration. "If people like me, I want to believe it's because I think people are marvelous, and maybe that part of my personality comes through on the screen."[810] Martin also had an opinion on the subject. In addition to calling his wife a national treasure, he expressed his thoughts about the connection between her good nature and public esteem. "She's great on TV because she's a nice honest person."[811] "All in all, she's a decent and useful citizen who tries to play her part and in so doing to give as much pleasure as she can."[812]

Much of that pleasure was had by the theater-going public, and it was always an anticipated delight when the Gabels came together on stage. One of their notable pairings was a week-long production of *The Lion in Winter* (1973) at the Westport Country Playhouse in Connecticut. The James Goldman play told the tale of Henry II of England and his wife, Eleanor of Aquitaine, in a dispute over which of their sons will inherit the throne. Interestingly, it was noted by some critics for being a medieval Virginia Woolf. Arlene and Martin were solid choices for the royal couple, bound by love yet divided by conflict. In reality, they worked well

---

807. Helen Keller Archive. Correspondence with Arlene Francis. American Foundation for the Blind. https://www.abf.org

808. *The Glen Falls Times*. Feb. 14, 1970

809. The *Miami Herald*. Aug, 8 1957 By Eleanor Darnton. TV's Darling Arlene Francis Says Stage is Her First Love. P. 30

810. *The Evening Sun*. Baltimore, Maryland. Aug. 25, 1965. By, Olga Curtis Arlene Francis Takes Care of the Men in Her Life. P. 44

811. *The Raleigh Register*. Beckley, West Virginia. Jan 8, 1954.

812. *Status Magazine*. Cira 1969. Duet for Two Stars.

together, and seldom clashed, an asset they attributed to being in sync. "We've been married so long, our minds usually work the same way,"[813] said Arlene. Still, Martin admitted that in the case of contention, his wife often prevailed. "When we disagree, I usually lose the dispute."[814]

In discussing their relationship, the Gabels both maintained that they were simply not argumentative. "I'm sorry if it sounds boring, Arlene conceded, but Martin and I just haven't had the kind of fights which make their way into gossip columns."[815] The mutual ease and comfort they felt with each other was clearly evident whenever they appeared in public. Arlene explained that the disagreements they did have were resolved through compromise. "It's knowing when you're wrong and admitting it. Martin and I have had our differences, but we've settled them."[816] Decades of marriage had also taught them quite a bit about the others' pet peeves, such as Arlene's request that the windows be rolled up when riding in a taxi cab. "She wants them closed so her hair won't blow, and I'm uncomfortable, Martin explained. Sometimes, we arrive at our destination in separate cabs."[817]

In 1972, they both appeared in the Hallmark Hall of Fame TV version of *Harvey (1972)*, starring James Stewart and Helen Hayes. Regrettably, Arlene and Martin shared no scenes together, but turned in fine performances individually. For audiences who preferred them as co-stars, there was a chance on stage the following year in a two-week run of *Who Killed Santa Claus* (1972) at Paramus New Jersey's Playhouse on the Mall. Arlene was something of a legend at the theater, where she had previously broken box office records for her run in *Old Acquaintance* (1967). Her appearance with Martin in *Santa Claus* (1972) that January was a revival. She had previously performed the play in the summer of 72, but the mystery thriller was plagued with behind-the-scenes tragedy.

---

813. *The Record.* Hackensack, New Jersey. Jan 28, 1973. By, Virginia Lambert. What's Arlene Francis's Line? TV, Radio, and Yes, the theater. P. 36
814. Ibid
815. Arlene Francis: A Memoir. (1978) By Arlene Francis with Florence Rome. P. 177
816. *Green Bay Press Gazette.* Jun. 20, 1978 by Marion Christy. Arlene is Back.
817. The *Orlando Sentinel.* Sept. 1 1963. By Christina Kirk. TV's Unlucky Star – Arlene Francis is Carefree on Camera but Tragedy pursues her Private Life.

Arlene's original co-star, Edward Zimmerman, succumbed to a heart attack during the play's run,[818] and her beloved mother, Leah, also passed away during that time. This performance marked a fresh start, and with Martin by her side, Arlene was surely strengthened by his support.

In the theatrical world, Martin was more than capable of commanding a starring role or supporting the leads. He did the latter in a production of Terence Rattigan's play, *In Praise of Love* (1974). Cast opposite Rex Harrison and Julie Harris, Martin played the role of an American novelist living abroad. He is friend and confidant of a married couple who both believe they are keeping a devastating secret from the other. The play debuted in November at the Kennedy Center Opera House, and early reviews predicted success. A write-up in the *Chicago Tribune* proclaimed it "a warm, gentle and old-fashioned English love story."[819] Martin offered his own kind words for the cast, saying that Rex Harrison "knows the stage" and calling Julie Harris "a great actress, and an angel by the way."[820] *In Praise of Love* (1974) opened on Broadway in December of 1974 and ran for 200 performances at the Morosco Theatre.

Martin spoke of the play briefly when he appeared as a mystery guest on the syndicated version of *What's My Line?* (1968) The episode is perhaps best remembered for showcasing the humorous side of the generally composed actor. Utilizing a Yiddish accent, he hilariously attempted to fool the panel, including Arlene, who after a few minutes of suppressed laughter asked: "Are you married?"[821] Afterward, she told the audience that she'd recognized Martin's disguised voice "As soon as he opened his mouth." But in her typical caring way, she gave her husband time to shine before revealing his identity. Martin was none too surprised that she guessed him. "I've been with this girl a long time, he said, she knows all my schtick."[822] The Gabels had not appeared together on *What's*

---

818. *The Bangor Daily News* (Bangor, Maine) Tony Award Winning Actor Dies at York. Jul 7, 1972

819. The *Chicago Tribune*. Nov. 14, 1974. Chicago, Illinois

820. *Courier Post*. Camden, New Jersey. Dec. 19, 1974. By Earl Wilson. Martin Gabel a White Knight in a Dark World. P. 57

821. *What's My Line?* (1974)

822. Ibid.

*My Line?* (1950) since the CBS finale in 1967. Nearly a decade later, the spark between them was just as evident.

Also enduring was their mutual love for the theatre. While they had different appetites for the stage during the 1970s (Arlene ravenous and Martin satisfied) each had made significant contributions. *In Praise of Love* (1974) would mark Martin's final performance in a play. But Arlene continued to accept roles, such as replacing an ailing Agnes Moorehead as Aunt Alicia in *Gigi*. Although appearing in several regional theaters throughout the late 60s and early 70s, the performance was Arlene's first on Broadway in eight years.[823] Martin once explained that his wife's preference for the stage had to do with the accomplishment of raw performance. no close-ups or cameras, just an actor's ability to interpret a character and transfer that emotion to a live audience.

Such was Arlene's attempt in the thriller, *Don't Call Back* (1975). Anthony Perkins was originally slated to direct the play, but Lou Cariou took the reins instead. Following 13 previews in New Haven and Philadelphia, it ran for only one performance at the Helen Hayes Theatre, unwittingly marking the last Broadway production to Arlene's credit. She called the experience "a one-night disaster"[824] and critics said much of the same. While chastising the play for being "a wrong number," one reviewer remarked on Arlene's committed performance: "The veteran actress moves through the alleged suspense melodrama. . . with resolute dignity beyond the call of duty. One can only sympathize with such devotion."[825] Her dedication to the role was characteristic of her professionalism, but she also had a few reasons to believe in the production. It had been written for her by novelist Russell O'Neil, and they had both approached the play with high hopes. "[826]Despite the disappointing reception, Arlene

---

823. *Daily News*. New York. Gigi Switch Jan 24, 1974

824. *The Boston Globe*. Sept. 2, 1979. Just What's Arlene's Line" Fate Keeps Putting Forks in the Road. By Kevin Kelley.

825. *New York Associated Press*. The Day. March 20, 1975. Critics Blast Play Starring Arlene Francis.

826. *The Boston Globe*. Sept. 2, 1979. Just What's Arlene's Line" Fate Keeps Putting Forks in the Road. By Kevin Kelley.

was undeterred. "That's the risk," she said, "I'd jump at the chance to do another play."[827]

This irrepressible resiliency is perhaps what made her career so durable. For actors who had worked as consistently as Arlene and Martin, the element of courage was essential. While Arlene was self-confident in her abilities, she harbored inner doubts about her career's future. Nearly 50 years in the business had not yet convinced her that she would remain perpetually in demand. "Martin can't believe I [still] feel insecure. He asks: 'Heavens, aren't you over that yet?'"[828] Despite her doubts, she continued to work and move gracefully with the unpredictability of a career in the spotlight. Time had taught her that no matter how popular the play or project, all success must reach its end, even a game show as established as *What's My Line?* (1968)

In 1975, the syndicated version of the game show was cancelled. In commemoration of the finale, Arlene appeared with Mark Goodson and John Daly in a two-hour retrospective, celebrating some of the best moments in the show's twenty-five-year history. *What's My Line? at 25* aired on May 28, 1975 and focused primarily on showing clips from the CBS version. During the program, John Daly noted that Arlene was even lovelier now than she was back then. When reminded of his comments during an interview, she humorously replied: "He's so gallant, but you can tell he was on *What's My Line?* rather than *To Tell the Truth*."[829] Arlene later expressed what she was feeling while the CBS video reels unfold, recalling the experience as "a storehouse of memories across the years."[830]

Among the most special moments for her were not shown as part of the retrospective, but likely included the times when her son appeared on the show. Peter joined his mother on the syndicated series for a two-week stint as a guest panelist and fooled her during both of his appearances as a

---

827. Ibid

828. *Green Bay Press Gazette*. Arlene is Back. By Marian Christy. Jun. 20, 1978

829. *Intelligencer Journal*. Lancaster, Pennsylvania. May 27, 1975. What's My Line Panelist Arlene Francis Has Special Charm. P. 11

830. Arlene Francis: A Memoir (1978). By Arlene Francis with Florence Rome. P. 102

mystery guest on the CBS version, and again on a syndicated episode. By the early 70s, the Gabels' son had achieved his own measure of success. Having already earned a degree in English literature, he graduated magna cum laude from Harvard Law School and served as Associate-In-Law at the University of California at Berkeley's Boalt School of Law.[831] By 1975, he was working as a law professor at New College of California in San Francisco (an institution of which he would later become president) and helping to create the school's public interest law program.[832] Peter's scholarship and ambition certainly imbued his parents with a sense of pride. For they, too, had reached many milestones.

Arlene had been the only one to remain on *What's My Line?* (1968) from its start in 1950 to the program's end in 1975. After over two decades on television, American audiences felt the absence of their beloved panelist. She was still a familiar voice on the east coast with her successful WOR radio show. Still, the woman who felt like every viewer's best friend, also missed being on TV. When Barbara Walters vacated her position as host of the NBC program, *Not for Women Only* (1976), Arlene was interested in the job. She inquired of the network's vice president, but was told that the position had already been filled. It was not uncommon for a coveted post to be occupied quickly, but disconcerting to Arlene was the fact that she had not been on NBC's radar as a potential replacement. Back in the 1950s, she would have likely been a first choice. This instance was one in a series of events which Arlene referred to as "hints. . . that I might no longer be the biggest thing since sliced bread."[833] Rejection was disappointing and dealt a considerable blow to her self-esteem. By the same token, television could be considered a compensatory activity for a stage actress. Arlene once provided her own rationale: "Naturally, one works in television because one is very well paid, but it is also lovely satisfaction to the performer's ego. It fills the need between plays."[834]

---

831. Peter Gabel Curriculum Vitae https://www.petergabelauthor.com
832. Ibid
833. Arlene Francis: A Memoir (1978) By Arlene Francis with Florence Rome. P. 195
834. *Sunday News* (Lancaster, Pennsylvania) Feb. 2, 1964. By Margaret McManus. Lovely Arlene Francis: Happy on a Perennially Popular Show.

Working on the stage was preferable, but not promised. The uncertainty of being cast in a part was something Arlene had to accept for the entirety of her career, and in an atmosphere of increasing ageism, it was becoming more difficult to secure roles. In 1978, she was urged by her agent to audition for a supporting part in the play *13 Rue de L'Amour* (1978). By this time, she had written her memoir with the help of her friend, Florence Rome, and further obligations left her with no time to commit herself to the play. Nevertheless, she did decide to audition—for a very specific purpose. "They like you, but they don't think you can do it,"[835] her agent told her. Those words made Arlene appraise her current position in the theatrical sphere and propelled the actress into action. She completed the audition and was offered the role. However, she declined the offer and explained her true reason for being there. "I've got news for you, she told them, I've written a book and have agreed to do a promotional tour. I did this reading for myself."[836] Reflecting back on the situation, she said: "How could they understand? I just had to see if I could still do an audition successfully."[837]

She could, of course, do anything with her signature finesse, known for winning the hearts of TV viewers and theatrical directors alike. In 1979, she was first in a series of actresses chosen to replace Hermione Gingold in *Side by Side by Sondheim* (1976), a revue celebrating the music of Stephen Sondheim. She served as narrator of the production in addition to performing a singing number. The play ran for a tryout before opening at the Charles Playhouse in Boston. Arlene could only commit to the role for two weeks due to the demands of traveling from New York City for her daily WOR radio program. "The evening really doesn't depend on me as the Narrator,"[838] she told *The Boston Globe*. But despite modest words about her contributions to the show, she garnered a welcoming response from audiences and critics. While calling her singing voice "rusty," one reviewer also noted the ovation she received following

---

835. *Green Bay Press Gazette*. Arlene is Back. By Marian Christy. Jun 20, 1978
836. Ibid
837. Ibid
838. *The Boston Globe*. Sep, 2, 1979. Just What Is Arlene's Line? Kevin Kelley.

her song and praised her for adding "warm professional gloss"[839] to the production. While no doubt pleased by the accolades, Arlene was also entering a reflective and introspective period in her career.

"I'm no longer a young woman,"[840] she said at the age of 71. It was during this time that Arlene began to speak publicly on the subject of professional regrets, and openly discussed what she believed stood in the way of a whole-hearted pursuit of the theater. Her musings thus far had leaned toward the fact that success on television was more secure and viable than taking her chances on the stage. "When I began in the theater I wanted to be like Lynn Fontaine, Tallulah Bankhead or Katherine Cornell. But later when I found it was so difficult to get stage parts, I began appearing on radio and then on television, always as myself. I got such recognition as everybody's friend that I stopped pursuing my own goal."[841] Getting lost in the vortex of television fame was one part of her perceived inability to achieve maximum recognition as an actress. But the allure of TV also extended beyond the perspective of the players themselves. When grappling with what-might-have-been, Arlene duly noted that the position she had attained as a television personality became difficult to shed for a character role. "You get locked into an image, and no one really thinks you can do anything else."[842]

There were also times when Arlene let her own doubts get in the way. Her appearance in *Side by Side* was a second chance of sorts. Back in the mid-1960s, Stephen Sondheim had been impressed by her performance in *Mrs. Dally* (1965) and asked her to star in his new musical *Anyone Can Whistle* (1964). At the time, she declined the role (despite urging from Sondheim) because she felt inept to perform the song and dance routines necessary for the part. In the end, the role went to Angela Lansbury. Arlene spoke about her decision to reject the musical during a candid interview with Kevin Kelley for *The Boston Globe* in 1979. "I adored

839. *The Boston Globe*. Sep. 14, 1979. Socko Sondheim. Kevin Kelley

840. *Green Bay Press Gazette*. Arlene is Back. Marion Christy. June. 20, 1978

841. The *Orlando Sentinel*. TVs Unlucky Star-Arlene Francis is Carefree on Camera but Tragedy Pursues her Private Life. Christina Kirk. Sept. 1, 1963

842. *The Boston Globe*. Just What Is Arlene's Line? Kevin Kelley. Sep, 2, 1979

it"[843] she said of the script. but "I was fearful and backed off."[844] She also gave a brief overview of her career, focusing less on the hits and more on the misses. "That's rather the story of my life, she said, preparation in one direction when the forks in the road take me in another."[845] She acknowledged her twenty-five-year stretch on *What's My Line?* (1950) and her then eighteen years as host of her WOR radio talk show. Yet, a summation of the acclaim did not take the sting out of her dissatisfaction where the stage was concerned. "It seems to me my longest runs have been outside the theatre! she exclaimed; do you think God is trying to tell me something?"[846]

Arlene's realistic take on her stage career by no means eclipsed her achievements across the board. She admitted being "in awe of accomplishment,"[847] so much so that she still considered herself insecure when it came to public acceptance, but there was no denying her impact in the industry. In 1978, she replaced the late Ben Grauer as radio's *Voice of America* (1978). "I'm particularly proud of that, she said, because I'm the first woman ever to do it."[848] She took on the position once a week, in addition to her regular radio program on WOR. The gaps in her theatrical goals were filled by a substantial stream of work in the entertainment sector, and above all, a loving and unbreakable family unit. When appearing at a lecture in 1980, she was asked the question: What is the best thing that has ever happened to you? Her immediate reply was her son, Peter. The esteem and affection Arlene had maintained both publicly and in private life made her a most fortunate woman. Her philosophies for living, she once said, were rooted in the golden rule and the Prayer of Saint Francis of Assisi.[849] She had chosen to end the *Home*

---

843. Ibid

844. Ibid

845. Ibid

846. Ibid

847. The *Orlando Sentinel*. Sept. 1, 1963. TVs Unlucky Star-Arlene Francis is Carefree on Camera but Tragedy Pursues her Private Life. By, Christina Kirk.

848. The *Odessa American*. (Odessa, Texas) May 28, 1978

849. The *Miami Herald*. Aug, 8 1957 By Eleanor Darnton. TV's Darling Arlene Francis Says Stage is Her First Love. P. 30 and Arizona Republic. Arlene Francis is rated Tops

(1954) show with that prayer in 1957, and although she professed no formal religion,[850] the record of her life reveals that she purposefully put into action the virtues of giving love, promoting peace, and extending pardon. Her exuberant spirit and genuine care for others might well have established Arlene as the other Saint Francis.

It would be sufficient to suggest that her likeability combined with capability kept her consistently employed. The abundance of job offers she had become accustomed to receiving during the 50s and 60s began to slow down in the late 1970s. Yet her presence was still requested by top directors like Billy Wilder. She appeared in a cameo in Wilder's film *Fedora* (1979), starring William Holden and Marthe Keller. Arlene played the part of a newscaster announcing the death of the film's main character. Although her screen time was brief, she conveyed the role with the poise and discipline befitting of a leading lady. Among the many attributes to her credit was a readiness to accept supporting as well as starring roles. This openness toward variety led to her appearance in a theatrical reading of George Bernard Shaw's *Don Juan in Hell* (1980). Opening at the Roundabout Theater in New York, Arlene portrayed Dona Ana in the production labeled a "conflict between flesh and spirit."[851] Her contribution was called "weary"[852] despite a favorable review overall by the *New York Daily News*.

Working in the entertainment industry since the late 1920s had strengthened her versatility as an actress and prepared her for the unpredictable. Her appearance in the 1980 Terrance Rattigan play, *The Winslow Boy* (1980), was another example. It's scheduled opening at the Paper Mill Playhouse in New Jersey was scratched due to the theater's destruction by fire. The production was then moved to the Royal

---

Because She Just Plays Herself. Jan Allison. May. 25, 1956

850. The *Orlando Sentinel*. Sept. 1. 1963. TV's Unlucky Star. Arlene Francis is Carefree on Camera but Tragedy Pursues Her Private Life. By. Christina Kirk.

851. *New York Daily News*. Dec. 22, 1980. A Devilishly Funny Evening of Shaw. By Don Nelson.

852. *The News* (Patterson, New Jersey) Dec, 26, 1980. Hell Loses its Virtue. Rachelle Cantlupe p. 17

Poinciana Playhouse in Palm Beach, Florida where rehearsals were played to a live audience. The show's interpretation of a British couple defending their son's honor failed to resonate with some critics. However, while the majority of the cast was scolded for lackluster performances, Arlene and co-star David O'Brien were noted as being "more comfortable in their roles"[853] than the others.

The stage was indeed like a second home to Arlene, but if the actress had her druthers, it could have been a trifle more advantageous. "When you come right down to it, she said in 1953, I've only been in one hit, *The Doughgirls.*"[854] If she had made that statement two decades later, she could easily have added *Once More with Feeling* (1958) and a litany of regional theatre productions. Throughout the years, she had achieved momentous feats, breaking attendance records for her off-Broadway performances in *Janus* (1963) and *Old Acquaintance,* (1967) and receiving countless glowing reviews for a plethora of plays. *The Boston Globe* once remarked that "Arlene managed to build a substantial theatrical career on the creaky foundation of a long succession of flops."[855] That double-edged compliment spoke to her talent and determination. While Arlene might have agreed with the Globe's remark, it would be substantially lacking to suggest that the actress was anything but proud of her lengthy career on the stage.

Martin was assuredly worthy of that same pride. He likely suffered insecurities and certainly experienced his share of disappointments. However, after over 40 years in showbusiness, he had developed an outlook which allowed him to see the larger picture of an actor's impact. During a speech he gave in 1970 at the American Academy of Dramatic Arts eighty-sixth graduation ceremonies, he said: "What is the overriding ultimate object of all these plays, this acting, these techniques, this long procession of great names in the ancient theatrical tradition?" Speaking for myself, I believe that its object, indeed, the object of all the arts,

---

853. *Fort Lauderdale News.* Jan 23. 1980. Winslow Boy could die in infancy. By Jack Zink. Wed.

854. *The Boston Globe* Sun. Aug. 15th 1953.

855. Ibid

is to deepen understanding, to broaden human tolerance, to play the leading role in our never-ending struggle to find a way of living together as civilized human beings."[856]

By the early 1980s, Arlene's tenure in theatre, radio, film, and television had taught her that achievement and acceptance meant her contributions mattered. She had also learned not to peg the legacy of a play solely on the length of its run, once referring to *Mrs. Dally* (1965)[857] as "a kind of personal success."[858] The scope of her work both on and off the stage was impressive. Continually achieving notoriety in a variety of mediums bolstered her level of satisfaction and fueled her desire to strive toward the next goal. "I have had an amount of success which means people care about what I do."[859] Arlene had long developed a special camaraderie with audiences, and they were as eager for her next adventure as she was. In contemplation of her career's future, she noted the support of her public as a driving force. "The critics may have rejected you, but somebody cares, and when the day arrives that nobody cares anymore, that's the time to hang up your eyelashes and retire from the arena."[860]

---

856. American Academy of Dramatic Arts. Eighty-Sixth Graduation Ceremonies. Tuesday, March 31, 1970. Transcript p. 23
857. Mrs. Dally ran for 53 performances at the John Golden Theater
858. *The Boston Globe.* Just What Is Arlene's Line? Kevin Kelley. Sep, 2, 1979
859. *Detroit Free Press.* Aug. 11, 1957 Now Arlene will Dance. That is, if her Foot is Healed in Time.
860. Arlene Francis: A Memoir (1978) By Arlene Francis with Florence Rome. P 7-8.

# Chapter Ten

"Women are moving ahead quite fast in television now; women in general have come further in the last ten years than we have in the previous hundred"[861]

– Arlene Francis in 1980

Over half a century had passed since Arlene first appeared on the Broadway stage. Her consistent presence on WOR radio and frequent television guest spots kept her a household name throughout the early 1980s. Having reached the point where past achievements threaten to outweigh future possibilities; Arlene strove to keep the balance in her favor. She was not alone in those efforts. In 1981, she returned to television with the NBC series *Prime of Your Life* (1981). The following year, she was inducted into the Broadcaster's Hall of Fame, commemorating a decades-long contribution to the medium. She once said that living life in the moment was her key to happiness. That outlook, combined with constant work, seemed a potent elixir for life's challenges. Yet, if audiences of a certain age were turning to Arlene for example or inspiration, they needn't look any further than her new TV program.

"Does NBC appreciate Arlene Francis"?[862] asked columnist Liz Smith in the mid-80s. She was referring to *Prime of Your Life* (1981), a series highlighting the accomplishments and challenges of adults in their golden years. When Arlene took the reins alongside co-host Joe Michaels, the five-year-old program was already in progress. It had first premiered

---

861. Arlene Francis Thinks Game Shows are Out of Line. (Mar 21, 2980). By Kathy Hoersten Quirk
862. New York daily News. 1986

in the mid to late 1970s, with Michaels and Ponchitta Pierce as the show's emcees. Pierce was eventually replaced by television journalist Pia Lindstrom who left the position in 1981 to broadcast *News for New York*, paving the way for Arlene. Unique to the show was the fact that it dealt with current issues facing mature citizens. In addition to celebrating the endurance of those forgoing retirement, surmounting inspiring feats, or making strides in the arts, the program shed light on issues such as grandparents' rights, continuing education, and employment opportunities for the aged.

Since its inception, *Prime of Your Life* (1981) was aired in the New York tri-state area. However, with Arlene as hostess, it was able to reach national syndication in 1983 and secure a 7:00pm timeslot on Saturday evenings. This triumph was attributed to the magnitude of her popularity and undeniable star power.[863] Featuring interviews with celebrities such as Lucille Ball, Van Johnson, Myrna Loy and Jack Lemmon, the show was able to generate interest on a broad level. In a sense, one could compare the program to a mature version of the *Home* (1954) show, except rather than targeting housewives and expanding on domestic issues, it dealt with concerns facing aging Americans. The component of travel and remote broadcast was present, although very much absent was product pitching or any sales angle. If the show tried to convince viewers of anything, it was that life after youth was a viable and worthwhile experience. "The prime of your life is whenever you are a grown up,"[864] Arlene said from the set. Her sunny approach to the idea of getting older was bolstered by her own active lifestyle. "It's what keeps the life juices flowing. You can't be static in your life. You've got to move on and readjust your sights as you grow older because the world changes. You must move with the times."[865]

---

863. *The Central New Jersey Home News*. Apr. 24, 1983. TV Data Service. Arlene Francis is in Her Prime. By, Ruth Thompson.
864. *Tampa Bay Times*. Regional Extra Page. Nov. 1, 1981. Show for Grown Ups Moves with Times. By Kenneth R. Clark.
865. *The Salina Journal*. Show for Over 50s may be Syndicated. Oct. 20, 1981. By, Kenneth R. Clark

She had learned that lesson while adjusting to the new syndicated version of *What's My Line?* back in the 1970s. Now, having a firm grasp on the evolution of years, Arlene was in good standing as a spokeswoman for embracing change, and *Prime of Your Life* (1981) was an effective vehicle for showcasing age as an art rather than a number. One episode[866] featured a motorcycle group for those over 65. Co-host Joe Michaels spoke to the riders as they described their passion and the sense of freedom gained from cruising the open road of life. Central to the program at large was that both men and women could grow older without losing ability or attractiveness. "Not one of today's glamour girls is under 30— not one," said Michaels, admitting to the possible exception of Brooke Shields.[867] Arlene had certainly sustained an ageless beauty which could in part be attributed to her lack of self-conceit. Once asked the question of how she managed to stay so young and beautiful, she replied: "I didn't know I did."[868] While such unassuming quality made her all the more lovely and endearing, she was at the same time concerned with maintaining an attractive appearance and quite conscious of her position as a positive model of maturity. "She cared about the way she looked, but not in a vain way at all, explained *Prime of Your Life's* (1981) executive producer, Karen Lee Cohen. "She knew that she was representing her community."[869]

Her position as hostess of a show that advocated for the aging was perhaps the only indication that she, herself, had joined the ranks of those over seventy. Although a champion for what could be accomplished in one's advanced years, she wasn't too keen on discussing the subject of chronological age, especially her own. "I don't understand where the years go. Why should I have to explain the business of age all the time?"[870] Perhaps curious about her peers' take on the subject; Arlene

---

866. *Daily Record.* Morristown, New Jersey. Dec. 18, 1983. Video Waves. By. John Southington

867. *The Salina Journal.* Show for Over 50s may be Syndicated. By, Kenneth R. Clark Oct. 20, 1981.

868. *What's My Line?* Cira 1970s (syndicated version) Honest Answers.

869. Telephone interview between the author and Karen Lee Cohen. November 21, 2020

870. Green Bay Press Gazette. June 1978.Arlene is Back. Marian Christy.

posed a similar question to actress Ruth Gordon in 1983 during an on-air interview[871] for *Prime of Your Life* (1981). Gordon was 85 years old at the time, and open about it. To this point, Arlene inquired: "Don't you ever get bored being called a zingy octogenarian? I mean, doesn't that annoy you for people to be constantly picking on the age problem?" Gordon responded by explaining that what was most important to her was a universal appeal "whether I'm sixteen or six thousand." She also gave Arlene and the viewing audience her personal secret to longevity: "I never face the facts," Gordon said, conceding that she would have never made it in show business if she would have accepted certain realities. "You have to kind of plan what you're going to have happen to you, and if it doesn't, you keep thinking it will. . . but it's never facing the facts."[872]

Many of the brightest stars in the theatre had reached a certain age by the 1980s. This only encouraged Arlene who still very much considered herself to be a working actress. Unlike certain entertainment-related professions, it was less difficult to age out of a stage career. "Even the theatre welcomes older people, Arlene noted, Katherine Hepburn fills a house anytime. Claudette Colbert, all the people who have managed to stay with their profession and work hard throughout the years and that's how it should be."[873] So, while a 92-year-old Cathleen Nesbitt was reprising her role as Rex Harrison's mother in *My Fair Lady* (1956), Arlene took to the stage in *The Inkwell* (1981) at the Pocono Playhouse. She played the lead character, a role originally performed by Gloria Swanson, portraying a Hollywood star returning to her old hometown for a visit. True to the changing of times, Arlene's character, Lila Lawrence, happened also to be a grandmother, albeit a very glamorous one. Called a "light comedy with a lesson,"[874] the play presented a capable assortment of cast members, including Anita Gillette, Jefferey Lynn, and Mary Cooper. It

871. Ruth Gordon, Arlene Francis – 1983 TV Interview. YouTube
872. Ruth Gordon quote. Ruth Gordon, Arlene Francis 1983 TV interview. YouTube
873. *The Salina Journal.* Show for Over 50s may be Syndicated. Oct. 20, 1981. By, Kenneth R. Clark.
874. *The Times Leader.* Wilkes-Barre Pennsylvania. July 7, 1982. The Inkwell: A Light Comedy with a Lesson. P. 14

also provided some thought-provoking dialogue, such as when Arlene's Lila stated: "Honesty has nothing to do with the truth."[875]

That line could loosely relate to the premise of *Prime of Your Life* (1981). While it might be true that one is older than they wish to be, the show demonstrated that seniors could honestly and authentically live life to the fullest. Every interviewee had a story to tell, and Arlene was heralded for giving guests an opportunity to express themselves without judgement or frequent interjection. That is part of what made her so revered. "She doesn't have to share a guest's opinion to give him or her a fair shake,"[876] noted a writer for the TV data service. Her skillful and caring approach to conversation made her something of an interviewer's interviewer. Such was proven when Jack Paar appeared on *Prime of Your Life* (1981) in October of 1981. Having already proclaimed Arlene to be the best in the business, he then related that hers was one of the only programs he would consider appearing on: "You are the last friend that I know of that has a show I would do."[877]

Arlene not only impressed her peers, but her younger colleagues as well. One of them was Chris Salvador. In his early thirties at the time, he worked as a producer for *Prime of your Life* (1981). "She helped shape my career,"[878] he said over three decades later. Speaking with all of the enthusiasm his vivid memories allowed, Chris related sincere and sentimental stories about his friend. "Arlene taught me a lot of things I still use to this day:"[879] from the special way to fold a dollar bill in four and hand it to a cab driver to marking certain words on a voice-over script for emphasis. He explained that Arlene had asked him to make "squiggly lines" underneath the words he wanted her to emphasize on or say all in one breath. This preference for precise diction likely stemmed from her work as an actress, but the full-bodied sound of her famously

875. Ibid

876. *The Salina Journal.* Show for Over 50s may be Syndicated. Oct. 20, 1981. By, Kenneth R. Clark

877. *The Tampa Tribune.* Apr. 24, 1983. Jack Paar to be a Guest of Johnny Carson's Show. By George Maksian -New York Daily News.

878. Telephone interview with Chris Salvador. November 20, 2020

879. Ibid

low voice was arguably an essential asset. "It wasn't an affectation, Chris noted, just refined."[880] Also remembered were her elegant mannerisms, "her body language. . . the way she moved her hands. . . ."[881] Everything Arlene brought to the show was part of her natural charm, and her easy-going and non-demanding nature made her a joy to work with behind the scenes.

Typically, each episode of *Prime of Your Life* (1981) was structured in three parts: a celebrity interview, a lifestyle segment, and an on-location filming. The producers divided the assignment of tasks between Arlene and Joe Michaels according to each co-host's particular strengths.[882] Michaels had a background in news media, and Arlene's popularity and experience with interviewing made her an ideal choice for the celebrity segments. One episode featured a conversation with Helen Hayes, filmed at the actress's home in Nyack, New York. Arlene strode through the rose garden with Ms. Hayes and visited the country estate's impressive rooms. A downstairs recreation suite contained original seats from the demolished Helen Hayes Theatre, and her Academy Award for *Airport* (1970) sat upon the mantel.[883] Intimate settings like these added to the engaging presentation, but a typical show could also take Arlene to broadcast sites like the Jefferson Memorial in Washington, D.C. or a rented ship in the New York harbor.[884] She was always willing to do whatever was necessary, even when she wasn't feeling her best. For example, Chris Salvador recalled a day on set when Arlene was contending with a painful abscess tooth. However, when filming began, one would have never known she was uncomfortable.[885] Her commitment to professionalism was a contribution to the program's success and an inspiration to those around her.

For Arlene's part, her interests were more aligned with the presentation of the show itself rather than ratings or production

---

880. Ibid

881. Ibid

882. Telephone interview with Chris Salvador. November 20, 2020

883. Ibid

884. Ibid

885. Ibid

processes. "She never came to an edit room,"[886] Chris explained. Her best work was done before the camera. That is where she was most comfortable and where she shined. One of Arlene's greatest strengths was being able to easily engage in a genuine conversation without prompts. She did "such a beautiful job" and was "very involved" during the interviews. "I never saw her with a [writing] tablet or clipboard."[887] She would educate herself about her guests prior to filming, but would occasionally learn inadvertent lessons on set. Once such occasion happened when preparing to film an interview with novelist Dame Barbara Cartland, who after making a dramatic entrance, requested that a low light be used to soften her face. Arlene must have made a mental note, because "After that, she always wanted a low light."[888] Taking pride in her appearance was part of her desire to be and give her best. But she was also bolstered by reassurance.

Each week after *Prime of Your Life* (1981) aired, Arlene would place a telephone call to Chris. "I always knew the phone was gonna ring Saturday night at 8pm,"[889] he recalled fondly. Arlene would usually offer a critique of the show, and ask how she looked and if her hair was alright.[890] Those questions expressed her vulnerability as a mature woman who was still very much in the public eye. Her concerns were not unusual for someone in her profession, but she needn't have worried. She consistently made a good appearance and was "always beautifully dressed"[891] in "gorgeous tweed suits"[892] in shades of blue and reddish tones.[893] The issue of aging and appearance was an unavoidable subject, and one commonly discussed by nearly every notable female personality. Even a fifty-year-old Sophia Loren appeared on *Prime of Your Life* (1981) to promote her 1984 book *Women and Beauty*. Arlene's level of comfort and ease as an interviewer

---

886. Ibid

887. Ibid

888. Telephone interview with Chris Salvador. November 20, 2020

889. Ibid

890. Ibid

891. Ibid

892. Ibid

893. Ibid

transcended any topic and fostered an open-hearted and welcoming environment for every guest on her show.

This gift for warmth and congeniality extended to her colleagues. Aside from a working relationship, Arlene and Chris Salvador also shared a sweet friendship. They spent many moments together "just shooting the breeze."[894] During one of their talks, she regaled him with stories of her early days as an actress. She reminisced about being directed by a young Orson Welles in the *play Danton's Death* (1938), recounting Welles's inventive use of rubber face masks to replicate the Parisian crowd scene. In addition to conversations, Chris sometimes visited Arlene at her apartment at the Ritz Tower. "She gave great parties and I can still see her front door in my mind."[895] But one of her most thoughtful gestures was that of giving gifts.[896] She once presented Chris and his wife Regina with a celery dish, engraved with the image of swans. "You and Regina are so in love,"[897] she said, explaining that since swans stay together for life, she wanted the two of them to have the dish bearing the lovebird's likeness. Also memorable was the time Arlene asked Chris to accompany her to the premiere of *The King and I* (1952). Yul Brynner was reprising his famous role for what would be the play's final run before the legend's death. "She rented a limo and it was just the two of us."[898] Upon arrival, "she took my arm and we walked inside the theater. "It was a big rush,"[899] he said, recalling the enormity of the moment for him.

Along with the memories made off-set, the show's guests sometimes provided their own unforgettable gestures. Such was the time Rock Hudson appeared on the program. Following the taping, the actor removed his large-frame 80s-style sunglasses and gave them to Chris, along with a pack of Tarrington cigarettes. It was a significant moment for the young producer. Although he had already achieved success as

894. Ibid
895. Telephone interview with Chris Salvador. November 20, 2020
896. Ibid
897. Ibid
898. Ibid
899. Ibid

production manager of WNBC TV for years prior to working with Arlene, the time spent on *Prime of Your Life* (1981) was simultaneously fun and rewarding. "These wonderful experiences were all because of her."[900]

In fact, so strong was Arlene's drawing power that sometimes guests even volunteered to appear on the show. In 1982, then first lady Nancy Reagan offered[901] to be a guest and discuss her book, *To Love a Child*, and promote The Foster Grandparent Program, a project engaged to aid the elderly facing poverty and loneliness. In an effort to explain the rewards of pairing the young with the older, she told Arlene: "I think that we have become so youth-oriented that we forget that there are a whole lot of people out there who have a great deal to give and want to give it."[902] In collaboration with the two-part interview, co-host Joe Michaels went on location to visit with a foster grandparent at New York's Center for the Blind.[903] It was this type of meaningful programming that set the show apart from the standard fare, and kept Arlene at the forefront of industry excellence.

During her tenure on *Prime of Your Life* (1981), she also hosted the occasional TV special. One program (co-hosted with Joe Michaels) was the WNBC TV presentation, *The Foxfire Glow* (1982). The Emmy-nominated[904] special aired in the New York market in 1982 and highlighted the stories of families living in Southern Appalachia. Shown throughout the program were re-created scenes from the play of the same name, starring Jessica Tandy, Hume Cronyn, and Keith Carradine. Arlene, looking radiant in a black and gold gown, interviewed Tandy and Cronyn in New York while Joe Michaels traveled to Georgia to talk with the local inspirations behind *The Foxfire Glow (1982)*. Told in an intimate

---

900. Ibid

901. *The Central New Jersey Home News.* Apr. 24, 1983 TV Data Service. Arlene Francis is in Her Prime. By, Ruth Thompson

902. *The Herald Stateman.* (Yonkers New York) October 29, 1982. First Lady on Prime of Your Life. By, Carmel Camise Marchionni.

903. Ibid

904. The Foxfire Glow received a New York Emmy nomination at the 27th annual NY Emmy Awards. https://www.nyemmys.org

documentary-style format, the show was well aligned with Arlene's talent for conversation, and at the same time, brought a bit of Broadway into the mix. The play itself was based upon the anthology, *Foxfire*. The volumes, written by local high school students, conveyed stories of their Appalachian grandparents. Giving voice to older citizens, the televised presentation was quite reminiscent of *Prime of Your life* (1981). However, the overall content provided a multi-generational appeal.

Undoubtedly, Arlene still possessed a strong public allure. Along with broadening the scope of informational programming, she had a sterling reputation for style and was a staple at fashion-themed charity events during the 1980s. In November of 1984, she served as mistress of ceremonies for an AIDS benefit and auction in Manhattan, raising funds for treatment and research. Dressed in a Scaasi gown of red taffeta, one of the many fashions up for auction that evening and valued at over $5,000,[905] Arlene joined a bevy of notable personalities, including chairwoman and former first lady Rosalynn Carter, actress and friend Claire Trevor, and past *I've Got a Secret* panelist Bess Myerson.[906] Also in attendance was Dr. Mathilde Krim, the renowned medical researcher and co-founder of amfAR, the Foundation for AIDS Research. Arlene interviewed Dr. Krim[907] on *Prime of Your Life* (1981), helping to bring much-needed awareness to the presence and impact of AIDS across the nation and facilitate a conversation about a disease widely feared and misunderstood in the early 1980s.

In addition to her public influence and visibility on television, Arlene maintained a consistent presence on WOR radio. According to a 1981 poll, hers was the most popular voice on the air.[908] She had received a coveted Peabody Award for her "meritorious service in broadcasting,"[909] and was inducted into the National Broadcaster's Hall of Fame in

---

905. Daily News, New York. Thursday November 8, 1984. Fashion Sets Fete to Fight AIDS. By Kathy Larkin.
906. Ibid
907. Email communication with producer Chris Salvador. April 6, 2021.
908. Ibid
909. *Daily News* New York. Mar. 6 1984

1982.[910] By then, it was common knowledge that she'd been hosting *The Arlene Francis Show* (1960) on WOR since 1960, conducting interviews with actors, authors, politicians and more. The program's high rating and faithful listenership made it an 11:10 am weekday tradition on the East Coast.

Aside from the theatre, her radio program was a beloved endeavor. She genuinely enjoyed the conversation and learning experiences that came along with engaging with guests from all areas of life and art. During special broadcasts, she welcomed her son Peter to the program. "She interviewed me once a year at Christmastime on her WOR radio show for decades, and would always take great interest in whatever I was thinking about or doing in each period of my life."[911] Having graduated with a Doctor of Jurisprudence from Harvard Law, Peter also earned a Ph.D. in Psychology from the Wright Institute in Berkeley, California. He taught college courses in law and psychology and co-founded the Institute for Labor and Mental Health in Oakland, which implemented programs geared toward lowering stress among workers and raising self-esteem.[912] By the 1980s, his efforts toward building and sustaining a more compassionate and humane world were just beginning to take shape. "He's given us every dream a parent could have for a son,"[913] said Arlene.

In the spring of 1984, the proud mother and loveable performer had been hosting her daily radio show for nearly twenty-four years. It came as a shock to her when WOR abruptly canceled the program in March. Peter was with his mother at her apartment on the day she received the news. "She was as blindsided as I've ever seen her."[914] Reeling from the cancellation, Arlene grappled with a loss of self-assurance and the stark realization that perhaps for the first time she had been disadvantaged by the decisions of her male bosses. "She didn't really get feminism until

---

910. *The Gazette* (Montreal Quebec Canada) Nov. 28, 1984
911. Email communication with Peter Gabel. May 31, 2020
912. Peter Gabel Curriculum Vitae. https://www.petergabelauthor.com
913. The *Orlando Sentinel*. Sept. 1, 1963. TV's Unlucky Star…By Christina Kirk.
914. Zoom conversation with Peter Gabel 2020

she herself was fired in her seventies from WOR,"[915] explained Peter. "She realized her charm could not save her from those men who ran the station. . . . ."[916] WOR offered no clear explanation except that Arlene's show would be replaced by news and commentary, presumably geared toward a younger audience.[917] In a comment to the press, the station's vice president Bob Biernacki stated: "Arlene has had a long history of popularity with both the staff of WOR and our listeners that continues to this day. We feel, however, that to keep pace with the demands of the ever-increasing competition, our programming must continue to evolve."[918] Biernacki also mentioned that he had asked Arlene to think about retirement.[919] "The last thing I would consider doing is retiring, Arlene said publicly, following the show's cancellation. "They gave [me] the weekend to think about a graceful way to leave. It's caused something of a furor, and I don't mean it to be that way, but it came to me as a terrific shock. My ratings are as good as ever. It's something I don't understand."[920]

Neither did her listeners. Mail flooded the New York City post office in opposition of WOR's decision. And Arlene expressed concern about losing connection with her public. "I don't know what's going to happen to all those fans, but I'll find them and they'll find me."[921] Many in the media also rallied around her, believing her ousting to be a direct result of ageism. "Arlene Francis Fired for Aging" was the headline of a news article written by columnist James Brady. Expressing blatant anger about the situation, Brady subsequently praised Arlene for being "a performer at the top of her form, shrewd, able, popular, and she has just lost her job. Not because she is too old, he added satirically, no one will ever say that."[922] Arlene, too, perhaps felt that her firing was age-related, and

---


915. Email communication with Peter Gabel August 20, 2020

916. Peter Gabel interview with W. Gary Wetstein, 2018

917. *The Herald News* (Passaic, New Jersey) Mar. 5, 1984

918. *Daily News* New York Mar 24, 1984

919. *Daily News* New York. Arlene Francis Loses Show. Mar. 3. 1984

920. Ibid

921. Radio Roundup. Other Shoe Hits Arlene. George Maksian. Mar. 24. 1984

922. *The Times Recorder*. Arlene Francis Fired for Aging. By, James Brady. Mar. 25, 1984

asserted that she was still a very capable woman. "I'm not crumbling or being wheeled around in a chair."[923] She was understandably hurt, but wanted to make it clear that she was not bitter. "Bitter is not the right word, she said. Disappointed, yes. I would have liked to stay on longer but the station obviously had other plans."[924]

In an attempt to lift her spirits, many of Arlene's friends and peers, including her radio producer Jean Bach, threw a star-studded party to say: "I Love Arlene Francis." In fact, that statement appeared on buttons worn by guests such as Claire Trevor, Walter Cronkite, Kitty Carlisle, fellow WOR luminary Joan Hamburg and many others. The event was held at Jean Lafitte Restaurant on West 58th in Manhattan and drew extensive coverage by media outlets. Despite the somber reason for the gathering, Arlene basked in the outpouring of affection. "It was the best party!"[925] she said afterward. "I wish I could do it again."[926] The event was perceivably an evening of mixed emotions. And because those in attendance knew their friend's invincible spirit, it was no place for pity. Declaring proudly that "Armenians are known to be survivors," Arlene held her own against the swift changes.[927] After over 50 years in the business, it would take more than a radio station to cancel Arlene Francis.

Following her program's cut, WOR settled her contract and offered her a position as "roving theatre critic" on John Gambling's *Good Afternoon New York*. She declined the job and reaffirmed her position: "I don't want to give up my show.[928] But alas, the final broadcast of *The Arlene Francis Show* (1960) aired on April 5, 1984. Barbara Walters was the in-studio guest while a bevy of call-in support and farewells came from celebrities like Lucille Ball, Phyllis Diller, and Rock Hudson, who had appeared as the show's first guest back in 1960. Friends like Jayne Meadows called

---

923. *Daily News* New York Mar 24, 1984
924. *Daily News* New York. Mar 24, 1984
925. Daily News (1984)
926. Ibid.
927. Other Shoe Hits Arlene. Radio Roundup. George Maksian. Mar. 24, 1984
928. Daily News New York. Mar 24, 1984

in to offer encouragement, and remarked on the growing number of industry professionals being released from their duties. "We're jealous of you, Arlene, Meadows said on the final broadcast, because you've been on the air so long, and now you're finally getting to join the ranks of those of us who have been canceled."[929] In the mid-eighties, WOR had terminated several longtime radio hosts including Jean Shephard, Stan Lomax, and Pegeen Fitzgerald.[930] According to *New York* Magazine's 1985 article, *Inside Radio's Battle for the Ages*, WOR had been struggling to compete with the onslaught of stations drawing younger audiences. Their problem wasn't necessarily ratings, reasoned writer Gigi Mahon, but demographics. "WOR has plenty of listeners, but—by the standards of Madison Avenue anyway—they're too old."[931]

The phrase "too old" was an unmentionable on *Prime of Your Life* (1981). After nearly eight years on television, it was continuing to prove society wrong about the limitations of age. In May of '84, Arlene and Joe Michaels were grand marshals at the Senior Olympics in East Hanover, New Jersey, presenting medals to the winners.[932] But heralding age and able as synonymous was not the show's only goal. It also took a realistic approach to the hardships endured by America's elderly, such as blockades to affordable housing and the threat of disease. Arlene had recently endured firsthand the ripple effects of ageism in the entertainment industry, and Joe Michaels voiced his views in a book aptly titled *Prime of Your Life* (1981). In addition to offering insight into financial planning and retirement, the book raised strong points about the evolution of society's ills where age is concerned. "I once wrote in an editorial that the worst crime one could commit in this country was to be old and poor, he expressed in the book's introduction, but as somebody else once wrote in another context, there's a new wind blowing."[933]

929. *Daily News*. New York. Apr. 7, 1984

930. New York Magazine. Jul. 22, 1985. Inside Radio's Battle for the Ages.

931. Ibid.

932. *Shopper's News*. (Paramus, New Jersey) Radio Stars will be Grand Marshals at Sr. Olympics. May 16, 1984

933. Prime of your Life (1981). By Joe Michaels. Quarto Marketing Ltd.

In November of 1984, an unexpected gale hit the Saturday night lineup. NBC cancelled the Emmy-nominated[934] *Prime of Your Life* (1981) and announced that the series would not be returning the following year. On the surface, it was another unexplained casualty, prompting the *Daily News* to call the popular TV program's cut a "mystery." However, the simple reason was that they had lost the syndication.[935] Arlene was understandably upset by the network's decision. "It's their business and they can run the station as they like. But it's shortsighted of them. . . of course, I'm sad about it. I did enjoy doing the program and it was an important service for our older viewers."[936] Also pressing the question of its cut was local viewership appeal. The show had enjoyed its highest ratings in New York since its premiere eight years ago, following closely behind the Channel 2 news.[937] With its send-off, NBC executive Bud Carey acknowledged the program's impact and success. "Thanks to Arlene and Joe, this show embodied a standard of excellence by which all future public affairs programming must be measured."[938]

Before *Prime of Your Life* (1981) officially concluded, a highly anticipated episode with Frank Sinatra was recorded and aired. The idea for the interview had been suggested a few years earlier by the show's executive producer, Karen Lee Cohen. "I have long been a fan of Sinatra, explained Karen, and knowing Arlene and Frank were good friends, I asked [her] early in our business relationship if she would ask Frank to do an interview and she promised she would. But alas, after a couple of years the show was canceled and Frank had not appeared. When I told Arlene about the cancellation she said, 'I'm sorry to hear that but I promised you Frank Sinatra and I will deliver before we are off the air."[939] Shaken by the upsetting news, Arlene still took the

---

934. Prime of Your Life received a New York Emmy nomination at the 27th annual NY Area Awards. https://www.nyemmys.org

935. Telephone interview with Karen Lee Cohen. November 21, 2020

936. *Daily News* New York. Mystery Over 'Prime' ax. Nov. 5, 1985

937. Ibid

938. *Daily News* New York. Nov. 3, 1985

939. Frank Sinatra! And Arlene Francis! And Me! May 6, 2019. Blog post by Karen Lee Cohen. https://www.Karenleecohen.com

opportunity to think beyond herself and her own circumstance. "That's the best example of who she was,"[940] said Karen. "She was a genuine authentic person of total integrity. She cared about people. There was nothing difficult about working with her,"[941] and, true to her word, she delivered Frank Sinatra. Producer Chris Salvador chose the Waldorf to film the two-part interview with introductions shot in the hotel's lobby. Before filming, Sinatra and a radiant Arlene, who was dressed in a blue flowing silk jacquard pant suit, exchanged warm greetings.[942] The mutual admiration they shared for each other was palpable, recalled Chris. During the episode, Sinatra discussed his Oscar-winning role in *From Here to Eternity* (1953) and his more recent decision to come out of retirement.

The interview was a success, a product of quality programming, and a promise fulfilled. However, the Sinatra episode was not the only time Arlene's thoughtfulness prompted a memorable moment. Karen Cohen told of attending a Christmas party at Rockefeller Center where she introduced Arlene to her date, David. Shortly after the party, she gave Karen a pair of rhinestone earrings in the shape of stars.[943] She said that she wanted her to have them because "They are like the stars in your eyes when you were dancing with David."[944] Behind the scenes gestures such as these revealed the genuine sweetness of her spirit, and testimonials from friends and colleagues tell of a woman who was just as admired off-screen as she was on.

"She was a trouper,"[945] said Chris Salvador of her willingness to meet any task set before her. The two of them worked together for the final time on a 1986 NBC television special called *Faces of the City* (1986). Some of the shots, such as the closing wrap up scenes, were filmed at night on the roof of the New York Marriot Marquis Hotel in Times

---

940. Telephone interview with Karen Lee Cohen. November 21, 2020
941. Ibid
942. Telephone interview with Chris Salvador. November 20, 2020
943. Telephone interview with Karen Lee Cohen. November 21, 2020
944. Ibid
945. Telephone interview with Chris Salvador. November 20, 2020

Square. Arlene didn't complain, braved the brisk and windy weather, and appeared smiling on camera in a fur coat and hat, with the city lights shining behind her. The program itself contained interviews with DKNY fashion designer Donna Karan, Tony-winning actor Robert Lindsay, renowned choreographer Robert Joffrey of the Joffrey Ballet, and legendary singer Peggy Lee. One very touching moment, remembered by Chris, was not seen on the program but occurred afterward. Peggy Lee invited the two of them to watch her perform at a nightclub, and while sitting in the audience together, Chris noticed Arlene crying while Lee sang the wistful song "I'll Be Seeing You." It reminded her of Martin, she explained.[946] Sentimentality was a part of her personality and goodbyes were particularly difficult to say.[947] When Chris left NBC in the late 80s, the station gave him a "beautiful going away party."[948] "She knew what was happening and came by,"[949] he recalled. Respectfully and without fanfare, Arlene quietly bade her friend and colleague farewell. "That was the last time I saw her. She is occasionally in my dreams and always looks the same as she did back then. I still have her swan celery dish and her phone number is still in my rolodex."[950] "Funny. . . I smile every time I see her name."[951]

By the winter of 1986, Arlene found herself without a steady job for the first time in her established career. In the notoriously fickle entertainment industry, remaining afloat that long was a commendable feat. Following the ending of a twenty-five-year era on WOR radio, *Prime of Your Life* (1981) had also come to a close. During the program's last year on television, Peter had returned to New York from San Francisco for a year-long teaching assignment at City University of New York Law School.[952]

---

946. Ibid

947. *Radio TV Mirror* July -Dec. 1956. Why do housewives hate to be called housewives? Too much to so? Or too little? Arlene Francis who enjoys being a housewife has an inspiring answer. By Gladys Hall.

948. Telephone interview with Chris Salvador. November 20, 2020

949. Ibid

950. Ibid

951. Email communication with Chris Salvador. November 2020.

952. Email communication with Peter Gabel. November 2020

"I was very occasionally there for a show,"[953] he recalled. At the time, Peter had also begun serving as editor for *Tikkun* magazine, a progressive Jewish interfaith periodical which title expresses the Hebrew word for to heal and repair.[954] Arguably, *Prime of Your Life* (1981) had made its own contributions for the greater good. The show was important for its time and raised awareness about the older percentage of the population, too often overlooked and underestimated. Demographically, Arlene, herself, personified the mature yet active citizen, but with age came an increased urgency to preserve her position in the public sphere. Her resolve to remain relevant was tied to an unwavering desire to contribute to her community, and whatever the future demanded of Arlene Francis, she was ready to defy the odds.

953. Ibid
954. Peter Gabel. https://www.petergabelauthor.com

# Chapter Eleven

"You have to rise above your troubles the best you can"[955]

– Arlene Francis

As the 1980s moved forward, life became increasingly unpredictable. Arlene had to navigate through a series of changes, facing them with resilience and characteristic determination. Before the decade's end, she would make her final appearance on the stage, celebrate 40 years of marriage to Martin Gabel, and wrestle with an unfolding of events that would shift the foundation of her personal and professional life. She had already endured the sting of WOR's decision to end *The Arlene Francis Show* (1960) in 1984, and as a result of the program's abrupt cut combined with the cancellation of NBC TV's *Prime of Your Life* (1981) in January of 86, she virtually disappeared from the two mediums she had dominated for decades. However, following a change of heart at WOR, her familiar voice would once again be broadcast live on the east coast, in a subtle yet triumphant return to the world of radio.

"She has graciously consented to rejoin our station,"[956] announced general manager Lee Simonson. In February of 1986, Arlene began making weekly Wednesday appearances on Joan Hamburg's show from 11:00 am –1:00 pm. The program consisted of interviews and live entertainment, courtesy of performers such as Marvin Hamlisch or Phyllis Diller.[957] Local listings heralded the news of Arlene's return.

---

955. *Toledo Blade*. (May 26, 1987). Arlene Francis Has a Line on Staying Young By Margaret Farnham
956. *Daily News*. December 28, 1985. For Old Time's Sake. New York.
957. *Daily News*. New York. Aug. 10, 1986. The Ladies Who Lunch. By Harry Haun.

And in addition to a full-color advertisement, word spread via numerous headlines, including one in the *New York Daily News,* which read in bold print, For Old Time's Sake. While Arlene might not have so closely associated herself with antiquity, the decision to bring her back to WOR was undeniably nostalgic. The station even decided to pay homage to radio's yester-year by broadcasting *Luncheon with Arlene and Joan* (1985), live, from Sardi's restaurant in Manhattan.[958] She had begun *The Arlene Francis show* (1960) at Sardi's East back in 1960.[959] So, in a sense, her career in radio was coming full circle.

Despite the reunion at WOR, Arlene was contending with personal concerns. "My husband was ill,"[960] she told an interviewer in the late 80s, and his failing health weighed heavy on her mind. In light of matters, she had initially been hesitant to accept the offer to return to radio. "I thought I just won't go back to anything else."[961] Yet, her decision to join Joan Hamburg likely helped boost her morale during Martin's decline. He had remained reasonably active following his final stage role in *In Praise of Love* (1974) and had subsequently appeared in two motion pictures. He was featured opposite Frank Sinatra in the televised movie, *Contract on Cherry Street* (1977) and paired again with Sinatra in the crime-horror thriller, *The First Deadly Sin* (1980). Acknowledged for his role as the museum curator Christopher Langley, he received a Saturn Award nomination for Best Supporting Actor in 1981.[962] Although he seldom expressed pride for such appearances,[963] the critics were often impressed. One reviewer referred to his efforts in *The First Deadly Sin* (1980) as being "Practically an Oscar-nominee type performance."[964] The role would mark Martin's last in a career spanning over fifty years.

---

958. Daily News. New York. February 1, 1986. Lunch with Arlene and Joan.

959. Daily News. New York. Aug. 10, 1986. The Ladies Who Lunch. By, Harry Haun.

960. Arlene Francis interview with Arlene Herson. DVD 1987

961. Ibid

962. Email communication with Peter Gabel and the 8th Annual Saturn Awards Winners and Nominees

963. Email communication with Peter Gabel. January 27, 2021

964. *New Pilot* San Pedro, California. Review. Oct. 24, 1980. The First Deadly Sin-atra.

"My father died in 1986, said Peter, having had cancer and a series of small strokes that would paralyze his legs. I am so moved in my memory by his dependency on my mother then, and her ease in caring for him, an expression of what bound them together."[965] Martin Gabel passed away on May 22, less than two weeks after he and Arlene celebrated forty years of marriage. He was laid to rest at Roosevelt Memorial Park in Trevose, Pennsylvania, a Jewish cemetery where other Gabel family members are buried. In the months that followed, Arlene found it difficult to speak about his death.[966] Over a year later, she was able to offer a few words during a televised interview with Arlene Herson. Reaching for the diamond heart pendant around her neck, she said: "I've never taken it off."[967] The gift her husband had given her on their first wedding anniversary was a tangible representation of their love. "He was an exceptional man, a brilliant man, she continued, holding back tears— very much missed."[968]

After losing Martin, Arlene was severely shaken. In time, she was able to find a certain amount of solace in being able to work. She credited a piece of advice with helping her garner the strength to move forward. "A doctor said to me: You've been working since you were eighteen years old, you really can't stop now. It will only make you more depressed."[969] Trusting those words, she continued her weekly position on WOR. She enjoyed the spontaneous atmosphere that broadcasting before a live audience allowed, and even compared it to being in a theater.[970] "It's just fun to see the enthusiasm in front of you."[971] Nevertheless, amidst the gaiety and familiar territory, Arlene was still quite fragile following Martin's passing. She recalled becoming emotional when a sentimental

965. Peter Gabel Facebook comment in What's My Line? (CBS) Facebook Group. April 27, 2020

966. *Toledo Blade.* Arlene Francis has a Line on Staying Young. By, Margaret Farnham. May 26, 1987

967. Arlene Francis Interview with Arlene Herson. 1987 DVD

968. Ibid

969. Ibid

970. Ibid

971. Daily News. New York. Aug. 10, 1986. The Ladies Who Lunch. By Harry Haun.

song such as "My Funny Valentine" was played on the piano during the live Sardi's broadcast. "I'd go to the ladies' room and mop up, and come back out and resume the show."[972] Ultimately, her decision to keep working helped a great deal. "It has made all the difference in the world," she said during a lecture for the Golden Care Plus program, a speaker series for those over 60. "If you stay home, you just get older and cranky. It's better to keep going."[973]

That is precisely what she did. In May of 1987, a tribute[974] was held in her honor. The event, benefiting the New York League for the Hard of Hearing, took place in the grand ballroom of the Waldorf Astoria Hotel. In a move that paid homage to *What's My Line?* (1950) guests including John Daly, Steve Allen, and Kitty Carlisle "signed in please" before giving glowing testimonials about their friend. "Some of the proudest moments of my life are when I'm mistaken for Arlene Francis,"[975] said Miss Carlisle from her platform as the evening's hostess. The gathering was punctuated by clips from a long and illustrious career, and raised over $150,000[976] for charity. Justly termed long overdue by several media journalists, the tribute perhaps came at the right time. It was held less than a week before the one-year anniversary of Martin's death, and no-doubt uplifted Arlene, bringing back her warm-hearted smile, and as Jack Paar described it, that "Wurlitzer" laugh. While the event celebrated past milestones, the enduring star was still working her way into the future.

In 1988, she began hosting a new weekend radio program, *Celebrity Hotline* (1988). Created by Earl Blackwell, the syndicated show was carried by over 100 radio stations.[977] Its interesting premise was explained in an article in the *Palm Beach Daily News*: "Arlene will call stars at

---

972. Arlene Francis Interview with Arlene Herson. 1987 DVD
973. *Toledo Blade*. May 26, 1987. Arlene Francis has a Line on Staying Young. By, Margaret Farnham.
974. *The New York Times*. May 18, 1987. Friends Sign in Please at Tribute to Arlene Francis. By, Ron Alexander.
975. Ibid
976. Ibid
977. *Daily News New York*. Jan. 1988

home, on set, wherever. . . to ask questions posed by listeners."[978] The first episode featured interviews with Donald Trump, Brooke Shields, and Neil Sedaka. In addition to radio, she continued to use her voice in support of causes related to aging well. In April of 88, she narrated *Sixth Sense*,[979] an educational film explaining how the development of heightened senses in the elderly can supplement decreases in vision and hearing. The reel was screened at the New Holstein Public Library in Wisconsin as part of a community film series.

For the better part of a decade, Arlene had become something of an advocate for the aging while gracefully accepting the changes happening in her own life. Just three years after her husband died, she endured another loss. Her trademark diamond heart pendant given to her by Martin over four decades earlier was stolen, callously snatched from her neck as she walked down Lexington Avenue in Manhattan. The assault shook her to the core. "I was so startled, I couldn't even yell, 'stop thief,'" she told the press.[980] Sometime later, famed jewelry designer Jose Hess created a reproduction of the necklace and presented it to her during a luncheon event. Arlene was overcome with emotion as Mr. Hess fastened the new diamond heart around her neck. The original pendant, which was never recovered, had become legendary. Above all, the heart had long been a symbol of love between Arlene and Martin. "He's gone, she said. And now it, too, is gone."[981]

At 80 years old, she pressed forward. In August of 1988, she performed in what would become her final play, *Social Security* (1988), at the Westport Country Playhouse in Connecticut. She appeared in the comedy alongside David Birney, portraying Sophie, the family matriarch who finds romance in her golden years. The role marked her 10th performance at Westport[982] and placed her among the theater's most elite

---

978. *Palm Beach Daily News.* Apr. 19, 1988

979. The *Sheboygan Press.* Apr. 6, 1988. Lunchtime Films Offered.

980. The *Cincinnati Inquirer.* July 7, 1989. Thief Snatches Keepsake.

981. *The Herald Statesman* (Yonkers, New York). Trademark Necklace Snatched from Arlene's Francis' Neck. The Associated Press.

982. *An American Theatre: The Story of the Westport Country Playhouse, 1931-2005.* (2005). By Richard Somerset Ward, Joann Woodward, and Paul Newman.

and enduring. At the time, she held a record (later broken by Betsy Palmer in 1998) for performing at the playhouse more than any other actress.[983] Her biography inside of the *Social Security* (1988) playbill ended with this anonymous quote: "Arlene is the only person I know who acts as though life were the best party she ever attended." That remained true, even when there was less to celebrate. For the majority of her life, she had maintained a youthful vitality, but as she entered her eighties, the onset of Alzheimer's disease began to counter her usual vibrant stride. A progressive type of dementia,[984] the illness is characterized as a disorder of the brain[985] by the *National Institute on Aging*. It causes memory loss and an eventual deterioration of physical ability.[986] It had claimed the life of her father in the 1960s, and she had raised public awareness about its threat during a 1984 broadcast of *Prime of Your Life* (1981).[987] Only a few years later, she herself would begin to struggle with symptoms.

"It's difficult to tell when it began,"[988] said Peter. Her emerging forgetfulness collided with the aftermath of Martin's death, likely masking illness with the expected fragilities of a heartbroken widow. Also, the disease was just beginning to reach public consciousness in the early 80s. Following the establishment of the Alzheimer's Association in 1980,[989] Congress designated a national awareness month in November of 83,[990] helping to lessen the stigma surrounding dementia. The social isolation once precipitated by the disease began to decrease as the faces of the illness became more well known. Actress Rita Hayworth was among the first celebrities to wage a public battle with Alzheimer's before her death in 1987. Yet its prevalence in society by no means eclipsed its devastatingly personal impact. Given Arlene's work-oriented identity, she had managed

---

983. Ibid

984. Alzheimer's Association. https://www.alz.org

985. What is Alzheimer's Disease? National Institute on Aging. https://www.nia.nih.gov

986. Alzheimer's Association https://www.alz.org

987. *The Times Recorder*. Arlene Francis Fired for Aging. By, James Brady. Mar. 25, 1984

988. Zoom conversation with Peter Gabel. 2020

989. Alzheimer's Association. Research and Progress. Milestones. https:///www.alz.org

990. Ibid

to remain active throughout the latter part of the 80s, continuing to work on WOR radio into the early 1990s. Alzheimer's disease would eventually ravage everything that she held dear. One foundation it could not shake was the bond she shared with her devoted and loving son. "Nothing changed my relationship with my mother. We had a solidarity and a bond that was constant."[991]

Arlene had always been proud of Peter, who by the 90s was president of New College of California in San Francisco and a professor of law at New College's public interest law school. She would often mention his achievements during an interview or public appearance, sometimes using wit and humor to divert other topics she preferred not to discuss, such as her age. "When someone asks my age, she explained, I just tell them that my son is twelve years old. Then I tell them he's a professor of law."[992] While working and living on the west coast, Peter was introduced to Lisa Jaicks, a lovely and bright young woman who would become his partner through life. An activist for social justice, she began as a waitress, formed a union with her co-workers at the restaurant where she worked, and went on to become an organizer for the hotel and restaurant workers union. Inadvertently, it was Peter's tenure at New College that brought them together by way of a fateful series of events. In 1987, the institution bestowed a posthumous honor upon Ben Linder, a young engineer who was executed, in the Nicaraguan Civil War, along with two colleagues, while attempting to work on hydroelectric systems that would provide clean water to the people of El Cua, Nicaragua.[993] Linder had been a friend of the Jaicks family, and Lisa's mother was among those in attendance at the ceremony at New College. Delivering the speech that day was Peter. He made such an impact on her that she decided, then and there, he was the perfect person for her daughter. She befriended him; and eventually, when the time was right, he and Lisa got together.[994]

---

991. Zoom conversation with Peter Gabel and his partner Lisa Jaicks. July 7, 2021
992. Green Bay Press Gazette. June 20, 1978. Arlene is Back. By Marian Christy.
993. Zoom Conversation with Peter Gabel and his partner Lisa Jaicks. July 7, 2021
994. Ibid

In 1991, they traveled to New York, where Lisa would meet Arlene for the first time. At this point, Arlene was still living in her apartment at the Ritz Tower and contending with the moderate stages of Alzheimer's.[995] "She was very welcoming, kind, and thoughtful," remembered Lisa. "I had decided to call her Miss Francis, but I was corrected. It would be Mrs. Gabel. So that's what I always called her, and she called me 'Peter's girl.'"[996] The two developed a sweet relationship and would spend time together. "Sometimes, when I was alone with her, we would go shopping. "We went to Bloomingdales, and the waves parted when she walked in, and people were asking for her autograph."[997] Later, when it became more difficult for Arlene to go out, she would send Lisa to the theater "recommending what plays I should see."[998] The only thing that worried Arlene was the fact that Peter and Lisa weren't married. She expressed her concerns, reasoning that marriage would provide certain protections should they ever have a baby. At this point, Lisa helped put her at ease by reminding her of something important. "We're talking about *your* son, I told her,"[999] emphasizing the fact that a man like Peter would not abandon his partner or his responsibility to a child. To that, Arlene realized the obvious and relievedly agreed: "Peter would never do that!"[1000]

Peter was also held in high esteem by Lisa's parents, Agar and Diana Jaicks. They were known and respected in the San Francisco political sphere. Mrs. Jaicks was a niece of Eleanor Roosevelt and her husband was active in the democratic party. Like his wife, he also possessed a deep fondness for his daughter's partner. Lisa recalled a memorable exchange with her father that occurred early on in her relationship with Peter. "In the beginning, we would go through ups and downs just like in any relationship,"[1001] she explained, and during one of those times, her father, Agar, made clear that should she and Peter ever part ways, he would still

---


995. Ibid
996. Ibid
997. Ibid
998. Zoom Conversation with Peter Gabel and his partner Lisa Jaicks. July 7, 2021
999. Ibid
1000. Ibid
1001. Ibid

want to remain friends with him. "He had never said anything like that to me before."[1002] His words further demonstrated the sincere affection her parents felt toward Peter, and the feelings were mutual. "I had a great affinity for Lisa's family."[1003]

In 1992, the Jaickses met Arlene during a visit to New York. They were in town for the Democratic National Convention in Manhattan, where Agar was a delegate that year for Jerry Brown. Unlike Lisa, who had not known the scope of Arlene's career, ("I'm ten years younger than Peter and wasn't allowed to stay up late enough to watch *What's My Line?*"[1004]) Agar and Diana were very much aware of her prominence over the years. "My dad said that he thought she was the smartest one on the panel."[1005] So meeting her for the first time would be a memorable event. When they arrived at her apartment, she "received them and was a lovely hostess."[1006] Agar was quite hard of hearing, and apologized for it. Still in command of her signature wit and candor, Arlene quipped: "You're lucky you're handsome."[1007] Missing from this important moment was, of course, Martin. "I wish my dad could have met Lisa; he would have liked her very much."[1008] Following their meeting, the Jaickses sent Arlene a bouquet of yellow roses. They had hoped to find the exact Arlene Francis rose variety, which are yellow, but were unable to locate them. Touched by their thoughtful gesture, she sent a thank you card in return, a token which remains in the family to this day.

As 1992 came to a close, Arlene was struggling with advancing Alzheimer's. The fact that Peter and Lisa were living in San Francisco made them worry about her all the more. She eventually required the care of a nurse[1009] and had the help of "Aunt Mildred,"[1010] who was Mildred

---

1002. Ibid

1003. Ibid

1004. Zoom Conversation with Peter Gabel and his partner Lisa Jaicks. July 7, 2021

1005. Ibid

1006. Ibid

1007. Ibid

1008. Ibid

1009. Peter Gabel Interview with W. Gary Wetstein

1010. Zoom Conversation with Peter Gabel and his partner Lisa Jaicks. July 7, 2021

Fairbairn, a relative on her mother's side. Also, part of Arlene's circle at that time were people like Carol Butz, her longtime secretary, and Yolanda Rey, her housekeeper. Yolanda, along with her daughter Xenia and son-in-law Jose Ramos, eventually moved with Arlene to California to help care for her. There were also friends offering companionship. Mary Cooper, one of Arlene's dearest confidantes, would visit often, and another close friend, Marian Shaw, wife of playwright Irwin Shaw, lived just upstairs at the Ritz and could check on her frequently.[1011] Another regular was Arlene's hairdresser, Eugene. He had been her beautician since she was on *What's My Line?* (1950) and he once regaled Lisa with a story about the old days, recalling how he would arrive at Arlene's apartment to do her hair before showtime. Then, she would leave for the theater, and he would dash home, trying to make it before the live airing of *What's My Line?* (1950) The reason for the rush was because he wanted to watch her hair on television![1012]

During her most challenging years, she received support from caring people, but none seemed to comfort her the way that her son's presence did. Lisa recalled how Arlene would lay her head on his shoulder. In those moments, her relief was palpable. "There was a beauty in it. . . and it was very heartfelt in a way,"[1013] said Peter, of the metamorphosis he watched his mother go through in the process of learning to live with her illness. "She was so innocent and well intentioned. She went from being a very charismatic person to being very vulnerable."[1014] Arlene had indeed been an impressive figure all of her life. Lisa aptly appraised her by saying: "She was extremely intelligent disguised as charming and attractive."[1015] She lived during a time when women weren't supposed to be smart, and while she never admitted to being a trailblazer, it is possible she inwardly acknowledged that designation.[1016] Upon reflection of her younger years,

---

1011. Ibid

1012. Zoom Conversation with Peter Gabel and his partner Lisa Jaicks. July 7, 2021

1013. Ibid

1014. ibid

1015. Ibid

1016. Ibid

she noted: "I wasn't a beauty; I was adorable."[1017] Certainly, many would attest that she was both. The person the public knew for over six decades was very much the same woman her family dearly loved. "She was warm and sweet to me always,"[1018] affirmed Lisa. "I felt that she was glad I was with her son."[1019]

Consistent with her buoyant and determined nature, Arlene made the effort to attend a few events in the early 90s. In May of '92, she helped honor her friend and former colleague, Hugh Downs, by taking part in a tribute gala at the Copacabana, sponsored by the National Academy of Television Arts & Sciences.[1020] Arguably, the most memorable of her final professional appearances came in January of that year, during a birthday tribute to Mark Goodson. In a brief segment, recorded at her apartment in the Ritz Tower, she graciously saluted her friend and *What's My Line?* (1950) dignitary with these words: "There have been many who tried to be like you. No one in the history of television has ever been like you in imagination and in your talents, and I don't think there will ever be."[1021]

True to form, Arlene never officially retired. She worked for as long as possible, and concluded a sixty-seven-year career on radio, stage, film, and television by quietly retreating from public view. During this period, Peter was frequently making urgent trips between San Francisco and New York City to be with his mother.[1022] As her illness progressed, it became necessary that she live closer to him., but because her fragile condition rendered her reluctant to leave home, initiating such a move would require gentleness and timing.[1023] Ultimately, an unforeseen accident set the events into motion. In 1993, Arlene took a fall in her apartment. She was admitted to Mount Sinai hospital, and would remain there for three

---

1017. Ibid
1018. Ibid
1019. Ibid
1020. *Daily News*. May 28, 1992. Tribute to Hugh Downs.
1021. Birthday Tribute for Mark Goodson. 1992. YouTube
1022. Zoom call with Peter Gabel. May 27, 2020
1023. Ibid

days following surgery to repair a badly broken leg.[1024] In that interval of time, Peter and Lisa decided it was the opportunity to bring Arlene back with them to California.[1025] "I knew my most important responsibility was to take care of my mother."[1026] In order to ensure her comfort and safety, they made the trip on a chartered private medical plane equipped with an attending physician.[1027] Once settled in San Francisco, Arlene would begin a new and profoundly personal chapter, one that would mark her most challenging and inspiring journey yet.

---

1024. Ibid
1025. Zoom call with Peter Gabel May 27, 2020
1026. Zoom Conversation with Peter Gabel and his partner Lisa Jaicks. July 7, 2021
1027. Zoom call with Peter Gabel May 27, 2020

# Chapter Twelve



In 1993, Arlene became a resident of The Heritage, an elder care community in San Francisco, California. Founded by the Ladies Protection and Relief Society in 1853, the establishment had a long-standing history of providing assistance to the vulnerable. During the early 1990s, new strides were being made in the field of art therapy, and organizations such as the Goldman Institute on Aging offered programs like ArtWorks. The benefits of stimulating creativity in those with Alzheimer's was central to the project's efforts, and it was while participating in ArtWorks that Arlene began a meaningful journey of expression, producing over 40 paintings and collages during a period of eight years. Those years would hold acute challenges, revealing days both bitter and sweet. Releasing her former life and embracing a new way of being, Arlene began an uncharted path, one that included becoming a grandmother. In each phase of living, she persevered. Naturally resilient, even as the past faded into the present.

When Arlene arrived at The Heritage, she was still recovering from her recent fall and subsequent surgery. Despite her fragile condition, she surpassed the expectations of her physicians. Initially, they cautioned Peter and Lisa about the usual patterns of complications that can arise when a person of eighty-five years suffers a broken bone. The possible onset of pneumonia was a concern, bringing her mortality into stark question. However, Arlene defied those odds. "She was so physically strong,"[1028] remembered Lisa. Coupled with her innate resolve, "strong spirit,"[1029] and "strong constitution,"[1030] she remained a survivor.

Her ability to live an independent life was stifled by advancing Alzheimer's, but a personal team of caregivers was assembled to help her navigate through a new and changing path. Among them was Peter's close friend, therapist Michael Bader. He was an accomplished clinical psychologist and former Dean of the psychology department at New College. His work with Arlene would help stimulate her creatively. It was a slow start, but in time, he was able to reach her. Dr. Bader recalled their first breakthrough. "One day, Peter brought in photo albums of old childhood pictures. When Arlene and I looked at them together, she lit up."[1031] "What's interesting about those experiencing dementia, he noted, is that while their short-term memory is impaired, their long-term memory often remains intact."[1032] Judging by Arlene's reaction to seeing photos from the past, "I thought, 'this is a way in.'"[1033]

Using pictures as a portal, he was able to get a glimpse inside her world. Because her speech was severely limited, any communication was precious. "If I pointed to a photo of Peter and asked: "Hey Arlene, who's that? She would answer: 'Peter.'"[1034] In fact, the bond that she shared with her son was something Dr. Bader found heartwarming. "He was so sweet and kind to her—*so* kind. Up until I started working with Arlene, I had thought of Peter as that cool guy walking around New College."[1035] This experience showed another side of his friend, one that he recalls with emotion to this day. "The most rewarding part for me was seeing the

---

1028. Zoom conversation with Peter and his partner Lisa Jaicks. August 4, 2021.

1029. Ibid

1030. Ibid

1031. Zoom conversation with Dr. Michael Bader. September 17, 2021

1032. Ibid

1033. Ibid

1034. Ibid

1035. Ibid

pleasure it gave Peter,"[1036] watching his mother come alive when looking at those old photographs. They would sit together and go through them, and he would do whatever it takes to make her smile or laugh."[1037] Because Arlene could not be as demonstrative as she once was, "the small things became the big things."[1038] "When Peter walked in the room, she would raise her eyes and smile."[1039] There was a connection and it was evident. Peter's gentleness and deep love for his mother was very affecting. "Watching him navigate through this wilderness with her was so moving, recalled Dr. Bader. "It kills me now just thinking about it."[1040]

Life for Arlene was unlike anything she had ever experienced. Yet, she lived it with an unchanging grace; the same grace that had carried her through all the days before. Despite the limitations, her naturally cheerful disposition was still present. This was especially noticeable when she was with Peter. "It was a very upbeat thing between us,"[1041] he said of their interactions. This positive rapport was supported by his loving and respectful approach to communicating with his mother during her illness. "I didn't believe in infantilizing her. I talked to her the same way I always had."[1042] Affording her this dignity, Peter was able to foster a consistency of positive energy that seemed to surround her regardless of the circumstances. Through the changes, there appeared to be an inner reservoir of strength and an unextinguishable light. "She always kept that glimmer in her eye."[1043]

It was perhaps Dr. Bader who provided a means to bring that light to the surface. The therapeutic family photograph sessions were the start of an awakening that would lead them to travel other "non-orthodox roads"[1044] of expression. His time with Arlene gradually waned over the

1036. Zoom conversation with Dr. Michael Bader. September 17, 2021
1037. Ibid
1038. Ibid
1039. Ibid
1040. Ibid
1041. Ibid
1042. Ibid
1043. Ibid
1044. Zoom conversation with Dr. Michael Bader. September 17, 2021

years. "I don't remember exactly when or how it ended."[1045] However, at one point, he discovered an approach that provided a level of skill and a new channel for communication. "I heard about this art program for people with dementia, offered by the Goldman Institute on Aging. I contacted them and they sent an art teacher to begin working with her."[1046]

That teacher was Nadine Gay, a visual arts instructor who specialized in art education for elders with dementia-related illnesses. A native of France and a graduate of the Pratt Institute in New York, she had taught in a variety of settings, and would eventually lead courses at New College. However, it was her association with the ArtWorks program that brought her together with Arlene in the mid-1990s. "I liked her right away,"[1047] remembered Nadine. Notwithstanding the challenges she faced, her innate warmth was still apparent. "Her graciousness. . . her gentleness. . . the dignity of this person. . . ."[1048] "I felt her sweet spirit."[1049] As she got to know Arlene, she also learned about her previous life as an actress and television personality. The height of her career was "before my time," she explained, "before I came to the States." When told of her extraordinary past, she decided to watch a few interviews and *What's My Line?* (1950) reruns, witnessing for the first time Arlene in her finest hours. "She was so sharp. She was remarkable for her generation."[1050]

Because she had been such a vital person, it was difficult to reconcile her past with her present. Still, there were certain things that illness could not destroy, things like feelings, and the positive exchange of energy. Those elements became foundational. Most beneficial to Arlene overall was the abundant amount of love she received. "Peter took good care of his mother,"[1051] and just like Dr. Bader, Nadine also noticed a heartwarming response in Arlene when her son was with her.

---

1045. Ibid

1046. Ibid

1047. Telephone conversation with Nadine Gay. October 22, 2019

1048. Ibid

1049. Ibid

1050. Telephone conversation with Nadine Gay. October 22, 2019

1051. Telephone conversation with Nadine Gay. October 22, 2019

Also included in this circle of support was Dr. Pierre Curtet, Nadine's husband at that time, and a psychologist, who Peter described as "The Alzheimer's whisperer."[1052] "He was remarkable with mom, and had a sixth sense about communicating with patients."[1053] Finding avenues of communication were challenging, and it was through art that Arlene found a new doorway of self-expression.

"I love to dabble around in paints a little,"[1054] she said back in 1966. Throughout her life, the performing arts were her greatest pursuit, but as the daughter of artist Aram Kazanjian, she did possess an appreciation for painting. Aside from completing an oil bouquet of flowers[1055] for her father's sixty-fifth birthday in 1940, Arlene never had much time for the making of art. Its impact on her was never as necessary as it would be during her years as a student of Artworks. The program's then director, Jeff Chaplaine, explained the approach to engagement: "Our artists attempt to transcend the barriers that result from age, cultural differences, language, and health."[1056] Because of Arlene's specialized needs, she worked one-on-one rather than in a group setting. Sometimes, students with Alzheimer's are resistant to participating in the artmaking process, but she was very responsive, so much so that for a time, sessions increased from one or two days a week to three. She was "happy and willing"[1057] to make art, said Nadine. "She would smile" and "I could tell she was content and the process felt good to her."[1058]

That process consisted of working with materials such as watercolors, fabric, and paper to assemble a colorful assortment of creations. It was

1052. Zoom conversation with Peter Gabel and his partner Lisa Jaicks. July 7, 2021

1053. Email communication with Peter Gabel. October 2, 2019

1054. Arlene Francis Interview with George Douth. 1966 YouTube

1055. The painting was reproduced by the General Electric Celebrity Art Reproduction series in the 1960s. Ms. Francis' original "Bouquet of Flowers" oil is in the author's collection.

1056. Advisory to the Media. Special Event: Private Art Show to Showcase Paintings of Arlene Francis in Honor of National Alzheimer's Month. Oct. 20, 1997. https://www.ucsf.edu

1057. Telephone conversation with Nadine Gay. October 22, 2019

1058. Ibid

"step by step"[1059] and "paced according to her rhythm,"[1060] with a typical session lasting for about an hour. "I would put some color on a brush for her and she would move it across the paper,"[1061] a remarkable feat given her physical limitations. Most important, was not so much the activity itself, but the exchange of energy. While working together, Nadine would talk to her throughout the process. "I was wanting to make her happy."[1062] This contact, interaction, and connection was paramount. "Once in a while, a little spark of her old personality, humor, and kindness definitely came through."[1063] Expression is an essential part of any art program geared toward those with Alzheimer's. According to art therapist Linda Lee Goldman, in her moving piece, *Art Therapy and Alzheimer's Disease: My Mother's Art*, "The process of making art assists patients to externalize the internal, to express what they cannot say and to anchor themselves. When we view their images, we are allowed a glimpse into their inner experience."[1064]

Several of Arlene's collages consisted of a lively blend of shapes and layers. One of them featured bright yellow sunflowers while another offered a kaleidoscope of abstract formations. Her paintings, with their swirls of pastel and primary color, provided a beauty and mystique all their own, an undiscernible roadmap of a very personal journey. Essential to this artistic process was the experience of being present. "Creating art in the moment gave her joy, "[1065]Nadine affirmed, also adding that she never saw Arlene in a depressed mood. This was likely due in large part to her participation with ArtWorks. "The quality of two people being together. It's definitely healing, healing to the heart and soul."[1066] Each

---


1059. Ibid

1060. Ibid

1061. Ibid

1062. Ibid

1063. Telephone conversation with Nadine Gay. October 22, 2019

1064. *Art Therapy with Older Adults: A Sourcebook.* Chapter 10: Art Therapy and Alzheimer's Disease: My Mother's Art. (n.d). Linda Lee Goldman. Counseling Creatively Chicago. Retrieved from https://www.googlescholar.com

1065. Telephone conversation between the author and Nadine Gay. October 22, 2019

1066. Ibid

piece would take two or three sessions to finish, and sometimes Arlene would add fabric and embellishments to a previously completed painting. Afterward, the art was displayed in the halls at The Heritage, providing observers with an outward representation of an inward strength.

Her strength was bolstered by an abundance of affection from her family and friends. During her last years, Arlene was surrounded by a life-enhancing source of support. She was occasionally in touch with caring people like her long-time friend Mary Cooper.[1067] "Arlene was the best friend I've ever known, said Ms. Cooper, whatever is good about me is partially because she has been my dearest friend."[1068] That sentiment likely echoed the feelings of anyone who had ever known Arlene. Throughout her life, she had assumed many titles: wife, mother, actress, game show icon, and more. One designation she had not yet attained, even by the age of eighty-seven, was that of grandmother. This would change, however, in July of 1995, when Peter and Lisa welcomed their son, Samuel Jaicks Gabel.

When Sam was just a few days old, they brought him to meet "Grandma Arlene."[1069] Peter was very eager to introduce them. "He wanted to rush him to her,"[1070] remembered Lisa, "He was so afraid that she would die without ever having met her grandson."[1071] The special meeting took place in the library of The Heritage. Arlene was brought in, and Lisa helped her hold Sam for the first time. "I put him in her lap and we held him together. I felt she knew that we belonged to her and she belonged to us."[1072] With Sam's birth came another source of love and a special bond. "He would visit all the time with either one of us."[1073] Sometimes, they would all sit outside together in the garden of

---

1067. *The Women I Have Dressed and Undressed!* 2004. By Arnold Scaasi. Simon and Schuster.

1068. Arlene Francis tribute site. Trivia. https://www.arlenefrancis.com created by Susan and Becky.2001. Retrieved from https://www.archive.org

1069. Zoom conversation with Peter Gabel and his partner Lisa Jaicks. August 4, 2021

1070. Ibid

1071. Ibid

1072. Zoom conversation with Peter Gabel and his partner Lisa Jaicks. August 4, 2021

1073. Ibid

The Heritage, decorated with its many water fountains. When Sam was a small boy, "He fell in one of the fountains and loved it!"[1074] For him, "visiting her also became visiting 'The Place,'"[1075] with its lush landscapes and elegant sitting areas. "He would run around in his superman cape."[1076] At one point, he was learning Capoeira, a form of Brazilian martial arts that incorporates dance and acrobatics. He wanted to show off his moves to his grandma, and as he began demonstrating a series of signature kicks, she unexpectedly spoke out and said: "No!"[1077] Since talking was difficult for her, Lisa felt that this gesture was her grandmother's instinct coming to the surface, as if to say: "This isn't the right place for that."[1078] Had circumstances been different, Arlene would have certainly played a very active role as a grandmother. "They would have had so much fun together," said Peter. "Sam loved Broadway and Sardi's"[1079] In spite of a relationship confined by the grips of her illness, and the fact that she would pass away when he was just six years old, Arlene and her grandson still made a connection.

"I remember her well,"[1080] said Sam two decades after her death. "She was really cool and nice."[1081] "I would sit on her lap. . . and I did feel connected to her."[1082] He even wrote an essay about her in school. "It was very endearing and it hung on my bedroom wall."[1083] Although Arlene didn't speak much during that time, a young Sam wasn't aware that this was a particular handicap. "I thought everyone's grandmother didn't talk."[1084] But I remember one time she said, "Hi Sam!"[1085] He was

---

1074. Ibid

1075. Ibid

1076. Ibid

1077. Zoom conversation with Peter Gabel and his partner Lisa Jaicks. August 4, 2021

1078. Ibid

1079. Ibid

1080. Zoom conversation with Sam Gabel. August 17, 2021

1081. Ibid

1082. Ibid

1083. Ibid

1084. Zoom conversation with Sam Gabel. August 17, 2021

1085. Ibid

the only one to hear her say those words, and that moment has remained a special and vivid memory for him. Because he had not known her before she became ill, her present state of being seemed quite natural. "I didn't know at the time that she had been famous."[1086] To him, "She was just Grandma Arlene,"[1087] and she lived in what he recalled as "a fancy old people's home."[1088] "I would sit in her room," and it didn't matter that illness had imposed limitations on what they could do together. "I was content just to be there."[1089] "When she died, what I remember most was my dad mourning her."[1090] As a young child, watching his father suffer such heartbreak was profound, and spoke volumes about the depths of love and loss. Clearly, Arlene's presence in her grandson's life was in its own way significant, and even though she wasn't able to express herself in the ways she would have wanted, her love was understood.

The ability to respond to love and creativity are among the most enduring senses in a person with Alzheimer's.[1091] It was through the process of making artwork that Arlene was able to form an acute avenue of expression. "Doing her painting was one of the only ways my mother could communicate and express her thoughts to all of us in her later years. "It gave her the strength to live with her disease and still be productive."[1092] When she turned ninety years old in October of 1997, a private exhibit of her art was held at The Heritage. Peter spoke at the event, relating how his mother's participation with Artworks had helped to improve her quality of life. "Apart from the love of those around her, no factor has played a more important role in her spiritual improvement than the work

---

1086. Ibid

1087. Ibid

1088. Ibid

1089. Zoom conversation with Sam Gabel. August 19, 2021

1090. Ibid

1091. *I'm Still Here: A Breakthrough Approach to Understanding Someone Living with Alzheimer's.* (2009).By John Zeisel. And I Remember Better When I Paint. 2009. Documentary.

1092. *The Noe Valley Voice.* Rumors Behind the News. By, Mazook. July -August 2001 https://www.noevalley.com

she has done with artist Nadine Gay through the Artworks project."[1093] Over the course of the next few years, she began to lose more mobility, making painting increasingly difficult.[1094] Yet, with an undiminished determination, she never gave up, a shining example of the endurance of the human spirit. "She was a sweet person," remembered Nadine. "It was quite a privilege to work with her."[1095]

On May 31, 2001, Arlene Francis Gabel passed away at the age of 93. A small memorial was held for her at The Heritage. Among those in attendance were residents who cared about her and had looked after her during the past eight years. At the service, Peter spoke and read aloud a tribute written by author Marsha Cassidy whose scholarly book, *What Women Watched: Daytime Television in the 1950s,* featured Arlene's extraordinary impact, transforming the role of women on television. For her entire life, Arlene had made an indelible impression on every person she encountered. Many were touched by her myriad talents, and others, by her friendship. Yet, only one person had the privilege of calling her mom. The special bond that she and Peter shared in life was strong enough to transcend death. Arlene left this earth 20 years ago as of this writing. Yet she lives on through her family—in the legacy of Sam, the memories of Lisa, and the unfailing love of Peter. "I wish she were still here. I was crazy about my mother."[1096]

---

1093. Advisory to the Media. Special Event: Private Art Show to Showcase Paintings of Arlene Francis in Honor of National Alzheimer's Month. Oct. 20, 1997. https://www. ucsf.edu
1094. Telephone conversation with Nadine Gay. October 22, 2019
1095. Ibid
1096. Zoom conversation with Peter Gabel and his partner Lisa Jaicks. August 4, 2021

# Chapter 13

"…As long as there is someone alive who loves you, you will never die. Arlene Francis shall always live."[1097]

– Oren Spiegler

Orson Welles called her one of the luckiest things that ever happened to show business. That statement, complemented by more than six decades in the field of entertainment, affirmed an undeniable love story between actress and audience. By the year 2001, the scope of her spirited charm had touched much more than television. While fighting a courageous battle with Alzheimer's disease, she won the admiration of her attendants and caregivers as easily as she had any producer or director before them. Her life to date had affected countless others in ways both tangible and immeasurable. Following her peaceful death on May 31, 2001, she was laid to rest beside her beloved Martin. "I want to live to be eight hundred, she once declared, I want people to say here comes Arlene and she's as old as Methuselah!"[1098] Ninety-three of those years were granted, in addition to a legacy that has since remained eternal.

Her first posthumous recognition came in November of 2001, when she was inducted into the Broadcasting and Cable Hall of Fame. Honored that evening were a select number of industry leaders including Katie Couric, Michael J. Fox, and Mary Tyler Moore. Arlene's award was accepted by actress Jane Powell, who, during her speech, spoke of a woman who broke barriers with a unique mixture of talent and grace.

---

1097. A Final Tribute (2001). By Oren Spiegler https://www.arlenefrancis.com via the WayBack Machine Internet Archive.
1098. Newspaper clipping circa 1950s.

"She was what really every woman wanted to be . . . the Arlene I knew was not afraid to make waves, [but] her waves were beautiful. Her waves were gentle."[1099] Noting her position as a pioneer for women on television, Powell continued: "She was the 'femcee' on the [show] *Blind Date* (1949). Can you imagine anybody being called a 'femcee' today?"[1100]

Indeed, she had changed the order of a woman's place on TV. Audiences saw for the first time the role reversal of the genders on the *Home* (1954) show in the 1950s: Hugh Downs as announcer while Arlene presided over the program as hostess and editor-in-chief. Largely ahead of its time, the groundbreaking show demonstrated that a woman could have both intellectual and domestic interests. She once gave an example of its dual format by saying: "We did interviews with Senator Humphrey and Senator Kennedy and, well, eventually you'd learn how to make a cream puff."[1101] In hindsight, the show's presentation of the enlightened woman was a gateway for future programming, and her presence as a capable fixture on TV was arguably inspirational. One anonymous writer stated: "When I was a young girl in the 1960s, Arlene Francis's work on television was proof to me that smart women could (sometimes) be appreciated in this world."[1102]

Her unique position made her a pioneer. In a time when women moved within the confines of societal rules, Arlene inadvertently became the exception. From her earliest days in radio, she was deemed capable by her male peers, thereby becoming the first woman permitted to announce a station break during a broadcast. She forged a feminine path through an otherwise male-dominated arena and paved the way for women whose names are now widely known. Barbara Walters noted Arlene as one of her early role models.[1103] When her rejection of the *Today* (1954) show anchor

----

1099. Broadcasting & Cable Magazine. Hall of Fame. Class of 2001. Nov. 19, 2001. P. 38

1100. Ibid

1101. Television in Review. Jul. 28, 1957. A New TV Format for Arlene Francis. By John Crosby. St. Louis Post-Dispatch.

1102. Anonymous. Jan. 2, 2019. Memorials. https://www.findagrave.com

1103. *Barbara Walters: An Unauthorized Biography.* 1990. By Jerry Oppenheimer. St. Martin's Press.

position opened the door to Walters' entrance in the 1960s, Arlene's track record on television had already proven that a woman could do a man's job and succeed. Because of the work she had done, it became possible for female talk show hosts and broadcast journalists such as Jayne Pauley, Diane Sawyer, and Oprah Winfrey to emerge with not just a voice, but one that even men would listen to and respect. In her time, Arlene held multiple and diverse positions with equal acceptance. Networks expected her to perform as effectively as a man and at the same time bring the warmth and empathy characteristic of her womanhood.

This feat required a delicate balance between the socio-cultural expectations of women's roles as defined by their male counterparts. In the days when the word feminine conjured an immediate archetype of the typical housewife, Arlene helped transcend fixed ideas of what a woman in a public position could offer. She gave television the "female touch" in a way that neither directly endorsed feminism nor questioned a woman's ability to be both sensitive and shrewd. Her credits include being the first woman to host a game show, portray a detective on radio, preside as mistress of ceremonies for the *Tonight* (1954) show, and open the New York Stock Exchange. Her admission that "We need a little help from the men"[1104] supported her ambivalent views on women's liberation, but she did, however inadvertently, create a shift in the gender perspective and expectations for women in public positions, clearing the way for a future of female leadership roles. In a time when men in media and power positions reigned supreme, Arlene was an anomaly and an inspiration. By the year 2001, she had left behind a lasting impression.

In the days following her death, several articles appeared in newspapers, written by those who felt compelled to share how she had personally touched them. One of the stories appeared in the *New Jersey Montclair Times*. It was written by a man named Jay Westfall, who told of being on the *Home (1954)* show in 1954 when Arlene visited the playground of the Edgemont Elementary School in Montclair. During

---

1104. What's My Line syndicated episode. Circa 1968. Honest Answers Segment. Q: Do you think the world political scene would be improved if the U.S. diplomatic corps was composed entirely of women?

the segment, Arlene interviewed the school's principal, Mr. Hartman, while Westfall, who was a sixth grader at the time, had been chosen for a simple on-camera task of delivering a note to Mr. Hartman alerting him that he was needed in the office. Westfall later wrote: "This little ruse, I was told, would bring a timely and convenient conclusion to the scene. But what I didn't know, and it may have been an impromptu idea by Ms. Francis, was that she would interview me briefly about my status as an 'upperclassman.'"[1105]

Taking the time to make a person feel special was a distinct part of her personality, and her legendary charm was absolutely unforgettable. In a brief article titled *Remembering Arlene Francis*, Mr. Alan Light of Iowa City wrote with nostalgia about watching *What's My Line?* (1950) as a kid. "It came on later than my bedtime, but I was permitted to stay up and see it. Francis was my family's favorite panelist, warm, gracious, charming, poised, engaging, entertaining, and beautiful. . . I am still sad at her passing. . . I like the idea that maybe somewhere she is playing *What's My Line?* (1950) again."[1106]

Her position as the third most famous woman in America in the 1950s solidified her impact as a distinctly feminine force. In her 1978 memoir, she humorously reminisced about the third most famous title while assessing her current popularity ranking. "I've got to admit that the poll was taken twenty years ago and I don't care to have anyone call to my attention more recent polls. I know a sinking ship when I see one!"[1107] In light of those comments, she would surely be delighted by a legacy that has remained afloat in a future of changing times and ever-evolving interests. In July of 2007, the Game Show Congress honored her memory by creating the Arlene Francis Legend Award for Lifetime Achievement.[1108] In October of 2021, she was inducted into the Radio

---

1105. *The Montclair Times.* June 2, 2001. Arlene Francis' Visit to Edgemont School in Montclair. By Jay Westfall.

1106. Remembering Arlene Francis. By Alan L. Light. The Des Moines Register. June 2, 2001

1107. *Arlene Francis: A Memoir.* (1978). Arlene Francis with Florence Rome. P. 189

1108. In Tribute: Arlene Francis Paved the Way for Women in TV. October 21, 2007

Hall of Fame, honoring her impact in the broadcast medium. Yet, above any professional recognition, Arlene is perhaps best remembered for simply being herself.

A magazine article in the 1970s remarked that if computers had to replicate one person for a new planet of inhabitants, Arlene Francis could potentially be the ideal model.[1109] Such admiration stood in contrast to her humble nature. She did not consider herself to be superior nor a leader among women. In fact, she was quite firm in her belief that no one possesses a magic recipe for perfection. "Even the greatest among men are simply fallible human beings, weighed down with the same physical, emotional, and ordinary human frailties that beset us all."[1110] Known for her humility, Arlene built a reputation on sincere goodwill and a genuinely welcoming appeal. For some, to watch her on television was like visiting with a friend; for others, there was a level of familial-like comfort that touched them most. "I received a letter after [mom] died, recalled Peter, [from] someone whose mother had died who looked upon my mother as his own, through the warmth she conveyed through the screen."[1111]

Arlene deeply affected her public and peers, and many of them wished to express their fondness for her in creative ways. At least two portraits were painted of her likeness. The first was done by artist Elizabeth Anthony in 1959. "I found Miss Francis to be very beautiful and tactful,"[1112] said Anthony, who had also painted the likes of Helen Hayes as Queen Victoria. The second portrait, painted by University of Utah artist and professor, Alvin Gittins, has become well-known. It was commissioned by the University in 1971 in honor of Arlene's longstanding participation with the institution (she even served for a time on the university's board of directors) and the painting was prominently displayed on the wall of her library at her Ritz Tower apartment. Interestingly, both the Anthony and Gittins paintings depicted Arlene in her famous *Once More with Feeling* (1958) Scaasi ensemble of silver gown and red cape.

---

1109. *Status Magazine.* Circa 1970s. A Duet for Two Stars.
1110. *McCall's.* August 1962. The Private Agony of Being in the Public Eye.
1111. Email communication with Peter Gabel. January 27, 2021
1112. The Record. May 4, 1959. Hackensack Artist Paints Broadway Star's Portrait.

Similar gestures of admiration occurred throughout the years, and one of the most significant was the documentary, *Arlene Francis – That Certain Something*, created by actress, entertainer, and research pioneer Jackie Sanders and narrated by Tony Award-winner Cherry Jones. The project began around 2002 and was the first film to chronicle Arlene's extraordinary career. Making the movie was no easy feat at a time when archival footage on the internet was scarce and YouTube search results yielded little.[1113] The film took four years of diligence and hard-won research to produce.[1114] Yet the story of how the documentary came to be is perhaps as interesting as the project itself.

It all started on the set of *Mona Lisa Smile* (2003), the romantic comedy starring Julia Roberts. Jackie Sanders was in wardrobe and makeup preparing for the role of band announcer when her hairdresser remarked that she looked just like Arlene Francis.[1115] She didn't know who Arlene was at that time,[1116] but as fate would have it, she was about to find out. Shortly after filming, Ms. Sanders returned home to her apartment in New York. Her son had left the television tuned to *the Game Show Network*, and lo and behold, *What's My Line?* (1950) was on the air,[1117] and there, in all her charming and radiant 1950s glory, was Arlene Francis.

It would have been difficult not to be taken by her. The eloquent voice, the glamourous gown, and quick wit were captivating. Following the broadcast, Jackie decided to read Arlene's memoir and was eager to find a documentary about her.[1118] She then contacted Ms. Francis's son Peter, and when he informed her that a film about his mother didn't exist, she set out to make one.[1119] Thus began an arduous journey that would include years of effort, interviews, and insight. Peter granted

---

1113. Interview with Jackie Sanders. August 4, 2022
1114. Ibid
1115. Ibid
1116. Ibid
1117. Interview with Jackie Sanders. August 4, 2022
1118. Ibid
1119. Ibid

Ms. Sanders permission to pull archives and transfer reels of tape into digital format. She was also permitted access to material held by the Museum of Radio and Television, and after scouring the nation for those who had known and worked with Arlene, Jackie landed interviews with people like Walter Cronkite, Arnold Scaasi, Kitty Carlisle Hart, Jean Bach, Betty White and others. Jackie recalled Ms. White's "complete adulation, love, and respect" for Arlene and her position as a trailblazer.[1120]

Production on the documentary concluded around 2006. The film was screened for the first time the following year at the Paley Center in New York City, commemorating Arlene's 100th Birthday. In attendance at the event were Peter, his partner Lisa, and their son Sam. They consider Jackie to be not only a skilled filmmaker and dedicated researcher but a treasured friend. Also at the premiere were Arnold Scaasi, columnist Liz Smith and others. The film has subsequently been shown at the Arlene Francis Center and was a selected feature at the 2019 Bozeman Film Festival in Bozeman, Montana. Jackie hopes to release the documentary in a streaming format in the future, enabling more viewers to learn about Arlene's noteworthy place in media. "Very few people did everything,"[1121] Jackie noted, reflecting on the scope of Ms. Francis's career. "Some actresses might work in radio or television for a while, but they don't do the news. Arlene did it all, and she really was the first lady of TV."[1122]

Along the way, she attracted people by the millions, but none more significant than Martin Gabel. An accurate appraisal of her life would not be complete without him, and his place, both individually and beside her, must be duly acknowledged. His legacy is one of undisputed talent and urbanity. From youth, he sought to make his mark in the theater. He did so with vigor and received the celebratory accolades befitting an actor of his superior skill. Throughout his life, the strength of Martin's talent most certainly prevailed. After his death in 1986, Norman Corwin wrote

---

1120. Ibid
1121. Interview with Jackie Sanders. August 4, 2022
1122. Ibid

a letter to Arlene[1123], expressing, along with his condolences, sincere admiration for Martin's narration of Corwin's VE Day masterpiece *On a Note of Triumph* (1945). His voice, remembered for its distinctive qualities, stirring, eloquent, refined, stood in a class by itself. He was called a renaissance man and a versatile actor. As one of the earliest members of Orson Welles's Mercury Theater, Martin has been long remembered for his role as Cassius in Welles's stage adaptation of *Julius Caesar* (1937), a portrayal heralded as perfection.[1124]

In 2008, he was characterized on screen by Irish actor Aiden McArdle in *Me and Orson Welles* (2008), a film about the making of Mercury's Caesar. The role was Martin's first in a Shakespearean play, and one that has since remained attached to his memory. He would discuss it proudly in retrospect, wryly recalling his portrayal of "the lean and hungry Cassius" "looking as though he'd eaten Dinty Moore's out of house and home."[1125] That was, if nothing else, a testament to the convincing nature of his performance. Whether he is best remembered for boldly embodying Cassius, assuming the persona of Professor Moriarty in *Baker Street*, or winning a Tony Award for a brilliant portrayal in *Big Fish Little Fish* (1961), he was, without argument, a great actor. Both Martin and Arlene shared their talents generously and genuinely. They were more than stars; they were exceptionally authentic human beings and the very definition of what it means to be "good people."

In the years since their passing, that goodness has been perpetuated. In 2009, The Arlene Francis Center for Spirit Art and Politics opened as a community gathering place and performance venue in Santa Rosa, California. Founded by Peter Gabel, it is "dedicated to carrying on mom's tradition of love and compassion in the public sphere."[1126]

---

1123. Norman Corwin's Letters. (1994). Edited by AJ Langguth [June 19. 1986. To Arlene Francis on the death of her husband Martin Gabel] p. 417. Barricade Books.
1124. St. Louis Democrat. Nov. 16, 1037. Lyons Den. Caesar. By Leonard Lyons.
1125. American Academy of Dramatic Arts. Eighty Sixth Graduation Ceremonies. Tuesday, March 31, 1970. Transcript p.20
1126. Peter Gabel's Facebook Post via the WML CBS Facebook Group. September 21, 2020

The non-profit center hosts a variety of events including concerts by local artists, live theater, cultural activities, fundraisers, workshops, and more. With a vision for unity, inclusion, and social change, the center has been continually acknowledged for its positive presence. The AFC or "The Arlene" as it is affectionately called, received a Boho Award for making "significant contributions to the arts in the North Bay."[1127] When discussing the center that stands in his mother's name, Peter said: "I think of what a smile it would bring to her face to imagine that I was carrying forward the spirit of love and generosity that she embodied."[1128]

That spirit lives vibrantly through her family. Called a "long-distance runner in the struggle for justice,"[1129] Peter has dedicated his life's work to fostering a more humane world. Drawing on his legal scholarship and passion for social transformation, he is a founding member of the organization PISLAP (Project for Integrating Spirituality Law and Politics) and is editor-at-large for *Tikkun* magazine. A respected public speaker and author, he has written several books, including his 2018 release, *The Desire for Mutual Recognition: Social Movements and the Dissolution of the False Self.* Peter, along with his partner Lisa, a union organizer, has made meaningful contributions for the greater good. Their son, Sam Gabel, carries on the legacy of entertainment through his career as a hip-hop emcee.

Clearly, Arlene's immortal essence continues to thrive. Thanks to television, film, and online media, she reaches new generations who are as swiftly taken with her signature qualities as were audiences decades ago. In that sense, she remains eternal. Her impact, both before and after her death has had an astounding ripple effect. Noted Peter: "I don't think mom or any of us grasped the influence she had playing "herself" as she put it, especially on *What's My Line?* (1950) With the second life that [the show] is having world-wide on YouTube, people from all over

---

1127. The Arlene Francis Center Facebook post. Dec. 10, 2013
1128. Article by Melody Karpinski. 2012 via the WML CBS Facebook Group
1129. Quote by Cornel West, professor of the practice of public philosophy at Harvard University https://www.petergabelauthor.com

the world are routinely writing to me about the impact my mother has on them."[1130] That second life is due in large part to W. Gary Wetstein, author of a forthcoming book on *What's My Line?* (1950). He has preserved nearly every existing episode of the CBS version on tape and cultivated a YouTube channel with over 100 thousand subscribers and counting. That labor of love exists as a companion to the popular *What's My Line?* Facebook group, bringing Arlene Francis before generations of new audiences daily.

Ironic, perhaps, that a woman who successfully sustained a career aimed toward the theatre is likely best remembered for her work on television. However, at the same time, numerous stage performances have been remembered in a wealth of favorable reviews, and two stars on Hollywood's walk of fame equally attest to her work on TV and radio.[1131] Her synonymous association with *What's My Line?* (1950) might prove an unlikely legacy for an actress. Still, her place on the popular panel program (both the CBS version and the syndicated show) brought her into the living rooms of America for the better part of 25 years.

By virtue of her great success, Arlene could never be defined by one singular achievement. From her earliest beginnings, she desired to be liked. She surpassed that goal, and became one of the most endearing personalities of all time. Her extraordinary life was full of beautiful exchanges of joy. She took pleasure in being in the spotlight as much as audiences enjoyed watching her shine. The special profession she chose opened her up to a world of public spectators, who, somewhere along the way, claimed her as their own. Many were in awe of her ability to bring out the best in people, instantly soothing nervous interview guests or game show contestants with a warm smile and a witty remark. Her effortless dance between love and trust was a hallmark of her professional and personal approach to living. At its core, the true nature of her impact was born from the spirit of her own credo: "My firm conviction, she once

---

1130. Email communication with Peter Gabel. February 25, 2021

1131. Arlene Francis's two stars on the Hollywood Walk of Fame were unveiled on Feb. 8, 1960

said, is that underneath its weaknesses, humanity is essentially decent and good and eager to believe the same about others. That's really why I love the life I have chosen."[1132] Arlene Francis earned her rightful place among the legends of entertainment. Few were as respected or worked as tirelessly. Even fewer were as loved.

1132. *McCall's.* August 1962. The Private Agony of Being in the Public Eye.

# Epilogue
## Spotlight on Sam Gabel: A Grandson's Legacy

Sam Gabel is Arlene Francis and Martin Gabel's only grandchild. He is also an entertainer, making his own impact and reaching a new generation. "I don't think a lot of people see it that way,"[1133] he said humbly, assessing his position of carrying forward his grandparent's legacy. Nevertheless, Sam, known professionally as the emcee "Professa Gabel," is the future of his family. Drawn to acting at an early age, he got his start in the community theatres of San Francisco. "My mom's brother, my uncle Scott, was an actor. I was really close to him and he got me involved in the Actor's Theatre."[1134] A natural on the stage, Sam landed a role in *Trip to Bountiful* (1953) and played Noah in the *Grapes of Wrath* (1988). These early performances fueled his passion for the arts. "I was so alive at the theatre and excited."[1135]

As a kid exposed to the magic of live performance, he reveled in both the process of performing and the ambiance surrounding the stage. It was "a circle of life moment,"[1136] he said of his early experiences in the theatre. "That's when I found out my grandparents were actors. I started to watch the movies they were in, and *What's My Line?*"[1137] He felt a fondness for the 1950s film and television era, possessing an affinity for Broadway and "old New York." For Sam, the source of

1133. Zoom conversation with Sam Gabel. August 17, 2021
1134. Zoom conversation with Sam Gabel. November 16, 2021
1135. Ibid
1136. Zoom conversation with Sam Gabel. November 16, 2021
1137. Zoom conversation with Sam Gabel. August 17, 2021

that love is clear. "It's all because of Grandma Arlene and Grandpa Martin."[1138]

In addition to theatrical performances, he began taking brief walk-on roles in movies. At the age of twelve, he appeared as a background actor in the film *Milk*, based on the life of Harvey Milk, the first openly gay elected politician in California. "I think I had one line."[1139] He recalled being on set with Sean Penn, Josh Brolin, and James Franco, enjoying the camaraderie and remarking on his own outgoing personality as a kid. "I would talk to everybody."[1140] One day, an actor on set said to him: "You're good!" That word of encouragement helped him gain more confidence. "It's hard to see that in yourself, but when someone else says you're good, you start to think: maybe I am."[1141] Along the way, it became clear that entertainment was Sam's chosen path. "I think my parents also wanted me to be an actor. They were always very supportive of whatever I wanted to do."[1142]

It was during his early teen years that he discovered rap. "I started freestyling"[1143] after meeting Cyph4, a mentor who would foster that talent. "I was home schooled in the seventh grade and I started going to a gym around that time, and that's where I met him. My mom introduced us because she thought it would be good for me to be around someone else besides my tutor all the time. He would just start freestyling and I was mesmerized."[1144] Before long, Cyph4 encouraged the skill in Sam, opening a new doorway of self-expression. During high school, Sam attended a theatrical arts academy, and for a time, studied the relationship between hip hop and globalization[1145] at San Francisco State University. From there, he forged his own musical path.

---

1138. Zoom conversation with Sam Gabel. November 16, 2021
1139. Zoom conversation with Sam Gabel. August 17, 2021
1140. Ibid
1141. Ibid
1142. Zoom conversation with Sam Gabel. November 16, 2021
1143. Zoom conversation with Sam Gabel. August 17, 2021
1144. Zoom conversation with Sam Gabel. August 17, 2021
1145. Peter Gabel Honorary Degree at San Francisco State -2015. YouTube. May 28, 2015

"I became known around the city as the kid that freestyles. Then I started writing and rapping."[1146] This new creative direction unfolded naturally and almost accidentally. "It was just something I could do and people started to notice."[1147] He recalled rapping in Dolores Park and the excitement of his first live show at the Boom Boom Room in the Filmore district. "Everyone stood in a line and would take turns rapping. It was like the Olympics."[1148] Early on in his career, Sam chose the name "Professa Gabel" as a way to pay homage to his father, a professor of law. "I love my dad, and I see myself as being very similar to him."[1149] As Peter imparted knowledge and wisdom to his students, so Sam speaks his own truths to the masses. "I think learning happens in different ways. Both of my parents try to make a difference through what they do. My mom is a union organizer, and I always felt that I also wanted to make the world a better place in my own way. . . I want to put stuff out there that makes people feel."[1150]

At the age of 26, he continues to pursue both music and acting. "I really want to do films. I love the theatre, but you have to dedicate months and months to one role. By acting in movies, I hope to accomplish more in less time."[1151] Of course, the stage is where it all began, and Sam credits his time at the Actors Theatre for awakening his creative instincts. "It was a blessing for that reason."[1152] In addition to his pursuit of acting, he is a full-fledged entertainer and emcee, performing shows across the nation. "I like the music scene in San Francisco and I want to start producing music for other artists, not just myself."[1153] So far, he has recorded and released several albums including *Ouch, Uneven Pavement, My Room Needs New Light Bulbs, Corner Booth,* and *Don't Forget You're Welcome,* a collaboration with his group The Watershed. If you listen and look closely, you will find cameo appearances by his grandparents in his work.

---

1146. Zoom conversation with Sam Gabel. August 17, 2021
1147. Zoom conversation with Sam Gabel. November 16, 2021
1148. Zoom conversation with Sam Gabel. August 17, 2021
1149. Zoom conversation with Sam Gabel. November 16, 2021
1150. Ibid
1151. Zoom conversation with Sam Gabel. November 16, 2021
1152. Ibid
1153. Ibid

A sample of Martin Gabel's intro from the *Baker Street* song *I Shall Miss You Holmes* opens his track "Cannot Be Touched", and footage of Arlene Francis playing the trombone was incorporated into his 2020 music video, *Don't Wait in Line.*

Although he never met Martin, and Arlene died when he was just six years old, Sam is grateful for glimpses of the past. "I visited their old apartment at the Ritz Tower about 15 years ago, and we even went back to the house she and my grandpa had in Mt. Kisco, New York. We knocked on the door and the people who lived there let us in. I think that was really fun for my dad."[1154] Over the years, he has also witnessed his grandparents through the legacy they left on film and television. "What I really like about my grandma is the impact of her character. The way people were drawn to her. She was sort of a brand before it was a thing. To hold that much strength of personality while the whole world was tuning in is so impressive. I seek to do that myself."[1155]

When asked how his grandparents would feel about his chosen profession, he said: "I really don't know. It's a different world now than when they were alive, but I think they would be proud of me and what I'm doing. . . because it's for them in a way."[1156] Sam's platform in entertainment has also allowed him to reintroduce his grandparents into popular culture, even in subtle ways. He smiles at the mention of Arlene Francis appearing in a rap music video. "I think she'd like it because it's her grandson's video."[1157] "It's hard for this generation to understand the impact she had."[1158] She was the first woman to do so many things and had shows on all three major TV networks at the same time. For Sam, that fact seems the simplest way to sum up the enormity of her popularity decades before him. "She was on all three channels back then," he said with a mixture of awe and pride, "That's what I tell people."[1159]

---

1154. Ibid

1155. Zoom conversation with Sam Gabel. November 16, 2021

1156. Zoom conversation with Sam Gabel. November 16, 2021

1157. Ibid

1158. Zoom conversation with Sam Gabel. August 17, 2021

1159. Ibid

# A Career Retrospective

Selected Plays of Arlene Francis

*La Gringa* (1928) role: Sister Felicidad (Broadway)

*Street Scene* (1929) role: walk-on (Broadway)

*A Very Good Man* (1929) role: Secretary

*Allison's House* (1931) role: unknown

*I Loved You on Wednesday* (1933) role: unknown

*Bridges to Cross* (1933) role: Ann Rowe

*The Body Beautiful* (1935) role: Sue Barnes (Broadway)

*Horse Eats Hat* (1936) role: Tillie (Broadway)

*The Women* (1936) role: Princess Tamara Helene (Broadway)

*Angel Island* (1937) role: Sylvia Jordan (Broadway)

*All That Glitters* (1938) role: Elena (Broadway)

*Danton's Death* (1938) role: Marion (Broadway)

*Michael Drops In* (1939) role: Judy Morton (Broadway)

*Young Couple Wanted* (1940) role: Catherine Daly (Broadway)

*Journey to Jerusalem* (1940) role: Miriam (Broadway)

*The Walking Gentleman* (1942) role: Doris (Broadway)

*The Doughgirls* (1942) role: Natalia Chodorov (Broadway)

*The Overtons* (1945) role: Cora Overton (Broadway)

*Blithe Spirit* (circa 1945) Elvira

*The French Touch* (1945) role: Jacqueline Carlier (Broadway)

*Burlesque* (1946) role: Bonnie

*Candlelight* (1947) role: Marie

*The Cup of Trembling* (1948) role: Sheila Vane (Broadway)

*My Name is Aquilon* (1949) role: Madeleine Benoit-Benoit (Broadway)

*Metropole* (1949) role: Carolyn Hopewell (Broadway)

*The Little Blue Light* (1950) role: Judith (Broadway)
*Road to Rome* (1953) role: Amytis
*Late Love* (1953) role: Constance Warburton (Broadway)
*Once More, With Feeling* (1958) role: Dolly Fabian (Broadway)
*Amphitryon 38* (1960) role: Alkmena
*Red Peppers* (1960) role: Lily Pepper
*Still Life* (1960) role: Laura Jesson
*Tchin-Tchin* (1962) role: Pamela Pew-Pickett (Broadway)
*Janus* (1963) role: Jessica
*Beekman Place* (1964) role: Pamela Piper (Broadway)
*Kind Sir* (1964) role: ADD
*Mrs. Dally* (1965) role: Evalyn Dally (Broadway)
*Dinner at Eight* (1966) role: Carlotta Vance (Broadway)
*Old Acquaintance* (1967) role: Katharyn Markham
*Pal Joey* (1969) role: Vera Simpson
*Who Killed Santa Claus?* (1972) role: Barbara Love
*The Lion in Winter* (1973) role: Eleanor of Aquitaine
*Gigi* (1973) role: Aunt Alicia
*Don't Call Back* (1975) role: Miriam Croydon (Broadway)
*Side By Side By Sondheim* (1979) role: Narrator
*The Winslow Boy* (1980) role: Grace Winslow
*Don Juan in Hell* (1981) role: Dona Ana
*The Inkwell* (1981) role: Lila Lawrence
*Social Security* (1988) role: Sophie

## Selected Radio Show Appearances of Arlene Francis

*King Arthur's Round Table* (circa 1932) role: various
*March of Time* (circa 1932) role: various
*American School of the Air* (circa 1932) role: (various)
*Roadways to Romance* (circa 1933) role: unknown
*The Columbia Dramatic Guild* (circa 1933) role: unknown
*Forty-Five Minutes in Hollywood* (1934) role: Mildred Rogers
*Cavalcade of America* (circa 1934) role: various
*Pepper Young's Family* (circa 1934) role: unknown

*The Beatrice Lillie Show* (1935) role: various
*John's Other Wife* (circa 1936) role: unknown
*Cartwheel* (1936) role: unknown
*Hour of Charm* (1935) role: Mistress of Ceremonies
*The Beatrix Fairfax Show* (1937) role: various
*Voice of Fashion* (1937) role: commentator
*Aunt Jenny's Real-Life Stories* (circa 1937) role: unknown
*Stella Dallas* (circa 1937) role: unknown
*Big Sister* (1938) role: Lola
*The Affairs of Anatol* (1938) role: unknown
*Around the World in 80 Days* (1938) role: Madam Aouda
*There Was a Woman* (1938) role: various
*What's My Name?* (1938) role: Mistress of Ceremonies
*The People's Rally* (1939) role: guest star
*Second Husband* (1939) role: Marion Jennings
*Now Playing Tomorrow* (1939) role: unknown
*Mr. District Attorney* (circa 1939) role: Miss Rand
*Daughters of Uncle Sam* (circa 1930s) role: unknown
*Betty and Bob* (1940) role: Betty Drake
*Beyond Reasonable Doubt* (1940) role: Gloria Wayne
*Helpmate* (1941) role: Linda Harper
*The Gorgeous Hussy* (1941) role: unknown
*Men in White* (1941) role: unknown
*Alaska Under Arms* (1942) role: unknown
*Gentleman From the Islands* (1942) role: unknown
*The Enemy is Listening* (1943) role: unknown
*The Lengthening Shadow* (1943) role: unknown
*Make Way for the Lady* (1943) role: unknown
*Stars in Khaki & Blue* (circa 1940s) role: Hostess
*Blind Date* (1943) role: Mistress of Ceremonies
*When it Comes to Dr. Morgan* (1943) role: unknown
*Straw Hat Documentary* (1946) role: Bonnie
*Leave it to the Girls* (1946) role: Guest Hostess
*The Affairs of Ann Scotland* (1946) role: Ann Scotland

*The Best Things in Life* (1947) role: unknown

*Quite By Accident* (1948) role: Ms. Merchant

*I Didn't Know it was Loaded* (1948) role: unknown

*It Happens Every day* (1952) role: Co-hostess

*Fun for All* (1952) role: Co-hostess

*What's My Line?* on Radio (circa 1953) role: panelist, moderator (once)

*Monitor* (circa 1950s) role: Commentator

*Family Living* (1959) roles: Hostess

*The Arlene Francis Show* (1960-1984) role: Hostess

*Flights of Angels* (1965) role: unknown

*Emphasis NBC* (1966) role: Commentator

*I Thought You Were Dead* (1974) role: Jenny

*NBC's First Fabulous Fifty* (1976) roles: Hostess

*Voice of America* (1978) role: Commentator

*Celebrity Hotline* (1988) role: Hostess

## Selected Television Show Appearances of Arlene Francis

*Blind Date* NBC (1949-1953) role: Mistress of Ceremonies

*What's My Line?* CBS (1950-1967) role: panelist

*Prize Performance* NBC (1950) role: celebrity judge

*Answer Yes or No* NBC (1950) role: panelist

*Saturday Night Revue: Your Show of Shows* NBC (1950) role: Guest hostess

*Sure as Fate* CBS (1950) episode: "The Dancing Doll" Role: unknown

*The Clock ABC* (1951) episode: "A Dream for Susan" Role: unknown

*Lights Out NBC* (1951) episode: "The Veil" Role: Sylvia Willis

*Suspense CBS* (1951) episode: "Her Last Adventure" Role: Eva

*Fashion Magic* CBS (1951) role: Hostess

*Lux Video Theatre* NBC (circa 1952) episode: Mr. Finchley Versus the Bomb. Role: Eddie Sloan

*Who's There?* CBS (1952) role: Moderator

*Visit* (1952) role: Hostess

*Lux Video Theatre* NBC (circa 1953) episode: Measure for Greatness. Role: Ann

*Talent Patrol/Soldier Parade* NBC (1953-1955) role: Mistress of Ceremonies

*The Home Show* NBC (1954-1957) role: Hostess -Editor in Chief

*The Comeback Story* CBS (1954) role: Hostess

*Person to Person* CBS (1955) role: Guest

*Playwrights '56* (1956) NBC episode: "You and Me and the Gatepost" Role: unknown

*Five Fingers* (1956) NBC episode: "The Man Who Got Away" Role: Cardin

*The Arlene Francis Show* NBC 1957-1958 role: Mistress of Ceremonies

*The Tonight Show* NBC (circa 1957 -1963) role: Guest hostess (multiple)

*The Mike Wallace Show* CBS (1959) role: Guest

*The Today Show* NBC (1959-1973) role: Guest and guest hostess (multiple)

*I've Got a Secret* CBS (1960-1966) role: Guest (multiple)

*United States Steel Hour* ABC (1960) episode: "When in Rome" Role: unknown

*United States Steel Hour* ABC (1961) episode: "The Big Splash" Role: unknown

*The Price is Right* CBS (1961) role: Guest hostess (multiple)

*The Gertrude Berg Show* CBS (1962) episode: The Mother Affair. Role: Mrs. Evans

*The Merv Griffin Show* NBC (1962-1968) role: Guest (multiple)

*Miss Universe Pageant* CBS (1962-1964) role: Co-hostess with John Daly (multiple)

*Missing links* NBC/ABC (1963-1964) role: Celebrity contestant (multiple)

*Get the Message* ABC (1964) role: Celebrity contestant (multiple)

*Girl Talk* ABC (1965-1966) role: Guest (multiple)

*The Mike Douglas Show* CBS (1967-1978) role: Guest and guest hostess (multiple)

*What's My Line?* (1968-1975) Syndicated. Role: panelist

*He Said She Said* CBS (1970) role: Celebrity contestant with Martin Gabel

*Password* CBS (1966-1975) role: Celebrity contestant (multiple)

*Match Game* CBS (1975-1976) role: panelist (multiple)

*Scarecrow and Mrs. King* CBS (1984) episode: "Double Agent" Role: Self

*Match Game/Hollywood Squares Hour* CBS (1984). Role: panelist

*Prime of Your Life* (1981–1986). Role: co-hostess

*As The World Turns* CBS (1986). Role: self

*Tattingers* NBC (1988). Role: self

*The Sally Jesse Raphael* Show CBS (1989). Role: guest

*The Maury Povich Show* CBS (1991). Role: guest

## Filmography of Arlene Francis

*Murders in the Rue Morgue* (1932) role: Streetwalker

*Too Much Johnson* (1938) role: Clairette Dathis

*All My Sons* (1948) role: Sue Bayliss

*With These Hands* (1940) role: Jenny

*Stage Door Canteen* (1943) role: uncredited

*One, Two, Three* (1961) role: Phyllis MacNamara

*The Thrill of it All* (1963) role: Mrs. Fraleigh

*Laura* (1968) role: Ann Treadwell (Made for Television)

*Harvey* (1972) role: Betty Chumley (Made for Television)

*Fedora* (1978) role: Newscaster

## Selected Awards & Honors of Arlene Francis

American Radio Woman of the Year (1939)

Emmy Award Nomination (1956) Best Contribution to Daytime Programming -The *Home* Show

Emmy Award Nomination (1957) Best Female Personality Continuing Performance

Peabody Award (1959) *Family Living* radio show -hostess

Hollywood Walk of Fame Star (1960) Radio

Hollywood Walk of Fame Star (1960) Television

National Father's Day Committee Husband and Wife Team of the Year (1961)

Golden Laurel Award Nomination (1963) Top Female Supporting Performance: *The Thrill of it All*

Plaque for breaking all attendance records at The Playhouse on the Mall in Paramus, New Jersey (1963) for her role in *Janus*

National Broadcasting Cable and Television Hall of Fame Inductee - posthumous (2001)

Radio Hall of Fame Legacy Inductee: posthumous (2021)

Emmy Award: Best Audience Participation Program Quiz or Panel Winner (1953) *What's My Line?*

Emmy Award: Best Audience Participation Program Quiz or Panel Winner (1954) *What's My Line?*

Emmy Award: Best Audience Participation Program Quiz or Panel Nomination (1955) *What's My Line?*

Emmy Award: Best Audience Participation Program Quiz or Panel Winner (1956) *What's My Line?*

Emmy Award: Best Audience Participation Program Quiz or Panel Winner (1959) *What's My Line?*

## Arlene Francis as First Lady of Television and more

The following is a list of Arlene Francis's selected achievements as "First Woman"

First woman to announce the name of a network during a station break radio (1935)

First woman (or one of) to co-host a game show on radio (1939) *What's My Name?*

First woman to portray a female detective on radio (1946) *The Affairs of Ann Scotland*

First woman to host a game show on television (1949) *Blind Date*

First woman to guest-host *Saturday Night Revue: Your Show of Shows* (1950)

First woman to guest host *The Tonight Show* (1950s)

First woman to host an informational TV program (1954-1957) The *Home* Show

First woman to host NBC radio's *Monitor* (1950s)

First woman to guest host *What's My Line?* during its brief radio run (circa 1950s)

First woman to open the New York Stock Exchange (1954)

First woman to guest host *The Price is Right* (1961)

First woman to perform William Hanley's script *Today is Independence Day* (1965)

First woman to host NBC radio's *Voice of America* (1977)

First woman's rights multi-media kit: *Silenced Minority* (Narrator) (1975)

## Selected Plays of Martin Gabel

*The Shannons of Broadway* (1930) role: unknown (Lehigh University)

*Paris Bound* (1930) role: James Hutton (Leigh University)

*Man Bites Dog* (1933) role: Emmet

*The Sky's the Limit* (1934) role: Fraser (Broadway)

*Dead End* (1935) role: Hunk (Broadway)

*Three Men on a Horse* (1935) role: Frankie

*Ten Million Ghosts* (1936) role: Peter (Broadway)

*Julius Caesar* (1937) role: Cassius (Broadway)

*Danton's Death* (1938) role: Danton (Broadway)

*Life With Father* (1939) co-producer

*Young Couple Wanted* (1940) co-producer (Broadway)

*Medicine Show* (1940) co- producer, role: statistician (Broadway)

*Charley's Aunt* (circa 1940) co-producer

*The Cream in the Well* (1941) producer, director (Broadway)

*Café Crown* (1942) producer (Broadway)

*The Survivors* (1942) producer, director, co-writer (Broadway)

*King Lear* (1950) role: Earl of Kent (Broadway)

*The Little Blue Light* (1951) role: The Gardener (Broadway)

*Men of Distinction* (1953) produced, staged (Broadway)

*Reclining Figure* (1954) role: Jonas Astorg, producer (Broadway)

*Will Success Soil Rock Hunter?* (1955) role: Irving LaSalle (Broadway)

*King Lear* (1956) co-producer (Broadway)

*The Hidden River* 1957 producer (Broadway)

*Once More, With Feeling* (1958) producer (Broadway)

*The Rivalry* (1959) role: Stephen A. Douglas (Broadway)

*Sweet Love Remembered* (circa 1959) producer

*Big Fish, Little Fish* (1961) role: Basil Smythe (Broadway)

*Children From Their Games* (1963) role: Melvin Peabody (Broadway)

*Baker Street* (1965) role: Professor Moriarty (Broadway)

*Mrs. Dally* (1965) producer (Broadway)

*Who Killed Santa Claus?* (1972) role: unknown

*The Lion in Winter* (1973) role: Henry II of England

*Sheep on the Runway* (1974) role: Joseph Mayflower (Broadway)

*In Praise of Love* (1974) role: Mark Walters (Broadway)

## Selected Radio Appearances of Martin Gabel

*Easy Aces* (circa 1930s) role: Neil Williams

*Big Sister* (1936) role: Dr. John Wayne

*Les Misérables* (1937) role: Javert

*Dracula* (1938) role: Professor Van Helsing (Mercury Theatre of the Air debut episode)

*A Tale of Two Cities* (1938) role: unknown

*Julius Caesar* (1938) role: Cassius

*The Magic Key* (1938) role: unknown

*Columbia Workshop* (1940) Episodes: various, role: various

*Suspense* (1942) Episode: "Devil in the Summerhouse. "Role: unknown

*Treasury Star Parade* (1943) Episode: "How Far That Little Candle." Role: unknown

*Theatre of Romance* (1944) Episode: "Love Song." Role: unknown

*Treasury Salute* (1944) Episodes: various

*Matinee Theatre* (1945) Episodes: various

*On a Note of Triumph* (1945) role: narrator

*Mollie Mystery Theatre* (1945) Episode: "Breakdown." Role: unknown

*That They May Win* (circa 1945) role: Narrator

*Arch Oboler's Plays* (1946) Episode: "Lust for Life." Role: unknown

*Inner Sanctum Mysteries* (1946) episodes: "Skeleton Bay," various.

*The Ford Theatre* (1947) "Connecticut Yankee on King Arthur's Court." Role: unknown

*You Are There* (1949) "The Trial of Burr." Role: unknown

*Crime Does Not Pay* (1949) Episode: "Glassy Finish." Role: unknown

*Pursuit of Peace: Fear Itself* (1950) role: narrator

*Anthology* (1950) "Murder from the Past and Merriment from the Present." Role: unknown

*Theater Five* (1965) Episode: "Flights of Angels." Role: unknown

## Selected Television Appearances of Martin Gabel

*With This Ring* (circa 1951) Master of Ceremonies

*Lights Out* (1951) Episode: "The Deal." Role: The Agent

*Mr. Lincoln: The End and the Beginning* (1952) role: narrator

*What's My Line?* (1956-1968) 168 episodes. Role: guest panelist

*To Tell the Truth* (1957-1963) various. Role: panelist

*The Tonight Show with Jack Paar* (1958 -1961) various. Role: guest

*Playhouse 90 CBS* (1959) Episode: "The Hidden Image." Role: George Barrow

*Martin Gabel's Roundtable* WNTA TV (1959) Host

*Play of the Week* (1960) "Tiger at the Gates." Role: Ulysses

*Have Gun Will Travel* (1960) Episodes: various. Role: Nathan Shotness

*Thriller* (1960) Episode: "The Watcher." Role: Freitag

*Cain's Hundred* (1961) role: George Vincent

The Americans (1961) Episode: The Rebellious Rose, role: Tim Mayhew

General Electric Theatre (1962) role: Hercule Poirot

Chronicle TV (1963) Fours Views of Caesar, role: Julius Caesar

Password (1962) role: celebrity contestant

*Get the Message* (1964) role: celebrity contestant

*Profiles in Courage* (1965) role: Daniel Webster

*Tarzan* (1967) Episode: "Mask of Rona." Role: Peter Maas

*He said, She Said* (1970) role: contestant

## Filmography of Martin Gabel

*Smash Up: The Story of a Woman* (1947) associate producer

*The Lost Moment* (1947) director

*Pictura: An Adventure in Art* (1951) co-narrator

*M* (1951) role: Charlie Marshall

*Fourteen Hours* (1951) role: Dr. Strauss

*Day of Deliverance* (1951) role: narrator

*Deadline USA* (1952) role: Tomas Rienzi

*The Thief* (1952) role: Mr. Bleek

*Tip on a Dead Jockey* (1957) role: Bert Smith

*The James Dean Story* (1957) role: narrator

*The Right Man* (1960) role: William Jennings Bryant (televised)

*The Power and The Glory* (1961) role: chief of police (televised)

*Vincent Van Gogh: A Self Portrait* (1961) role: narrator (televised)

*The Crime Busters* (1962) role: George Vincent

*The Making of the President* (1963) role: narrator

*Marnie* (1964) role: Sidney Strutt

*Goodbye Charlie* (1964) role: Morton Craft

*Lord Love a Duck* (1964) role: T. Harrison Belmont

*Divorce American Style* (1967) role: Dr. Zenwin

*The American Dreadnought* (1968) role: narrator

*Lady in Cement* (1968) role: Al Munger

*There Was a Crooked Man* (1970) role: Warren LeGoff

*The Front Page* (1974) role: Dr. Max Egglehofer

*Harvey* (1972) role: Judge Omar Gaffney (televised)

*Smile Jenny, You're Dead* (1974) role: Meade De Ruyter (televised)

*Contract on Cherry Street* (1977) role: Bob Waldman (televised)

*The First Deadly Sin* (1980) role: Christopher Langley

## Selected Awards & Honors of Martin Gabel

Tony Award Winner for Best Performance by a Featured Actor: Basil Smythe in *Big Fish, Little Fish* (1962)

National Father's Day Committee Husband and Wife Team of the Year (1961)

Academy of Science Fiction, Fantasy and Horror Film Nomination for Best Supporting Actor: Christopher Langley in *The First Deadly Sin* (1980)

# Summaries of Selected Plays

*Burlesque* (1946)
*Once More, With Feeling* (1958)
*Beekman Place* (1964)
*Mrs. Dally* (1965)
*Social Security* (1988)

*Burlesque*,[1160] (1946) a play in three acts by Arthur Hopkins and George Manker Watters
 Arlene Francis as Bonny (August 12 – 17)
 Bert Lahr as Skid

## Background

In August of 1946, Arlene joined actor Bert Lahr in a revival of *Burlesque*, at the Greenwich Playhouse. Arlene was cast as Bonny; a role originally played by Barbara Stanwyck in the show's 1929 London debut. Nearly two decades later, it ran for a successful week's tryout in Connecticut. Arlene was pregnant when she performed in Burlesque, and she was replaced by actress Jean Parker when the show opened on Broadway, on December 25, 1946.

## Summary

Bonny (Arlene) and Skid are married entertainers. The talented pair headline a burlesque troop in the mid-west. Bonny is a friendly woman,

---

1160. Reference for background and Summary: *Burlesque* (1926). By George Manker Watters and Arthur Hopkins. Samuel French, Inc. (1935). Tamron Manker Watters (1963).

savvy by nature, and hopelessly in love with her husband. Skid, the comedic tour de force, returns his wife's affections, but regrettably shares them with liquor, and a certain chorus girl.

Bonny badgers her husband about his reckless ways. She knows he has talent to make the big time but fears his penchant for strong drink will be detrimental to a future on Broadway. When Skid receives an offer to appear in a New York production, Bonny encourages him to take the job, despite the fact that his chorus girl lover has already been cast in the show.

Skid's Broadway gig takes a toll on his marriage, and a separation is in order. Bonny moves to New York with a wealthy admirer whom she intends to marry. While in town, she hears rumors of Skid's failure. As she once feared, his drinking is affecting his ability to work. Hoping to talk some sense into him, Bonny calls and asks him to visit her hotel suite. When he arrives, she is unable to conceal her heartache, both over his condition and the breakup of their union.

Seeing Bonny again made Skid hit the bottle even harder. He returned to burlesque, and could not come to terms with the fact that his soon-to-be former wife would marry another man. While in rehearsal for a new show, his drinking renders him ill. Bonny hears the news of his sorry state and rushes to his side.

After nursing him back to health, Bonny helps Skid prepare for opening night by reviving some of their old song and dance routines. The duo eventually realizes they were made for each other, regardless of the troubles that had passed between them. During the show's final act, the newly reunited couple vow to never again let the curtain come down on their marriage.

*Once More, With Feeling,*[1161] (1958) a play in three acts by Harry Kurnitz
    Produced by Martin Gabel and Henry Margolis
    On Broadway (October 21 - June 6)
    Arlene Francis as Dolly Fabian
    Joseph Cotton as Victor Fabian
    Walter Matthau as Maxwell Archer
    Paul E. Richards as Chester Stamm
    Ralph Bunker as Mr. Wilbur
    Rex Williams as Luigi Bardini
    Leon Belasco as Gendels
    Dan Frazer as the interviewer

## Background

*Once More, With Feeling* ran for 263 performances at the National Theatre, marking one of Arlene's longest runs in a starring role on Broadway. She had her eye on the part from the beginning. But Martin was not one to easily let her appear in a play he was producing, and writer Harry Kurnitz was extremely choosy about the actors selected to bring his characters to life. When Arlene finally landed the lead at the behest of Kurnitz, she was delighted. She later recalled: "When Martin said to me, 'Listen, Arlene, Harry has suggested that you ought to play the part of the wife,' I knew Harry hadn't been persuaded because I was sleeping with the producer."[1162]

## Summary

Dolly (Arlene Francis) is a charming harpist, married to the brilliant yet tyrannical conductor Victor Fabian (Joseph Cotton). Victor's volatile temperament and complete disregard for the feelings of others has driven Dolly away. His insufferable behavior is often directed at his orchestra, and has threatened to prevent his success as a conductor. The only reason Victor Fabian's antics have been tolerated thus far is because of Dolly.

---

1161. Reference for Background and Summary: *Once More, With Feeling*. (1959). By Harry Kurnitz. Random House. NY.
1162. *Arlene Francis: A Memoir* (1978). By Arlene Francis with Florence Rome

Her graciousness and sparkling manner have always managed to persuade Victor's trustees in his favor, and to beg forgiveness when he heaps abuse upon yet another weary violinist. When news circulates that Dolly and Victor have separated, he is denied a position as orchestra leader of the Chicago Civic Symphony. So, in an effort to change their minds, Victor selfishly decides to woo her back into his life.

His manager, Max archer, dishonestly promises the Chicago trustees that Mr. and Mrs. Fabian have reunited. And they agree, on that premise, to offer Victor the Civic orchestra. Dolly is subsequently summoned to the apartment that she and Victor once shared. She arrives, after having received several dozen roses from Victor. However, she does not come with reconciliation in mind. Since striking out on her own, she took a position as a music teacher at a college, and has become engaged to its president, Mr. Hilliard. She cautiously tells Victor about her engagement.

He is outraged. And an argument ensues in the presence of Max Archer. It is then revealed that Victor and Dolly were never actually married. This unique situation provides an opportunity for both parties to achieve their desires. Dolly must provide proof of a divorce in order to marry her fiancé, and Victor wants Dolly to reunite with him for the sake of her influence and his reputation. It is agreed that the two will marry in seclusion and quietly divorce soon after. However, they will live together as a married couple for the duration of three days.

The two initially agreed upon sleeping in separate rooms, but in a moment of weakness brought on by drinking and reminiscing, Dolly prepares to give in to Victor's advances. Their romantic interlude is broken, however, by the arrival of Dolly's fiancé, Mr. Hilliard. Victor had sent for him in a fit of rage when he first learned about the engagement. Now, his plan has backfired.

As a result of the incident, Dolly decides to call off her engagement to Mr. Hilliard and promptly divorce Victor as planned. Max Archer, the observant manager, tries to make Dolly see that Victor only sabotaged her engagement because he couldn't bear the thought of her being with someone else. Dolly agonizes over the situation, but she isn't the only one whose nerves are on edge.

Victor is opening at the Civic that night. His normally intolerable ways have softened since Dolly's arrival, and his newfound attitude surfaces in an interview before the opening. As Dolly listens backstage, Victor tells the interviewer that he is rejecting an opportunity for a tour in order to spend more time with his wife. This endears Dolly to him once more, and the two decide to stay together–this time, as a real married couple. When showtime arrives, Victor goes on stage and leads the orchestra with surprising tenderness.

*Beekman Place*,[1163] (1964) a play in three acts by Samuel Taylor
    On Broadway (October 7 - October 31)
    Arlene Francis as Pamela Piper
    Ferdinand Gravet as Christian Bach-Nielson
    Leora Dana as Emily Bach-Nielson
    Carol Booth as Augusta Piper
    Laurence Luckinbill as Simon Holt
    George Coulouris as Samuel Holt
    Mary Grace Canfield as Mildred Kelsey

## Background

After an out-of-town run and two Broadway previews, *Beekman Place* opened at the Morosco Theatre and ran for 29 performances.

## Summary

Pamela Piper (Arlene Francis) has been living abroad in London for a number of years. She is widowed and has a 21-year-old daughter, Augusta. On short notice, Pamela and Augusta have arrived in New York, where they will be staying at the Beekman Place apartment of Pamela's dearest childhood friend, Emily. The head of the household is Emily's husband, accomplished violinist, Christian Bach-Nielson. He is in a state of self-imposed retirement. And Emily, is in the process of writing his memoirs, which he dictates to her through snippets of selective memories.

They are just beginning to flesh out a curious story about Christian being injured during the war when a billiard table fell on his foot, but dictation is put on pause when Pamela and Augusta arrive. After usual pleasantries, the true reason for their sudden visit is revealed: They were expelled from London after Augusta kicked a policeman during a protest to ban the nuclear bomb. Once *that* secret is out, more revelations follow. Unbeknownst to Pamela, her daughter, Augusta is pregnant. The father, Simon, is a young man she met during one of the protests in

---

1163. Reference for Background and Summary: *Beekman Place: A New Comedy by Samuel Taylor*. By Samuel Taylor. A Random House Play. Random House. NY

London. They are in love and intend to marry, but Augusta has kept the relationship a secret because the young man's father was a former lover of Pamela's.

The news of Augusta's pregnancy is eventually revealed after Christian overhears a long-distance conversation between her and the unborn baby's father. Matters are further complicated when a startled Pamela, upset about her daughter's condition, is consoled by Emily. During drinks and conversation, the two discuss old times. Pamela begins to rehash her past failed relationships, telling of spending a weekend with a man only to have it abruptly end when a billiard table fell on his foot. Emily immediately makes the connection between Pamela's rendezvous and the dictated story in Christian's memoir. She is livid and feels betrayed.

During the ensuing chaos, Augusta's prospective fiancé, Simon, arrives from London. The two openly profess their love and plans for marriage. Pamela defeatedly accepts the situation, but she is quite disturbed after learning that Simon's father is none other than her latest former love. However, a reconciliation between them is on the horizon and hints of a double wedding in Switzerland began to permeate the atmosphere. Emily also relents, coming to terms with the long-ago weekend affair between her husband and her best friend, and Christian, shaken but wiser, picks up his violin and vows to resume his career.

*Mrs. Dally*,[1164] based on two one act plays by William Hanley
    Produced by Martin Gabel
    On Broadway, from September 22 – November 6, 1965
    Arlene Francis as Evalyn Dally
    Robert Forster as Frankie (The Lover)
    Ralph Meeker as Sam (Mr. Dally)

## Background

On September 22, 1965, *Mrs. Dally* opened at the John Golden Theatre in New York and ran for 53 performances. Playwright William Hanley was honored in 1963 for his original production of Mrs. Dally Has a Lover, winning the 1963 Drama Desk Award. Two years later, Hanley re-constructed the play for Arlene by merging it with his sequel titled: Today is Independence Day. The entire dramatic piece was divided into a two-part, one act play, retitled: *Mrs. Dally*.

## Summary

**Part one: *Mrs. Dally Has a Lover***

Evalyn Dally is an unfulfilled housewife, engaged in an affair with her neighbor's eighteen-year-old son Frankie. She feels rebuffed by her husband Sam, (who we don't meet until part two of the play) and is reveling in the attention of a much younger man. The illicit couple meet regularly for an afternoon tryst in her apartment.

The play's setting finds the pair in the kitchen, engaged in a post-rendezvous conversation, punctuated by a gamut of emotions. Evalyn's vulnerabilities are revealed through Frankie's ignorance about love, and its complicated nature. The pair's May-December romance is fueled by regret and immaturity.

Eventually, Evalyn reveals a secret she has kept from Frankie. She and her husband Sam had a three-year old child who drowned as a result of

---

1164. Reference for Background and Summary: *Mrs. Dally and Other Plays* (1963). By William Hanley. The Dial Press. New York. Apollo Edition.

Sam's negligence. Frankie is sensitive toward the matter, but the idea of motherhood brings the Mrs. Dally's thirty-eight years into sharper focus. The topic of age clearly bothers her, and she is troubled by the forbidden nature of their affair.

The heaviness of the mood is lightened when Frankie asks her to play him a song on the trombone. She used to perform in a nightclub act but gave it up when she married. After some convincing from Frankie, she plays a song, and is met with his sincere compliments. The serious mood of the play returns, however, when Mrs. Dally confesses that she is in love with Frankie. Her young beau clearly does not understand the weight of her revelation. She knows that their relationship is hopeless, and fears that their next afternoon together could be their last.

**Part two: *Today is Independence Day***

Evalyn and Sam Dally are a married couple going through the motions. A typical July 4th afternoon finds them scarcely speaking to each other from across the kitchen table. Mrs. Dally makes conversation with her husband, trying futilely to rouse him from the self-imposed stupor in which he has settled. Sam has been drinking heavily and has taken to sleeping outside on the fire escape. He attributes this unique arrangement to the warm temperature in their apartment, but Evalyn clearly takes it as a personal rejection.

Contrary to his absence in the bedroom, Sam has been at home more than usual lately. He is recovering from an attack he endured while driving a cab, and his daily presence around the house might be a reason why Evalyn no longer seems emotionally attached to Frankie (who is not mentioned in this portion of the play). In fact, she appears quite determined to reignite her seemingly doomed union with Sam.

She continues to probe her husband in an effort to find out how he really feels about her and the state of their marriage. Eventually, Sam reveals his guilt over the death of their son. Evalyn tries to console him, but is not successful. Talking about the past brings them closer together for a brief moment, but Sam announces that he thinks a divorce is best for them both. This stuns Evalyn who refused to believe Sam would actually leave her. She implores him to stay, and a fight ensues.

The sound of their bickering is broken by the ringing of the doorbell. It is a delivery for Mrs. Dally: A bouquet of flowers for her birthday. They are from Sam who had ordered them earlier that morning. She is touched and surprised that he remembered. Sam closes the open door and decides to stay.

*Social Security,*[1165] a comedy in two acts by Andrew Bergman
    August 15–August 27, 1988
    Arlene Francis as Sophie Greengrass
    David Birney as David Kahn
    Christine Healy as Barbara Kahn
    Jack Aaron as Martin Heyman
    Laurie Heineman as Trudy Heyman
    Paul Lipson as Maurice Koenig

## Background

Social Security was the final play of Arlene's career. She performed in an off-Broadway production at the Westport Country Playhouse in Connecticut, from August 15, 1988–August 27, 1988. Actress Olympia Dukakis played the same role on Broadway two years prior with Marlo Thomas and Ron Silver in the starring cast., but Arlene's summer theatre performance in Westport would set a record at the time for most appearances by any actress at the playhouse.

## Summary

Sophie (Arlene) is an 80-ish widowed matriarch of a Jewish family. Her two daughters, Barbara and Trudy are in dispute over her care and wellbeing. The eldest of the two is Barbara. She is married to David, an art dealer. The childless couple lives comfortably in a high-rise Manhattan apartment that looks similar to an art gallery. This situation is slightly envied by Trudy, the younger sister who lives in Mineola with her husband, Martin, and with Sophie, whom they have been "taking care of" for years.

When Trudy and Martin pay an unexpected visit to Barbara and David, the couple senses that trouble is afoot. During a strained visit, Trudy complains at length about how difficult it has become to live with

---

1165. Reference for Background and Summary: *Social Security: A Play in Two Acts by Andrew Bergman* (1986). By Andrew Bergman. Nelson Doubleday, Inc. Garden City, New York.

Sophie, who apparently refuses to be left alone or to be looked after by strange caregivers. Trudy also reveals that she and her husband are on their way to rescue their daughter (who is away at college) from an unsanctimonious lifestyle of promiscuity. Soon, the reason for their visit comes into sharper focus.

Trudy and Martin have come to drop mother Sophie off with Barbara and David while they attempt to solve their daughter's problems. They are leaving town tonight and will be gone for as long as it takes to settle the issue, and, to ensure their plan would not be foiled, they already brought Sophie with them—she is waiting in the car outside of the apartment. To Barbara and David's dismay, they are now, like it or not, the newly designated overseers of the family matriarch, who immediately insists on a cup of tea.

Sophie's arrival has caused Barbara's nerves to become frayed, and her constant doting leaves her with less time for David. When he calls to say that he's bringing an important artist home for dinner, Barbara scrambles to prepare a small buffet while pleading with her mother to remove her frumpy housecoat and change into a nice evening dress. Uninterested in her daughter's request, Sophie instead begins to reminisce about days gone by. An ongoing exchange of memories ensues, punctuated by Barbara's insistent pleas. Sophie finally agrees to ditch the housecoat and begins to disrobe just as David and his distinguished guest walk through the front door.

In short order, Sophie is ushered into the bedroom to dress, while Barbara and David cater to their guest, a ninety-year-old artist named Maurice Koenig. Soon, Sophie emerges in an elegant gown, pleasing all present, especially Maurice, who seems immediately taken with her. In a matter of days, the two become a couple. The romance turns serious and Sophie accepts Maurice's offer to purchase an apartment for her. She is enlivened by the new relationship, and her newfound independence has allowed Barbara and David time to grow closer.

When Trudy and Martin finally return to pick her up, they have news of their own. Their daughter is decidedly out of danger and planning to marry a rabbi. But they, however, have decided to divorce. Trudy is especially troubled by the sudden change of events. Her daughter is grown, her husband has just left her for another woman, and her mother has fallen in love. Alas, with Sophie living on her own, Trudy realizes that she is the one alone.

# About the Author

Jennifer Bitman is an author and freelance writer from Los Angeles, California. Her debut biography, *Joan Crawford: A Talent for Living*, was self-published in 2018. The book was well-received by readers worldwide. It reached the number-one position on the Amazon free book charts during a promotional period and was accepted upon review into the L.A. County public library system. Jennifer has earned a bachelor's and master's degree in psychology in addition to a master's degree in Christian studies. She has been invited to appear as a guest on classic film-related podcasts, and in 2021, she wrote the biography that accompanies Arlene Francis's profile on the Radio Hall of Fame website.